To my teachers

Liz and Dave.

Thank you.

Mom

CONTENTS

FOREWORD

Forward March!

By Toni Hager (www.kidscanlearn.net)

Our FAScinating Journey started as the continuation of Liz Kulp's book *The Best I Can Be Living With Fetal Alcohol Syndrome or Effects* to explain Liz's growth after one year of neurodevelopment therapies. Somehow, with the Lord's guidance, it became more. This book became an introduction to neurodevelopment and other therapies written in simple language families can understand.

Families who adopt a 'healthy' baby or toddler may discover by fourth to sixth grade the child has learning differences the school can not manage and behavior the parents do not understand. One parent may read, search and scour for information. Another may retreat into hobbies or work to keep life as normal as possible. Some pray for miracles. Some ask for a cure. Families may withdraw from the community avoiding 'public' statements and misunderstandings. They mourn the dreams for the child. In isolation they can handicap themselves and their child's development. I also am the parent of two special needs daughters.

Alcohol consumption during pregnancy is one of the leading preventable causes of birth defects and childhood disabilities in the United States.[1] It is a lifetime permanent medical diagnosis. There is no cure.[2] Prenatal exposure often goes under-diagnosed or misdiagnosed.

Children with Fetal Alcohol Spectrum Disorder (FASD) can have serious lifelong disabilities, including mental retardation, learning disabilities and behavioral problems.[3] Children and their families are left isolated and without services. The family struggles to do the best it can. Undiagnosed adults with FASD try to raise children and find themselves involved in child protection. The circle continues. Families are exhausted, depressed and hopeless.

1. Centers for Disease Control and Prevention (1995) Update: Trends in fetal alcohol syndrome – United States, 1979-1993. *Morbidity and Mortality Weekly Report*. 44:249-251
2. Centers for Disease Control and Prevention (2003) *CDC: Fetal Alcohol Frequently Asked Questions*. Online: http://www.cdc.gov/ncbddd/fas/default.htm (Accessed January 13, 2004)
3. Centers for Disease Control and Prevention (2003) *CDC: Living with Fetal Alcohol*, Online: http://www.cdc.gov/ncbddd/fas/default.htm (Accessed January 13, 2004)

Statistics show that more than 85%[4] of families with a disabled child end in divorce. This is a travesty. Parents feel hopeless when 'something is not right'. They may drain their insurance and savings looking for a miracle. Still their child has difficulties. The family crumbles, leaving one parent primary care responsibilities with no relief and both parents feeling exhausted, rejected and angry. It is a vicious circle. Raising a child with a learning disability or developmental delay is complex. It is difficult for parents to determine which professional to see first. Going from professional to professional can be demoralizing for both the parents and the child. At each stop families gain additional labels (FASD, OCD, ODD, APD, VPD, LD, ADHD, RAD, SI, etc.). Sadly, very few families find solutions other than medication to help the child.

The emotional cost of raising a child with brain damage is taxing. There is little energy left to search for answers. Traditional therapies don't always work, as they tend to address only one part of the body, while the child's damage is more global. To complicate things many doctors and other professionals don't recognize or accept FASD as a diagnosis. The daunting task remains to continue to rear the child. The financial cost to the United States based on the 10th Special Report to the U.S. Congress on Alcohol and Health estimated the annual cost of FASD to be $2.8 billion in 1998![5]

I was recently told by an adoptive case manager that she believes more than 90% of children in North American foster care and older adoptions have prenatal exposure to alcohol, drugs, chemicals or experienced some form of malnourishment. That means during part of the child's life in the womb or early childhood brain development, there is a high probability of brain or other hidden metabolic damage. Children with FASD (Fetal Alcohol Spectrum Disorder) who are undiagnosed and not helped face extreme challenges and misunderstandings. Unlike children who are deaf, blind or physically impaired, they are often accused of being obstinate or willful. Many times they are unable to do something not because they will not but because they are neuro-logically incapable. Their self-esteem plummets and without help social problems escalate. Early pregnancy, chemical abuse, violence, promiscuity, reactive outbursts, suicide, running, school dropout and gangs become commonplace.

I had not worked knowingly with children exposed to alcohol in the

---

4. Bridge Builders c/o Valley Life Center, 3421 Monroe St, Santa Clara, CA 95051 408-246-4881
5. Centers for Disease Control and Prevention (2003) CDC: Fetal Alcohol Frequently Asked Questions. Online: http://www.cdc.gov/ncbddd/fas/default.htm (Accessed January 13, 2004)

womb. In the fall of 2000, Jodee sent me Liz's manuscript for her future book *The Best I Can Be: Living With Fetal Alcohol Syndrome or Effects*. Liz had painstakenly written her own history — each page taking 30 minutes. Jodee and Liz were fun and energetic. Thinking of Liz makes me smile. She reminds me of a stick of lit dynamite. Jodee was willing to research, test and try new things. We joined forces. We would see if we could make a difference.

Since the initial printing of *Our FAScinating Journey*. We have duplicated the program we began with Liz researching, testing and adapting therapies from around the world. The diversity of prenatal injury requires an individual neuro-educational plan for each child. We have seen varying improvement with the over sixty children we have worked with. We continue to progress. The CanLearn Center and School for children prenatally exposed to toxic substances in Spokane, Washington is now in it's third year.

Our FAScinating Journey will introduce a path to readers to work with prenatally exposed children. The Kulp family illuminates this path with lights shining with hope for possibilities for a future for these special children.

On your journey through these pages you will:

- Discover creative approaches in reaching and loving children with attachment issues.
- Understand how alcohol affects the growing brains of children.
- Become familiar with brain terminology.
- Uncover ideas to help a child nutritionally.
- Wade through school and behavior issues with tears, laughter and strategies you may not have tried.
- Meet professionals who have helped the Kulp family help Liz grow.
- Loose yourself in a myriad of ideas within the appendix.
- Smile as you get to know Liz, a very real teen who is determined to be the best she can be despite FASD.

Our FAScinating Journey: The Best We Can Be, Keys to Brain Potential Along the Path of Prenatal Brain Injury is written for families, professionals and the community. It's goal is to open the door to possibilities for our citizens who have sustained brain injury due to toxins in the womb.

While this is Liz Kulp's story, our hope is to open doors for you and your child. We want to help your family become strong and united rather the divided and fall. We want to provide your child 'a chance to grow!'

PREFACE

A LETTER TO PARENTS
OF CHILDREN
WITH PRENATAL BRAIN INJURY

from Karl and Jodee Kulp

Karl, Liz and I hope you enjoy *Our FAScinating Journey: Keys To Brain Potential Along the Path of Prenatal Brain Injury.* We open our hearts and home to professionals, friends and parents hoping that by sharing our lives we can improve the lives of others. *Our FAScinating Journey* is written to provide information for families of children with prenatal brain injury, specifically FASD (fetal alcohol spectrum disorder). We have worked diligently to translate professional language into easy-to-understand vernacular for families and non-professionals. This does not mean the work is less than, we hope it becomes more than. We hope our work bridges understanding and provides for other children's futures.

Our daughter, Liz is a teen with a twist, a senior in high school looking forward to adulthood. With tenacity and perseverance Liz passed state math, reading and writing exams. She is qualified for graduation and is mainstreamed in a public high school of 1,700 students. In December 2003, she passed her business college entrance exam. These achievements did not come without support and a step-by-step plan.

Our FAScinating Journey does not show you how to fix fetal alcohol brain damage. It does, however, provide understanding and insight into the life of persons with FASD and strategies to improve futures. At the second printing of this book Liz (age 17) struggles with normal teen, young adult transitioning and FASD issues. We walk alongside Liz, guiding and picking her up as she transverses secondary disabilities and the dangers of adult transition. She is a very real teen with very real permanent issues resulting from exposure to alcohol in the womb.

As Liz's peers acquire higher level thinking and abstract reasoning, she is left behind stuck in concrete operations. IQ testing does not make adaptations for a child unable to acquire abstraction. As with many children with FASD her IQ of 79-84 at ten-years-old decreased to just above 70 at age 17 qualifying her for adult developmental support services.

We began working with Liz's brain and body issues in a strategic wholistic and therapeutic way at thirteen-years-old. We hope the processes we discovered can be duplicated in centers and schools to help children with FASD reach their fullest potential. We hope the exercises and knowledge we used with Liz as a young teen can be used for younger children and provide access to additional abilities and adult success. Our journey was exhausting mentally, physically, spiritually and financially. The discoveries we made in the process shed light on opportunity we hope can be replicated.

It was worth the cost if we can decrease secondary disabilities for other young people and if additional training and support systems become available for families raising these young people (See MOFAS's *SOS: Seeds of Success* available at www.mofas.org.)

We continue to speak to whoever will listen. Liz continues to write inspirational lyrics. She is a courageous young woman struggling with her own realities in a complex world. She is writing a sequel to *The Best I Can Be: Living with Fetal Alcohol Syndrome or Effects*. We offer the first workbook in our young adult series called *Heart Break* free at www.betterendings.org.

"The Whitest Wall" - a novel to expose the general public to the realities of young adults with fetal alcohol is currently in manuscript form. It is my dream that this work will break down barriers of misunderstandings for future generations. Perhaps we can lay bare the realities of the damage alcohol does to babies, to families and to the socio-economics of the world.

Sharing Our Hope — The Kulp Family
Jodee, Karl and Liz Kulp

"The brain is happy to do what the brain is ready to do"
Toni Hager

ACKNOWLEDGEMENTS

"May my cry come before you O Lord;

give me understanding according to your Word."

Psalm 120:169

*W*e would like to thank our Heavenly Father who listened to my prayer in helping to find the original blueprint of development for Liz and the tools to reorganize, rewire and rebuild her spirit, mind and heart.

We are grateful for our courageous daughter Liz, who is truly a survivor — creating her life to become the best it can be. May her mission to change the course of history and prevent this birth defect succeed. And to David Magnuson, the son of my heart, for his innovative way of understanding Fetal Alcohol from the inside out. I thank you both for all the laughter, all the tears and all the growth you have given me.

We are grateful for the professionals and families who are living and loving, working and doing research for children and persons who have been prenatally exposed to alcohol in the womb. We would especially like to thank the following persons for investing their time and efforts into helping our daughter Liz grow: Cathy Bruer-Thompson, Nancy Liebeg, Norman and Beverly Benson, Dr. Carrie Kulp, Lauren and David Runnion-Bareford, Kathy Kienzle, Jay and Jeanne Patterson, Jeff and Kathy Haley, Greg and Diane Olson, Robin and Jim Hokanson, Liv Horneland, Judy Howell, JoAnn Kraft, Dr. Jeff Brist, Dr. Elizabeth Reeve, Toni Hager, Dr. Don Sealock, Dr. Travis Johnson, Dr. John Nash, PEASE Academy, MOFAS, Karen Johnson, and Thunder Spirit Center, Linda Lee Soderstrom, Dr. John Brick.

We are indebted to the developmental pioneers who provided the stepping stones along the path in discovering Liz's brain potential. We are indebted to their years of work and the thousands of clients who came before us.

We are also indebted to the tireless efforts of all the experts in the field of Fetal Alcohol research among them: Ann Streissguth, Ph.D.; Edward Riley, Ph.D.; Sterling Clarren, M.D.; Larry Burd, Ph.D.; Teresa Kellerman, Susan Carlson; Joyce Holl,

Lisa Brodsky, Lois Bickford, Pinian Chang, Ph.D.; Jocie DeVries; Susan Doctor; Barbara Morse; Diane Malbin; Kathleen Shea; Lydia Caros, M.D.; Lynne Frigaard.

We especially thank those adults with FASD who are surviving and living fruitful lives despite having been prenatally exposed. We have discovered in our journey wonderful people with FASD who are parents, business owners, restaurateurs, and service people who have offered their successes in hope that our daughter and many other children will also be successful.

We thank all the current front line parents and families who love children who have been prenatally exposed. Together we truly can make a difference. Tomorrow can be better for our children.

Most importantly, I would like to thank my life partner, Karl, who has joined me on this journey from its very inception. His differences in perspective, wisdom and strength have continued to add lights to the paths of brain potential we have discovered for Liz. Without our differences this journey would never have been possible.

God Bless To All
Jodee Kulp

May this book bless you with
understanding and vocabulary.

_____

I think I heard right . . .
Let's see the thing-a-ma-jig is connected
to the heepsbody next to the hisbody. It
hooligigs around the wham-o-room.
Yep, I got it.
Parent of child with FASD

OUR FAScINATING JOURNEY

A LIGHT

FOR FAMILIES

FOR CHILDREN

FOR PROFESSIONALS

ABATES DARKNESS.

1 . Introduction

Later

Snuggled together on the sofa, Liz[6], Dave[7], Karl and I quietly watched a movie on New Years Eve 2001. We had come so far! Thank God for a diagnosis. Recognition of FASD (Fetal Alcohol Spectrum Disorder) was the key to open the door that had been locking Liz's life. My entrepreneurial business spirit flourished in the chaos of FASD fragmented knowledge. Our FAE (Fetal Alcohol Effects) diagnosis was the clue that told us we were dealing with brain injury. If we had been wiser we could have seen the flashing red lights and sirens along the way – failure-to-thrive, SID (sensory integration disorder), dietary issues, ADHD, LD, motor planning, language, visual and auditory processing problems – each had pointed to neurological dysorganization.

Karl, Liz and I rolled up our sleeves 'to be the best we could be.' We enhanced Liz's biological systems in the same order she was created - tiny step-by-step. We changed our lifestyle to invest in Liz's future. Her future would become our future.

Today, we know Liz's organic neurological-based developmental disabilities will probably require a continuum of services throughout her lifespan – changing as she changes. We also know her brain could be rewired; we watched it happen.

We asked questions and found answers. We asked questions that still have no answers. We laughed and played and danced and sang. We jumped and stomped and screamed and cried. We tried and failed. We tried and succeeded. Like a revolving spi-

Liz's thinking reminded me of a tangled fishing line with a thrashing fish or a tangle of flashing Christmas tree lights we couldn't turn off. Knowing where to start in the untangling process was the solution to help Liz's learning and emotional issues.

6. Liz is our adopted daughter who was prenatally exposed to toxic substances in the womb.
7. David lived with us as a foster baby and has continued to be a part of our family even after he was adopted by his next foster family.

Liz's diagnosis of FAE did not change Liz. It changed Karl and I, and because of how we changed Liz had opportunity for new potential.

ral we continued to layer tiny piece upon tiny piece, trying to follow a sequential developmental pattern.

Liz's antics opened the hearts and minds of the public to the realities of prenatal exposure to alcohol. She became a role model and though she gained that title, we did not avoid the secondary disabilities of FASD. Liz struggles daily with the results of exposure to alcohol as a tiny developing human being. She is a very real teen with very real FASD issues. For her own safety, she quickly shares that she has FAE if she acts inappropriately. Liz's book *The Best I Can Be: Living with Fetal Alcohol Syndrome / Effects* written when she was thirteen-years-old triggered this book to further help families and professionals.

We met families dealing with FASD from around the world working together and providing online support. We no longer felt alone in the middle of this FASlane. We had a reality-based perspective we could add to with our love, experience, education, and tenacity. We penetrated the murk and began understanding how to parent Liz. Because of that Liz gained opportunities to grow.

Liz is an advocate for herself and others with FASD. She encourages young people with FASD to believe they are not alone. She believes in her "abilities" and does not let her differences hold her back. She boldly spoke on national television telling pregnant moms to quit drinking and represented FASD at the Young Women's Health Summit in Washington, D.C.

For two years, Liz's MoAngels performed inspirational hip-hop & rap at community events. The Tiger Woods Target Start Something Scholarship provided the seed money for public relations efforts. Liz was honored as the Adopted Child of the Year by the Minnesota Foster Care Association. She spoke, passed out hundreds of FASknots on International FASday and Spirit Free Recipe booklets over the holidays and received the Girl Scout Silver Award for her efforts. She lives her dream that each person can begin to change the world.

We have been asked what made the difference for Liz? Could we duplicate a program? Karl, Liz and I cannot give you answers for the person you love with prenatal brain injury. Every person is different. We can, however, share with you our journey.

It is a journey of hope.

BETTER ENDINGS NEW BEGINNINGS

*We exposed Liz to a rich and varied environ-**ment*** from the moment she arrived in our home at five months of age. She was failing to thrive. Our job was to keep her alive and love her with consistent invested care. Our neighbor Nancy, an RN, became her nanny who focused her attention on Liz's health and development eight hours per day while I worked four days a week. Working provided me the energy and stamina I needed to take the baton in the evening to care for a baby who could not deal with human touch, cried often, was easily overstimulated and failed to sleep through the night for almost three years. Karl, Nancy and I loved her unconditionally. We invested every bit of time, money and opportunity we could and Liz grew. She thrived. We attributed her early difficulties to attachment disorder. We were wrong.

We worked with a clinical nutritionist to develop a diet to help her grow. Reading, classical music, massage, experiences she could tolerate and a play room that looked like a therapeutic day care center encouraged her development.

Liz grew happily through her preschool and kindergarten years. She failed miserably in first grade and by the end of the year she was withdrawn and angry. Stomach and headaches became a daily occurrence. We transferred her from a small private school to a public school with special needs support services and trained teachers. Liz continued to fall through the cracks. By fourth grade, she was joyless, sad and sullen. At home she was rageful, impulsive and violent. It appeared the work she had accomplished was unraveling and an independent adulthood unattainable.

My online FASD buddies around the world: You keep trucking through situations that would make other people give up, and you still have the energy to help and encourage others. You've kept Brian and me sane for years, as we've struggled with the knowledge that our daughter is NOT going through a phase and not willfully acting-out, but is a person with permanent brain damage. She is NOT doing this against us. You've taught me so much. You make me laugh and cry. You inspire me with your courage and devotion to your children. You make this fight worthwhile.

Love, Bonnie Buxton
(FASD mom and FASworld International co-founder)

It has been seven years since Liz (then age ten) and I jumped into homeschooling to help her catch up with her peers. We began on April Fool's Day with laughter and smiles reading the book *Living With Learning Disabilities: A Guide for Students* by David E. Hall, M.D. Liz crossed out every "DIS" in the book with a black marker. Soon the book was filled with "abilities" instead of DISabilities. We collected DIS

At three Liz lay on the sofa quietly listening to her favorite composer — Vivaldi. She told me she was eating his music.

words — *(Dis means without, separated from)* — disappointed, disagree, disaster. And then we replaced them with "eX" words — *(Ex means beyond, upward, out of, proceeding)* — eXcel, eXamine, eXhibit, eXcite, eXceptional, eXcellence, eXpectations, eXample. "X" symbolized for us the cross of Christ and became the cornerstone in our school — we focused on hope, order, love and restoration instead of defeat, chaos, hatred and destruction. We watched *"The Miracle Worker"* and decided if Helen Keller and Anne Sullivan could do it we could too.

We eXposed her knowledge and abilities, jumpstarting with a preschool curriculum. We enjoyed life and played. We spent hours biking, jumping rope, and learning to rollerblade. We raised baby chickens and ducks. Together we walked the long road back to "abilities". *(We invite you to visit our homeschool at www.betterendings.org)*

We found areas she had missed and developed interactive and exciting ways to relearn. We removed the grading system. Liz progressed (P) or mastered (M) a task. We removed failure. We focused on neatness, creativity, accuracy and attitude.

It has been five years since Liz mistakenly thought to have friends you needed to please them at all costs. She became popular in our urban neighborhood with fearless, outrageous and dangerous behaviors. We sought a therapist who discovered as we had that talking, coaxing and normal training did not make a difference — something else was wrong. At age 12.5 we discovered Liz had FAE — fetal alcohol effects or prenatal exposure to alcohol — the damage had been hidden behind her normal loooking exterios. Liz adapted well in many areas and no one put the pieces together. We were told she would peak in learning and need to be taught horizontally once that peak occurred. Translated

*We played
"I am thinking
of something"
challenging Liz
to ask questions.
She loved
challenging us
with her own
ideas.*

that meant she could learn to do the wash, but probably not learn to fix the washer. Liz's brain was damaged and the injury was permanent.

A week after our FAE diagnosis, I met with a clinical nutritionist. We removed processed foods from our diet and increased fresh vegetables and fruits. We learned to provide Liz with nutrition her body could process and added supplements to help her brain and circulatory system.

A year later we met Toni Hager, a neurodevelopmentalist. She evaluated Liz and developed a brain training program. We were surprised how little we understood the daily struggle our daughter faced. Our hearts broke as we learned what we had overlooked. Prenatal and early infant issues caused developmental delays. Crucial steps were halted, skipped or interrupted. Infant reflexes were operating even though they should have disappeared. Later reflexes had never engaged. She suppressed her vision in one eye, and suppressed her hearing in her opposite ear. She processed only three pieces of information at a time. These inefficiencies directly impacted her ability to utilize "learned" skills. Many of her skills were awkward or inadequate since learned behavior is when neuro connections have connected properly. Until her brain developed connections, progress in reading, math and general life skills would be difficult.

It was our job to help Liz build a solid developmental foundation. We developed a brain-friendly learning environment for Liz. We learned how to empower her brain before we expected performance. We kept our environment and structure stable. Toni's program took about one hour a day and we broke up her exercises into three time periods - morning wake up, academics and just before bed. Liz referred to the morning program as plugging in her brain. In the evening it helped her fall asleep. The change in her demeanor and learning abilities was drastic. I began looking forward to teaching her. My little fighter was building a neural highway back to her brain. This time the roadwork was being laid correctly and in sequential order.

*Liz
subconsciously
used most of
her energy to keep
herself appearing
like others.*

Karl and I studied child development and the brain to help Liz. We found health specialists with experience, equipment and tests to isolate Liz's individual issues. Just as an athlete learns new skills and improves old ones, Liz was back in the race and gaining academic, emotional and kinesthetic ground.

We could not separate biology from intellect, they were the same. Repeat . . . repeat. . . repetition built reliability. Learning through repetition produces permanent neurophysiological change. The circuitry gets more efficient.

FIVE SIGNIFICANT PARENTING CHANGES:

1. **Paradigm shift from bad behavior to brain injury.**
2. **Unconditional love, humor and attention.**
3. **Adequate nutrition, sleep and a functioning metabolism.**
4. **Sequential tiny developmental steps.**
5. **Our daughter is a normal child with a disability, not a disabled child.**

The more integrated Liz's brain became, the more she was able to think and do. Her eyes sparkled. Her brain worked with her instead of against her. Liz has grown into a dynamic young woman and we believe she will have an independent or semi-independent adulthood. We are working with developmental disability services, the public school system and community support services to make that transition as smooth as possible. We expect we will continue to see results. We expect we will start, progress, regress, and start again. It is a repetitive lifetime process of growth.

Liz's High School
Graduation picture
age 17.

Karl, Liz and I are honored to give you our life map. We begin by introducing you to the brain. You will need this information to help your child. For professionals who question this book's simplicity, I have tried to make the following pages clear for families who are loving children affected by prenatal brain injury by translating medical, educational and pyschological vernacular. I use terminology and language families will understand and build a vocabulary for communicating with you.

We hope within the following pages families find lights along their trail for *a better ending and a new beginning* for the person they love.

2. THE BRAIN

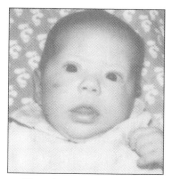

Liz at four months prior to joining our family.

TERATOGENS
THE TYRANT-A-SAURAS WRECKS
OF A BABY'S BRAIN

Your brain is a little bigger than your two fists, yet it is the control center for your whole body. There is no computer system presently on earth that compares. It is projected that neurons multiply at a rate of 250,000 nuerons per minute during early pregnancy and number over 100 billion in the three pound adult brain.[8] The human cerebral cortex has an area of about 2.5 square feet, has 25 billion nuerons, is interconnected by over 100,000 kilometers of axons and receives 300 trillion (yes trillion) synapses.[9] There are about 3 mil-

Liz 3 years old and Dave 18 months with Jodee.

8. Kandel, E.R., Schwartz, J.H. and Jessell, T.M. *Principles of Neural Science,* New York: McGraw Hill, 2000
9. Nolte, J., *The Human Brain. An introduction to Its Functional Anatomy*, 4th edition, St. Louis, Mosby, 1999.

Dave 14 years old and Liz 17 years old.

lion miles of axons in the human brain.[10] The brain is the 21st Century's new frontier. We still have much to learn.

The substances that cause damage to a baby during pregnancy are called **'teratogens'** — from the Greek word teraton which means monster. Teratogens are poisons. Different kinds affect different parts of the body or brain. For example, the sleeping pill thalidomide had an effect on the babies of women who took the drug between the 34th and 50th days after their last menstrual cycle. Between days 39-44 the baby's arms were shortened. Between the days 42-48 the baby's legs were shortened. Between days 41-43 the baby's hands were not properly formed. Babies of mothers who took thalidomide before the 34th day or more than 50 days after their last period showed no damage. The same rule applies to other drugs.

Many types of substances can harm a baby's brain — medications, street drugs, alcohol, nicotine, cocaine to name a few. Viruses such as German measles, viral hepatitis and herpes simplex also can take their toll. The exact damage depends on the time of exposure. Luckily for a baby, everything that gets into the mother's bloodstream does not

> **SPECTRUM** — a child with fetal alcohol spectrum disorder (FASD) can have damage ranging from mild to extreme.
>
> **VIABILITY** — affects will be different in each baby due to:
> a. amount and timing of alcohol exposure during pregnancy
> b. mother's nutrition
> c. parity – first pregnancies have less damage than subsequent pregnancies
> d. fetus – how strong it is, genetic factors (father's sperm)

reach the brain of her child. There is a barrier of tissue that acts like a filter to protect the brain against some toxins. Many toxins that can enter cells of other tissues such as muscles, can not enter the brain because of this filter called the **blood-brain barrier**. During early stages of pregnancy, however, the filter is not as powerful a sentinel as later in the pregnancy. Therefore, some toxins cause more harm during pregnancy's earliest months. In addition, when a toxin crosses the blood-brain barrier, not all parts of the brain are damaged in the same way. The amount and kind of damage depends on what cells in the brain are developing at that very instant.

More than one in ten women report current alcohol use and of the

10. Conlon, R., States of *Mind: New Discoveries About How Our Brains Make Us Who We Are,* New York: Dana Press, 1999

women who reported drinking during their pregnancy, 23% reported drinking during their first trimester, 6% reported drinking during their third trimester. The Centers for Disease Control and Prevention (CDC) estimate that more than 130,000 pregnant women per year in the U.S. consume alcohol at levels shown to increase the risk of having a baby with FAS or other alcohol related condition[11]

Alcohol exposure can cause devastating effects. It is a teratogen that CAN CROSS the brain barrier! In some cases whole parts of a brain may be missing. Alcohol deprives oxygen to the brain. Brain cells die and they cannot be replaced after only four minutes without oxygen.

Occasional **binge drinking**[12] can cause buck-shot-like damage. These scattered holes in the brain affect whatever area happened to be developing at the time. Brain cells die or migrate to the wrong place. Neurons are in tangles with incorrect or incomplete connections. The most common effect is permanent brain damage causing learning disabilities, behavior problems, memory deficits, attention deficit hyperactivity disorder, and/or mental retardation. This unchanging physiological damage to the brain is called '**static encephalopathy**' and these

Some days John can control his impulses to be wild, silly or rude, other days he cannot. I try to help his job place understand that even though he can control his impulses 90% of the time (on meds anyway), it's that 10% of the time that I worry about. I never know when that will happen. I have to be ready at any given time for that inconsistency to show its face.

Teresa Kellerman

(Mom to John with FASD)

structural abnormalities can be documented with MRI and CT scans. Brain functionality can be viewed with SPECT scans and qEEGs. For individuals with FASD these tests can help discover where damage has occurred.

Teresa Kellerman an adoptive mother to young adult John Kellerman has worked tirelessly on educating professionals and families on the issues surrounding fetal alcohol brain injury. Her organization Fetal Alcohol Community Resource Center located at *www.fasstars.com* provides information to help families and professionals. I am honored to have been permitted to add her Fetal Alcohol and The Brain to this publication.

11. Flynn, H.A. et al (2003). Rates and correlates of alcohol use among pregnant women in obstetric clinics. Alcoholism: Clinical and Experimental Research. 27 (1):81-87
12. Binge Alcohol Use: 5 or more drinks on one occasion Heavy Alcohol Use: 5 or more drinks on 5 or more occasions within the past month   (Source: Center for Science in the Public Interest, Nov. 2003)

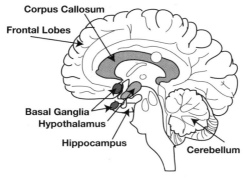

Corpus Callosum
Frontal Lobes
Basal Ganglia
Hypothalamus
Hippocampus
Cerebellum

FETAL ALCOHOL AND THE BRAIN
(simplified for families)

by Teresa Kellerman
Fetal Alcohol Community Resource Center — www.fasstars.com

The regions of the brain that are most seriously affected by prenatal alcohol exposure in terms of ability to function are:

1   **Frontal Lobes** - control impulses and judgment. The most noteworthy damage to the brain probably occurs in the prefrontal cortex, which controls what are called the Executive Functions.[13] (See page 12)

2   **Corpus Callosum** - passes information from the left brain (rules, logic) to the right brain (impulse, feelings) and vice versa. The Corpus Callosum in an individual with FASD might be smaller than normal, and in some cases it is almost nonexistent. (See page 21)

3.   **Hippocampus** - plays a fundamental role in memory.[14]

4.   **Hypothalamus** - controls appetite, emotions, temperature, and pain sensation

5.   **Cerebellum** - controls coordination and movement, behavior and memory.[15]

6.   **Basal Ganglia** - affects spatial memory, behaviors like perseveration and the inability to switch modes, work toward goals, predict behavior outcomes and the perception of time, puts brakes on actions.[16]

13. http://www.washingtonparent.com/articles/9906/executive-functioning.htm
14. http://www.niaaa.nih.gov/about/council6-99-text.htm
15. http://webmd-practice.medcast.com/Z/Channels/2818/article3280
16. http://unisci.com/stories/20011/0227013.htm

Alcohol is a 'teratogen' (substance that is toxic to the baby's developing brain). Since the brain and the central nervous system are developing throughout the entire pregnancy, the baby's brain is always vulnerable to damage from alcohol exposure. Damage can occur in various regions of the brain.

Children do not need to have full FAS to have significant difficulties due to prenatal exposure to alcohol. According to research done by Drs. Joanne L. Gusella and P.A. Fried, even light drinking (average one-quarter ounce of absolute alcohol daily – see page 30) can have adverse affects on the child's verbal language and comprehension skills. *[Neurobehavioral Toxicology and Teratology, Vol. 6:13-17, 1984]* Drs. Mattson and Riley in San Diego have conducted research on the neurology of prenatal exposure to alcohol. Their studies show that children of mothers who drank but who do not have a diagnosis of FAS have many of the same neurological abnormalities as children who have been diagnosed with full FAS. *[Neurotoxicology and Teratology, Vol. 16(3):283-289, 1994]*

Damage to the brain from alcohol exposure can have an adverse affect on behavior. Alcohol exposure appears to damage some parts of the brain, while leaving other parts unaffected. Some children exposed to alcohol will have neurological problems in just a few brain areas. Other exposed children may have problems in several brain areas. The brain dysfunction is expressed in the form of inappropriate behaviors and behavior problems should be viewed with

Alcohol Exposure During Stages of Pregnancy

1 During the **first trimester**, as shown by the research of Drs. Clarren and Streissguth, alcohol interferes with the migration and organization of brain cells. *[Journal of Pediatrics, 92(1):64-67]*

2 Heavy drinking during the **second trimester**, particularly from the 10th to 20th week after conception, seems to cause more clinical features of FAS than at other times during pregnancy, according to a study in England. *[Early-Human-Development; 1983 Jul Vol 8(2) 99-111]*

3 During the **third trimester**, according to Dr. Claire D. Coles, the hippocampus is greatly affected, which leads to problems with encoding visual and auditory information (reading and math). *[Neurotoxicology and Teratology, 13:357-367, 1991]*

From the College of Cognitive and Linguistic Sciences at Brown University, Providence, RI.

Executive Functions

Executive functions of the prefrontal cortex:	Effects of alcohol exposure on behaviors related to executive functions:
• inhibition	• socially inappropriate behavior, as if inebriated
• planning	• inability to apply consequences from past actions
• time perception	• difficulty with abstract concepts or time and money
• internal ordering	• like files out of order, difficulty processing information
• working memory	• storing and/or retrieving information
• self-monitoring	• needs frequent cues
• verbal self-regulation	• requires "policing" by others
	• needs to talk to self out loud, needs feedback
• motor control	• fine motor skills more affected than gross motor
• regulation of emotion	• emotions: moody "roller coaster", exaggerated
	• apparent lack of remorse
• motivation	• needs external motivators

respect to neurological dysfunction. Although psychological factors such as abuse and neglect can exacerbate behavior problems in FAS, we are looking primarily at behavior that is organic in origin. When it comes to maintaining good behavior, it is not a matter of the child 'won't' but 'can't.' (Diane Malbin[17]) Sometimes the person's behavior is misinterpreted as willful misconduct (Debra Evensen[18]), but for the most part, maintaining good behavior is outside of the child's control, especially in stressful or stimulating situations.

Almost all children with FASD disorders have some attachment issues, display inappropriate sexual

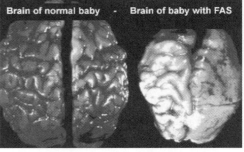

Brain of normal baby - Brain of baby with FAS

Brain of a normal baby and the brain of a baby with FAS. This child lived ten days. (Photo: Clarren)

Most sorrowfully, we found that the combination of their superficially good verbal skills and their behavior problems made them unacceptable candidates for most traditional treatment programs. The girls were often teenage mothers, the boys in trouble with the law.

Ann Striessguth, Ph.D.

17. http://www.come-over.to/FAS/cantwont.htm
18. http://www.fasalaska.com/interps.html

behaviors, show poor judgment, have difficulty controlling their impulses, are emotionally immature, and need frequent reminders of rules. Behavior problems in children with FASD are often blamed on poor parenting skills. Yet even alcohol exposed children raised in stable, healthy homes with exceptional parenting can exhibit unruly behavior. The most difficult behaviors are seen in children who were prenatally exposed to alcohol and who also suffer from Reactive Attachment Disorder (RAD). As a result, many will require the protection of close supervision for the rest of their lives.

Special thank you to *Teresa Kellerman*

Director FAS Community Resource Center for her contribution to this section

Secondary disabilities

(May developed as a result of failure to properly deal with the primary disabilities.)

■ Education
– Learning difficulties
– Disruptive
– Disrespective
– Poor peer relationships
– Chemical use
– Disobedience
– Droppping out
– Expulsions
– Suspensions

■ Confinement
– Jail
– Mental health
– Alcohol or drug treatment

■ Legal
– Run away
– Delinquency
– Violence
– Property crimes
– Theft
– Sexual misconduct

■ Mental Health
– Depression
– Anxiety
– Attachment
– Eating disorders
– ADHD/ADD
– Hallucinations
– Mental illness
– Suicide

■ Independence
– Social problems
– Poor peer selection
– Victimization
– Addiction
– Alcoholism
– Behavioral problems
– Reactive outbursts
– Chronic unemployment
– Conduct
– Poverty
– Homelessness

■ Sexuality
– Promiscuity
– Prostitution
– Inappropriate touching or advances
– Voyeurism
– Obscene phone calls
– Compulsions
– Early pregnancy
– Sexual acting out

Sources: Striessguth, Malbin, Morse, Ritchie, Burd.

12 years and over

60%	Attentional problems
65%	Male trouble with law
50%	Female trouble with law
50%	Inappropriate sexual behavior
	18% sexual advances
	17% sexual touching
	16% promiscuity
	14% exposure, compulsion
	9% voyeurism
40%	Depression
38%	Drug/alcohol
30%	Behavior Problems
12%	Suicide attempts

21 years and over

90%	Mental Health problems
90%	Difficulty independent living
82%	Employment problems

(Source: *Streissguth, et. al, 1988*)

Protective Factors

■ Early Diagnosis

■ Special Education Services

■ Stable, Nurturing Home

■ Absence of Violence

(Source: National Center on Birth Defects and Developmental Disabilities)

BRAIN BASICS FOR FAMILIES

The brain consists of three regions: the **brain stem**, the **cerebellum** and the **cerebrum**.

It has been found that areas of the brain are designated to perform different tasks. However, brain scans have shown that when completing a task many areas of the brain are engaged, with some areas being stronger than other areas. From loving to living – our brains make us human.

Main regions of the brain

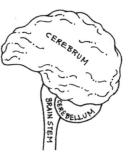

Work areas of the brain

Pre-motor

Sensory Motor

movement
leg
trunk
arm
neck
face
tongue

eye

touch

executive
functions,
judgment,motor
impulse
control

speech

hearing

taste

smell

vision

cerebrum

brain
stem

internal organs

muscle
movement

cerebellum

The brain is shaped not only by its biology but also by its experiences and education. It is your education and experience that give your brain **plasticity** – the ability to learn new things.

It is what makes the same child growing up in Japan different from growing up in New York City or a jungle in Africa.

The brain is the only organ that can analyze and study itself. The brain does not work in isolation, it is interconnected, each part collaborating with another. It is the medical frontier for this century.

The Brain Stem

The normal brain grows orderly beginning in the **brain stem** (sometimes referred to as a reptilian brain it resembles the whole brain of a reptile). The brain stem lies deep in the brain and controls automatic actions of your internal organs. It is located between the cerebrum and the cerebellum and leads to the spine. Originating in the brain stem are twelve cranial nerves.

These nerves control smell, hearing, vision, eye movement, facial sensations, taste and swallowing. They also control muscle movements in the face, neck, shoulders and tongue.

The **brain stem** area of the brain is wired and streamlined (myelinated) in the womb. Myelin allows axons in the organs, limbs and face to quickly send information for survival skills – breath, heartbeat, cry, suck, root, use of eyes and ears. Myelination takes up considerable space and accounts for a lot of the brain's four-fold increase from birth to adulthood. At birth a baby's brain is myelinated enough to jump start the baby.

The brain stem contains four distinct neural systems each with its own separate neuro-transmitter. They are:

1. medulla
2. pons
3. midbrain **(reticular activating system)**
4. thalamus

1. The medulla is located in the lowest part of the brain stem that merges with the spinal cord – our brain's vital link to the rest of our body. It regulates breathing and circulation, helps maintain some aspects of muscle tone, and like the spinal column helps in reflex behaviors such as swallowing and salivation (hiccups, sneezing, vomiting, coughing). Sensory and motor nerve fibers connecting the brain to the body cross over to the opposite side as they pass through the medulla.

2. The pons (meaning bridge) relays impulses within the brain and the spinal cord and lies between the medulla and the midbrain. Its key location implicates it in its functions of the sensory (internal sensation - receptive - sensory)

Brain Stem Functions:

- Breathing, heartbeat
- Swallowing
- Reflexes to seeing and hearing (Startle Response)
- Alertness and ability to sleep
- Automatic nervous system: sweating, blood pressure, temperature, digestion

When a midbrained injured person (cerebral palsy) is under pressure their symptoms become worse. They breathe faster and breathe away their carbon dioxide. This constricts their blood vessels and delivers less oxygen to the brain inhibiting the ability to function.

and motor systems (internal survival functions - heart-beat, breathing, etc.).

3. The midbrain acts like a relay station to transmit signals to higher levels of the brain. These tracks of nerves go upward to the cerebrum and downward to the spinal cord. These tracks called the **reticular** (network like) **activating system** sifts through masses of incoming information from the senses and decide what part is important enough for your attention. Though tiny, it is a powerhouse. It is in charge of your level of consciousness, alertness maintenance, perception and regulation of pain, breathing and some reflex actions. It is the center for the pupils response to light and controls the actions of the eye (blinking, opening and closing pupils, lens focusing). It helps us to coordinate the movement of our head and trunk in response to sound, to understand where our body is in space, and to integrate our movements. No conscious thought occurs in the midbrain; instead pressure from the midbrain is transmitted to the cortex, where it registers a conscious thought – "I am thirsty," "I am sleepy." The cortex may appear to be running the show, but the midbrain wields deceptive power.

The core functions of Liz's brain were damaged — the ability to sense, perceive, act, process and store, but unlike a child with cerebral palsy it was almost invisible.

Liz looks capable, yet a simple skill like skipping or sweeping at age 13 created a frustrating rage.

4. The thalamus receives sensory input – from the eyes, ears, nose, touch (skin and hair) and movement. It is thought to affect our motivation and emotions. The thalamus also acts as a relay station and is located just above the **hypothalamus** that is involved in hunger, thirst, flight or fight reaction, bodily temperature, sex and sleep. It works closely with the pituitary gland. Several times in life, at puberty, for example – the midbrain rearranges the way we see the world.

Brain Stem Injury Observed Problems:

- Sleeping difficulty (**Insomnia, Sleep Apnea**)
- Dizziness and nausea (**Vertigo**)
- Swallowing food and water (**Dysphagia**)
- Problems with balance, movement
- Decrease vital capacity in breathing, important to speech
- Environment organization and perception problems

Our initial neurodevelopment work with Liz began at the most basic levels, stopping her infantile reflexes, engaging normal reflexes, stabilizing her emotions and building her sensory highway.

Note: Data regarding observed problems has been compiled from TBI Traumatic Brain Injured persons and the resulting loss of functions due to specific injuries.
Visit www.neuroskills. com for TBI resource information.

A child or adult who sustains a traumatic brain injury (TBI) is provided with a team of professionals for rehabilitation. Can't the same support services help a child with prenatal traumatic brain injury?

The Cerebellum

The **cerebellum** is a 'little brain' which lies below the back part of the cerebrum at the base of the skull and acts as an assistant to the cerebrum (motor cortex) in the coordination of movement. It compares what you thought you were going to do with what is actually happening at the limb level and corrects the movement if there is a problem. It coordinates the impulses from the motor area of the cerebrum. Your desire to walk, run, bike, or perform any muscular activity may become a series of disorganized muscle contractions no matter how hard you try without this coordination and timing of motor programs, attention and classical conditioning. The nerve pathways of the cerebellum cross over, so the left side of the cerebellum helps us move the right side of our body and the right side of the cerebellum helps us move the left side of our body. The cerebellum helps with maintenance of muscle tone, balance and strengthening impulses for muscle activity.

Cerebellum Functions:

- Balance
- Coordination of voluntary movement
- Muscle tone
- Motor planning
- Fine motor skills
- Gross motor skills
- Attention
- Classical conditioning
- Some memory for reflex motor skills

Cerebellum Brain Injury Observed Problems:

- Inability to reach out and grab objects, **(Tremors)**
- Dizziness **(Vertigo)**
- Slurred Speech **(Scanning Speech)**
- Inability to make rapid movements
- Loss of ability to walk and/or coordinate fine movements

The Cerebrum

Through the **cerebrum** (cerebral cortex) we express our intellectual, moral and spiritual values as it integrates and processes sensory information. It is the cerebrum that makes us different from other animals.

The cerebrum is made up of six layers of brain cells and contains 75% of our brain cells (neurons) even though it is only 25% of the brain's volume. Its ridges and crevices increase it's surface capacity. The cerebrum is divided into four distinct regions called lobes:

1 Frontal lobe   3 Occipital lobe

2 Temporal lobe   4 Parietal lobe

The cerebrum in general is divided into three areas: **sensory** (receive, interpret sensory data); **motor** (muscle control, movement); and **association** (memory, emotion, reasoning, will, judgment, personality traits, intelligence).

Four lobes of the brain

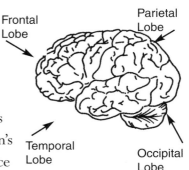

Frontal Lobe

Parietal Lobe

Temporal Lobe

Occipital Lobe

Words don't mean much unless they are put into action Talk therapy is a lot of hot air when there is neuro — anatomical or chemical — damage.

1. The Frontal Lobe (front of the brain)

The **frontal lobe** is the most evolved part of the brain and lies right under our forehead. Unfortunately this area is the most sensitive to trauma, neurotoxin effects, stress and nutritional insufficiencies. It is the last region of the brain to develop and it appears many of our children who are mildly FASD affected have frontal lobe issues. Frontal lobe injury has been shown to hamper creativity, flexibility and inventiveness in facing new problems while allowing the IQ performance ability. Damage can result in the inability to switch problem-solving strategies as a problem evolves.

The frontal lobe provides our consciousness and tells us how we are doing within our environment. It

Frontal Lobe Functions:

- Executive functions
- Planning
- Reasoning
- Thinking
- Inhibition
- Judgment
- Self-control
- Concentration
- Conscience
- Speech/motor skills

controls our expressive language, assigns meanings to the words we use and involves word associations. It helps us initiate activity in a response to our environment and allows us to make judgments about our daily activities.

If we wish to voluntarily move a muscle, an impulse from the cerebral cortex stimulates the motor area of the frontal lobes. The motor area controls the feet, legs, trunk, shoulders, hands, neck, face, tongue and larynx. The sensory strip that controls the five senses (sight, smell, taste, touch, hearing) lies next to the motor strip. Damage to the frontal lobe affects our motor activities and memory for habits.

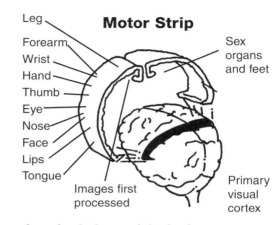

The frontal lobes are the centers of emotion, judgment, will-power and self-control. They translate the feelings of the limbic system (that controls mood and libido) into recognizable feelings, emotions and words such as love, passion or hate.

Development of the frontal lobe happens later in infancy. The frontal lobes of the brain (that also help in the retrieval of information) connect with the emotional center of the brain called the limbic system by about age nine months. That is why it is not unusual for an older infant to cry when a parent leaves or when a stranger appears. The child fears change.

Prenatal brain injury is deceptive even to trained professionals. The more I learned, the more I realized Liz's damage was global. I studied every developmental chart I could find. Where was Liz was on the developmental scale? What came before? Next? We strengthened the lower skills before introducing new skills.

Liz remains unable to regulate her emotions and reactions to life. Living in the moment, she reacts impulsively without understanding or care of her actions or others' feelings. Change to Liz's routine or plans sends her into a tailspin even at seventeen-years-old. To help you understand this feeling, imagine yourself in an elevator that suddenly jerks or driving your car in the middle lane down the freeway, during rush hour when a strange noise suddenly begins and there are no exit ramps near by. Persons

MRI and CT scans can show the physiological damage a person has incurred due to prenatal alcohol exposure.

who sustain traumatic frontal lobe brain injury later in life have provided us a myriad of information of just how important the frontal lobe is.

EMOTIONALITY CHANGES WITH GROWTH

The two-year-old is aware of choices, but is not yet aware that errors can be prevented. A child this age begins to understand right from wrong. The child begins to think "what will mommy think if I throw the pizza?" As the child grows she becomes aware of her intentions, her name and the enjoyment of the event. Finally her language skills develop so she can categorize her world into groups. It seemed we had to teach Liz everything. It wasn't enough to explain that we don't throw food. We explained it in detail, "We don't throw food at home. We don't throw food at a restaurant." Rules did not seem to translate from one place or event to another.

A three-year-old cannot associate what happened 'an hour ago', but a four-year-old can. Understanding the concept of time develops around age four and can usually be noted when a child uses verb tenses appropriately. The child is able to make connections between her past and her present. Liz lives in a time void, although she uses correct verbs, any recent occurrence vanishes or becomes history.

Our ability to 'go with the flow', think (concentrate and pay attention), plan ahead and communicate with others is housed in our frontal lobes. Five- to seven-years-old children begin formal schooling and are able to relate to responsibility in social situations. They can understand even if something is boring, they must try to sit still to learn; when someone is talking you try to keep your mouth shut and if you are mad you try your best not to hurt yourself or someone else. Liz, struggles with these concepts. Angry at being caught where she was not supposed to be, she threw

The behavioral effects associated with damage to the frontal lobe include:

- difficulty with transitions, distractibility, sequencing problems
- poor problem solving skills, motor planning, understanding of cause/effect
- problems generalizing
- concrete thinking (math problems)
- trouble interpreting social cues from peers
- difficulty regulating response to sensation
- difficulty following and understanding directions
- temper tantrums

her purse violently at the glass window, clawed her face and bit her arm in frustration. She was mad she got caught, there was no guilt.

Myelination in the frontal lobes happens during the teen years, providing improved behavioral control and risk assessment. We hoped Liz' would also benefit from this growth.

Observed Problems Due to Frontal Lobe Brain Injury (TBI)

- Mood changes (**Emotionally Labile**)
- Persistence of a single thought or activity (**Perseveration**)
- Inability to express language (**Broca's Aphasia**)
- Inability to focus on a task (**Attending**)
- Inability to plan a sequence of complex movements needed to complete a multi-stepped task, (making a sandwich, following a recipe) (**Sequencing**)
- Difficulty with problem solving
- Loss of flexibility in thinking,
- Loss of spontaneity in interacting with others
- Loss of simple movement of various parts of body (**Paralysis**)
- Changes in social behavior and personality

The frontal lobe and cerebrum is divided into two hemispheres – the right and the left – that are connected by the **corpus callosum.**

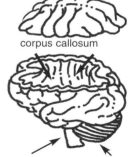

cerebrum

corpus callosum

brain stem   cerebellum

Corpus Callosum Connections

The corpus callosum is a fiber tract that integrates the right and left sides of the brain and provides a communication path for learning and memory. It contains more than 300 million axon but only transfers about three percent of the information our brain processes.[19] For most human beings the brain hemispheres do not function in isolation.

One hemisphere may dominate, but the other usually has some capability and contributes. In other words "the right hand does know what the left hand is doing." Under stress we tend to react from our dominant hemisphere.

Hemispheric asymmetry theory has its origin in work that Roger

19. Dr. John Nash, Behavioral Medicine www.qeeg.com

Sperry performed in the 1960s. Sperry studied patients whose corpus callosum had been surgically cut so that the two hemispheres were completely separate. Each hemisphere acted like an independent brain, but some functions were performed best by only one of the two hemispheres. This led to the pop psychology work of right brain /left brain theory, now under scrutiny.

Right Hemisphere — Left Hemisphere

Top View
front of head

Children with extreme seizure activity who have had a hemispherectomy (a radical treatment removing up to half of the brain) have been found to perform on a single hemisphere what both hemispheres were doing before. The younger they are at surgery the faster neuron pathways reroute.

Sometimes Freudian slips make sense. "The corpus Columbus allows passage of data between each hemisphere of the brain." I laughed as I pictured a little ship filled with information struggling to get from one side of the brain to the other. I wonder if the "Hippo" campus has a different kind of memory than an elephant and what happens if the Basal Ganglia gets slippery.

Research in Germany[20] has discovered through MRI's that the corpus callosums of musicians who play instruments with both hands is larger than normal. Hopefully Liz's Suzuki Harp lessons exercised to her corpus callosum.

For persons prenatally exposed to alcohol the corpus callosum may be missing, deformed or intermittent in its communication. This can cause difficulties in social functioning.

Each hemisphere performs different functions more efficiently. *For example, a graphic designer will use the right brain to conceptualize a design and the left brain to figure out how to execute the production.*

• **The right hemisphere controls left motor and sensory activity** and is more active in intuitive and abstract thought, spatial relations, humor, artistic expression and visualization. It draws its information on qualitative patterns that are not organized into sequences and clusters around images. It sees correspondences and resemblances.

20. FAS TIMES - Fetal Alcohol Syndrome / Family Resource Institute, FAS/FRI, PO Box 2525, Lynnwood, WA 98036. Call 1-800-999-3429 to request article. Visit www.fetalalcoholsyndrome.org

- **The left hemisphere controls right motor and sensory activity** and is more active in rational and logical thought and deductive reasoning, reacting, language and handwriting. It draws on previously accumulated, organized and sequential information and can see cause and effect. It tends to look for differences and prefers certain established information.

Your face

2. The Temporal Lobes (underside of brain)

The **temporal lobe** (auditory cortex) is located just above the ears on each side of the head, alongside the frontal and parietal lobes. We process sounds, tastes and smells in our temporal lobes. The temperol lobes store our experiences, memories and images. They allow us to categorize objects. They are involved with our hearing, memory, learning and language interpretation. They helps us to recognize objects and faces. They perceive 'what' forms in visual images.

"What do you mean I can think about my feelings. I can't think when I am feeling."

Liz

Damage to the temporal lobes in the brain can produce behavioral effects such as:

- hyperactivity
- memory problems
- difficulty in coping or regulating self
- impulsivity
- temper tantrums
- poor sense of time
- lack of motivation

Temporal Lobe

- Emotional responses
- Hearing (auditory)
- Memory
- Learning
- Speech
- Motivation

Observed problems due to Temporal Lobe Brain Injury

- Difficulty in recognizing faces (**Prosopagnosia**)
- Difficulty in understanding spoken words (**Wernicke's Aphasia**)
- Difficulty with identification of, and verbalization about objects
- Inability to categorize objects (**Categorization**)
- Short term memory loss
- Interference with long term memory
- Right lobe damage – persistent talking
- Increased aggressive behavior
- Increased or decreased interest in sexual behavior
- Selective attention disturbance to what we see and hear

3. The Occipital Lobes (back of brain)

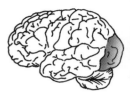

The **occipital lobes** (visual cortex) rest at the back of the cerebrum and are our vision center. Their location was no surprise to me. I always knew mothers had eyes in the back of their heads.

Damage to the occipital lobes may affect the a perceiving and understanding of visual information.

Occipital Lobe

- Controls vision
- Color recognition

Observed problems due to Occipital Lobe Brain Injury

- Production of hallucinations
- Visual illusions - inaccurately seeing objects
- Difficulty recognizing drawn objects
- Difficulties in reading and writing
- Difficulty in identifying colors (**Color Adnosia**)
- Defects in vision (**Visual Field Cuts**)
- Difficulty with locating objects in the environment
- Inability to recognize the movement of an object (**Movement Agnosia**)
- Word blindness - inability to recognize words

A developmental visual examination revealed a myriad of causes for Liz's difficulties.

4. The Parietal Lobes (center of brain)

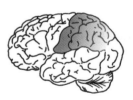

The **parietal lobes** (motor cortex) sits just behind the frontal lobe. They are responsible for our sensory interpretation by receiving and processing the sensations of touch (pain, heat, cold, pressure, size, shape, friction and texture). They provide the integration of these senses to help us understand a single concept. This is where the brain monitors our body's position in space so we know where we are and in what position, allowing us to manipulate our bodies and objects. It is through the processing in the parietal lobes we can direct our voluntary movements.

Parietal Lobe

- Cognition
- Information processing
- Pain and touch sensations (tactile)
- Spatial orientation
- Speech
- Language comprehension
- Visual perception

The parietal lobes integrate visual data from the occipital lobe and perceives 'where' images are. In combination with the temporal lobes they help us see quickly, understand and respond to a visual scene. They are closely linked to writing and speech fluency.

Observed Problems Due to Parietal Lobe Brain Injury

- Difficulty with drawing objects, uncoordinated gross/fine motorskills, distinguishing right from left, doing mathematics (**Dyscalculia**)
- Poor body scheme,lack of awareness of some body parts and/or surrounding space (**Apraxia**) difficulties in self care and social boundaries.
- Inability to attend to more than one object at a time, to name an object (**Anomia**), to locate words for writing (Agraphia), to focus visual attention
- Problems with reading (**Alexia**) decreased receptive language skills

The more I learned about neuroanatomy, the more I realized Liz had subtle global damage in her body (**metabolic**), brain (**nuero**) and central nervous system (**CNS**). And it occurred not just in utero but also during the early months of development in infancy.

The more I needed to know – the more I realized no one knew.

No two persons with prenatal brain injury are the same. Damage to developing cells is complex. Knowing where the damage is helps to choose medications, rehabilitation methods and academic strategies.

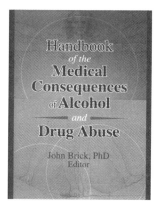

WHERE DID YOU SAY HIPPOPOTAMUS WAS? OUT ON A LIMB 'IC?

A number of significant processing centers that are important to our prenatally exposed individuals lie deep within the brain.

Limbic System

The deep limbic system (that includes the hypothalamus and thalamic structures) lies near the center of the brain and processes our sense of smell, stores highly charged emotional memories, and affects sleep and appetite cycles, moods, sexuality and bonding. It is about the size of a walnut, but it packs a wallop. It is the part of the older mammalian brain that allows animals to experience and express emotions. The deep limbic system adds spice to our life — both positive and negative. It provides the passion, emotion and desire to make something happen. This part of the brain is intimately connected with the prefrontal cortex and seems to act as a switching station between running on emotion (the deep limbic system) and rational thought and problem solving (cortex). When the limbic system is turned on, emotions tend to take over. When it is cooled down, more activation of the cortex is possible and the emotions are regulated with problem solving, planning and rational thoughts.

Liz operated directly out of her limbic system as she charged through our lives. Her responses to the world were immediate and spontaneous, without a thought of who or what was standing in front of her or the damage her behavior or reactions would cause. Could we connect the two?

Basal Ganglia

The area of the brain surrounding the limbic system is called the basal ganglia. It is a processing center and sometimes described as a braking system. It integrates feelings and movements (such as swinging your arms while walking), stores patterns of learned behaviors, programming from the past and is involved in the body's anxiety

The basal ganglia and hippocampus are known to be affected in some persons with prenatal exposure to alcohol.

levels. The system is complicated and small disturbances can cause unwanted movements, emotions or an absence of or difficulty with intended movements or emotions.

An individual with damage in the basal ganglia may have difficulty with inhibition, problems with planning, verbal fluency, working memory, perseveration, cognition and abstract thinking.

For example: *Sitting still is one of the highest levels of balance. You must put the brakes on all movements except those reflexes that maintain upright posture to sit still. You apply a brake to some postural reflexes and release the brake on voluntary movement to move. Liz had a long, long — where is she anyway? — way to go.*

Hippocampus

The hippocampus is involved in the complex forming, storing and sorting of memories. It receives partially processed information and packages it in a way that can be used as memory and then sends the package to a storage location in the brain. The hippocampus (shaped like a little seahorse) is the memory gateway that lies adjacent to the brain modules responsible for the generation of emotions: the limbic system. **It is not surprising that we learn best about those things we care about.**

Why did Liz react so angry to change? Then if she played a video game she laughed when a change occurred?

Teresa Kellerman provided a possible answer: There is no pattern in jumping through life. Video games are concrete and predictable. Real life is abstract and unpredictable. There is no way in a family home to keep the circumstances the same. The "characters" change (clothing, attitude, location, statements) and the "background" (counters, clutter, mail, laundry, dishes) changes. The phone rings, the mail is laid in a different spot, the dog barks, something is always different. And every action that the child takes produces a different reaction. In the game the guy always gets up after he is killed.

"Everyone has a reason for the way they behave, and that reaon is consistent, even though it is different from our perceived norm. We need to show respect, love and compassion to these children, rather than consider them to be 'problems' that need to be controlled."
                                                                    Roland Mann

3. ATTACHMENT

BRAIN NEW BEGINNINGS

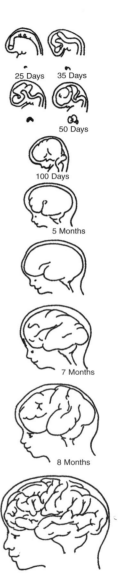

25 Days 35 Days

50 Days

100 Days

5 Months

7 Months

8 Months

Seven to twelve days after fertilization, mom and embryo begin to share blood supply. Fetal alcohol damage can occur any time now . . . mom has not missed a period.

Three weeks after conception the brain begins its lifelong journey of development. Genetics establishes the basic cells and wiring plan for connection between different regions of the brain. Experience fine-tunes those connections helping each person adapt to the particular environment they live in. Each is important in the development of a human being. Our brains are far more impressionable in early life than they are in later years. This has a good side and a bad side. It is good because young brains are open to learning and are positively affected by enriching influences. It is bad because young brains are more vulnerable to problems in their environment — malnutrition, toxicity, neglect, impoverishment, abuse, and abandonment.

One of the most sensitive periods in brain development occurs shortly after conception, when the neural tube is closing during the fourth week. If the tube fails to seal in the head end of the embryo, anencephaly (lack of cerebral cortex) results. If the tube fails to seal at its lower end, part of the spinal cord may develop outside the spine known as spina bifida. A simple dosage of 400

Our brains are continually reshaping themselves throughout our lifetimes — adapting and learning from our environment.

9 months at Birth
Illustrations adapted from Tom Prentiss, Scientific American (1979)

micrograms of Folate (folic acid) a day beginning one month **before** conception and continuing at least until the end of the first trimester can prevent 60% of neural tube defects from developing in the first place. Curious, I needed to know how much 400 micrograms was. Karl and I counted out 100 grains of table salt and measured them on his grain scale. We discovered 400 micrograms was equal to less than 2 grains of table salt! If something so seemingly insignificant can make such a difference, what did toxins like alcohol, tobacco, pesticides, solvents, drugs, lead, mercury, other chemicals or depravation of oxygen do to our children? What could viruses, infections or medications do to little developing brains?

Alcohol is often viewed as the 'good drug of choice' when compared with the 'bad street drugs'. Yet alcohol seems to have more devastating and longer lasting effects on children exposed prenatally than street drugs do. Some effects of cocaine tend to diminish over time, and long term damage may not be as severe as originally predicted. Test scores of children prenatally exposed to heroin show their physical and psychological development are usually within normal range. However, these illicit drugs are often used in combination with alcohol.[21]

A 12 oz. beer, a 12 oz. wine cooler, a 4 oz. wine or a 1.2 oz. of liquor contain the same alcohol content. An embryo or fetus does not have liver function or enzymes available to digest alcohol or process chemicals like an adult. One hour after a pregnant mother drinks alcohol fetal blood alcohol levels are higher than the mother's. An inebriated fetus is not getting adequate oxygen, is not exercising healthy developmental movements and is metabolically concentrating on survival instead of growth. Damage to early cell development damages future development of that cell.

Our brains mature from the tail (spinal column) to the head (cerebral cortex). In the fifth week of conception the synapses are already beginning to form in the fetus's spinal cord. By the sixth week, ultra sound has shown that these early neural connections provide opportunity for the first fetal movements — spontaneous curling and arching of

1st Trimester (Months 1-3)

- Arms bend
- Legs kick
- Head rotates
- Mouth opens, reflex yawn
- Toes curl
- Suck/swallow reflexes
- Reflex action to touch
- Reflex breathing motions

www.zerothree.org

21. US Department of Health and Human Services, 1994

Effect	ALCOHOL[1]	Amphetamines/[1] Methamphetamine[4,5]	Cocaine[1]	Marijuana[1]	Tobacco[1]	Heroin[1,2,3]
Pregnancy						
Spontaneous Abortion	■		■			
Increased Stillbirth	■	■	■			
At Birth						
Low Birth Weight	■	■	■	■	■	■
Facial Malformations	■					
Small Head Size	■		■			■
Respiratory Problems	■				■	■
Organ Damage	■	4,5				Increase Risk HIV and AIDS
Birth Defects	■	4,5				Increase Vision Hearing Problems
Infant						
Poor Feeding	■	4,5	■			■
Excessive Crying	■	4,5	■	■		■
Higher Risk SID			■	■	■	
Impaired Growth	■	4,5				
Sleeping Problems	■	4,5	■			■
Developmental Delays	■	4,5		■		
Child – Adult						
Intellectual Delays	■	4,5		■		Speech Difficulties
Inattention	■	4,5			■	■
Hyperactivity	■	4,5		■	■	■
Behavioral Problems	■	■				Mood Swings
Learning Problems	■	■				■

1. Chart designed with data from National Institute on Drug Abuse (2001) www.drugabuse.gov and www.babyparenting.about.com (2001) .
2. Harrison, D. *Drug Exposed Infants*, Growing Together. 4 (8): 1, 4
3. *Bruised Before Birth*, Amy Bullock, Elizabeth Grimes, and Joan McNamara
4. *Methamphetamine Use During Pregnancy* (10/2002), Affects development of baby's brain, spinal cord, heart and kidneys. North Dakota Dept. of Health, www.ndmch.com
5. Because Meth can be made with materials readily available in the US, it is sometimes called 'poor man's cocaine' Illinois Department of Public Health (2003) www.idph.state.il.us

I discovered embryology was not a subject to which a great deal of attention was given in medical school. This made me wonder if perhaps many unsolved medical mysteries had their roots in this period of greatest learning, most rapid growth, and greatest vulnerability. When the body is first learning how to be a body and the brain is learning the vast majority of what it will know about being a brain.   Julie Motz (1998)

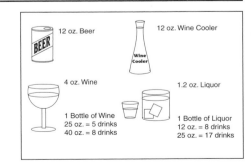

All have the same alcohol content.

What Kinds of Damage Can Occur From Alcohol Exposure In Utero?

Primary disabilities attributed to prenatal alcohol exposure
(Possible disabilities a child may be born with)

- Death
- Heart failure
- Heart defects
- Renal (liver) failure
- Height and weight deficiencies
- Asthma
- Immune system malfunctioning
- Mental retardation
- Developmental delay
- Developmental speech and language disorder
- Developmental coordination disorder
- Tremors
- Tourette's traits
- Autistic traits
- Deafness

- Central auditory processing disorder
- Loss of intellectual functioning (IQ)
- Little or no retained memory
- Severe loss of intellectual potential
- ADD/ADHD
- Attention deficit disorders
- Extreme impulsiveness
- Cerebral palsy
- Tight hamstrings
- Rigidity

- Complex seizure disorder
- Epilepsy
- Mild to severe vision problems
- Dyslexia
- Adaptive esotropia (cross-eyed)
- Serious maxilo-facial deformities
- Cleft palate
- Dental abnormalities
- Sensory Integration
- Hyper sensitivity
- Night terrors

- Sleep disorder
- Precocious puberty
- Sociopathic behavior
- Poor judgment
- Cognitive perseveration
- Higher than normal to dangerously high pain tolerance
- Little or no capacity for interpersonal empathy
- Little or no capacity for moral judgment
- Echolalia (repeat words sans understanding)

And I have to live with it

Sources: Malbin, Steissguth, Morse, Ritchie

the whole body. Two weeks later, at the eighth week, the limbs are able to move, and by the tenth week the tiny little fingers grasp. The developing baby can yawn, stretch, hiccup, swallow and suck its teeny thumb, toes or fingers. The fetus takes its first breath, though it may do so only once every 24 hours. Though most women can not feel it by the end of the first trimester, the fetus has varied ability to move. These early movements are the rudimentary beginning of sensory and motor development.

In the second trimester, critical reflexes develop including continuous breathing movements (rhythmic contractions of the diaphragm and chest muscles), and coordinated sucking and swallowing reflexes that are controlled by the brainstem. The eyelids can open and the taste buds function. The brainstem is mostly matured by the end of the second trimester, which is

2nd Trimester (Months 4-6)

- Arms, legs, fingers move in patterned reflex combinations
- Suck reflex matures
- Whole body reacts reflexively to touch by 14 weeks
- Taste buds began to form by 16-20 weeks

3rd Trimester (Months 7-9)

- Plays with fingers
- Breathes in rhythm
- More coordinated sucking and swallowing
- Sees light
- Hears sound

www.zerotothree.org

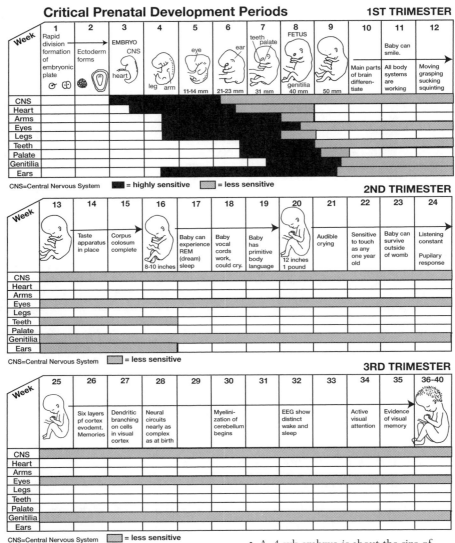

Critical Prenatal Development Periods

SOURCES:
1. Adapted from K.L. Moore, The Developing Human, W. B. Saunders Co. 1977
2. www.brainconnection.com (2001) Prenatal Brain Development

- A 4 wk embryo is about the size of President Roosevelt's ear on a dime.
- A 9 wk old fetus is about the size of a quarter.

when babies can begin to survive outside of the womb.

In the last trimester, the cerebrum (cerebral cortex) begins developing. At the time of birth it has only just begun to function. Premature babies show basic electrical activity in the sensory regions of the cerebral cortex (touch, vision, hearing) and in their primary motor region. Though primitive even at birth, late term fetuses are capable of simple forms of learn-

The period of early infant development is significant in laying a foundation for future intellectual, fine and gross motor skills.

Liz lived with us for four weeks without making eye contact. I prayed. I rocked. I sang. One day I sang Jesus Loves Me Liz's eyes lit up. Could her mother have sung this song to her in the womb?

ing, like habituating (decreasing their startle response) to a repeated auditory stimulus, such as a loud clap outside of the mother's womb. They may recognize familiar voices and common environmental sounds such as pets or music played or sung to them while in the womb.

Once in the world, every experience excites certain neural circuits and leaves others inactive. Anytime we make any sort of mental activity one of our ten billion neurons reaches out with its dendrite across the vast expanse of the brain connecting to another dendrite. The possibilities of creativity and connectivity are endless. Neural circuits process information through the flow of electricity like computer circuits. Circuits that are constantly turned on will be strengthened and those that are rarely excited will be pruned away. Each neuron may have hundreds of dendrites, but the dendrites are still relatively simple in design.

Pruning the dendrites streamlines a child's neural processing; making the remaining circuits work smoothly and efficiently. Without synaptic pruning a child could not walk, talk or even see properly. As neuroscientists say, "Cells that fire together, wire together." [22]

Adult dendrite

These neural connectors allow us to see, hear, feel, talk and move — they also allow us to love — or not to love. The caregiver snuggles, rocks, smells, gazes and coos at the infant. Our early beginnings set the stage for our future ability to form and maintain emotional relationships. This very vulnerable developmental period is critical in shaping the capacity to love and develop into a healthy, happy and productive person — to attach or not attach. Embraced in love the infant grows.

Newborn dendrite

Brain development is most sensitive in its earliest period. Children who are malnourished — deprived of calories, vitamins, minerals, fats and protein in their diets — between mid-pregnancy and two years of age do not grow adequately physically or mentally. Their brains may be smaller because of reduced dendrite and myelination growth, and the production of fewer glial. Inadequate brain growth is one explanation of why children who were malnourished in the womb and as infants often suffer lasting behavioral and cogni-

22. ZERO TO THREE Brain Wonders (www.zerotothree.org)

tive deficits – slower fine motor and language development, lower IQ and poorer academic performance.

At birth the brain of a newborn is still relatively small – one quarter the size of an adult brain – and only the lower levels of the nervous system are very well developed (the spinal cord and brain stem). Though the newborn's brain works sixteen times slower than an adult when processing information, it is growing at an incredible rate as new neural connections are made and others are pruned away. The speed of neural processing dramatically increases during infancy and childhood, as areas of the brain connect and myelinate.

Babies synchronize their heart beats to their mothers and fathers. They can see, hear, and move to the rhythm of the mother's voice in the first few minutes and hours of life. They prefer the human face to other shapes and can feel emotions from others.

During the first month of life, the number of connections or synapses increases from 50 trillion to 1 quadrillion. If an infants body grew comparably, the 8.5 lb. infant would weigh 70 lbs. at one month old.[23]

Newborns come into the world with a wide array of reflexes despite their apparent helplessness. These reflexes are an early indicator of nervous system functioning. The lower brain controls all of the newborn's behavior – grasping, kicking, crying, sleeping, rooting and feeding. These brain stem functions are reflexive to gain information about the environment, seek nourishment and protect the infant. Infant reflexes provide the basics for balance and muscle tone. They are the training wheels to develop gross and fine motor skills. The higher regions (limbic and cerebral cortex) are still quite primitive.

Immediately following birth, the newborn is given an Apgar score that evaluates the infant's heart, breathing, muscle tone, body color and reflexes. When doctors conduct reflex tests on a newborn they try to assess lower level functions. Are they equal on both sides of the body? Is the central nervous system functioning properly?

A brain of a newborn weighs:

350 gms - birth

500 gms - 3 months

660 gms - 6 months

925 gms - 12 months

The Reflex Chart (on the next page) lists some of these early reflexes. A child with a normal central nervous system **(CNS)** develops in an orderly, sequential manner from a being with mass movements of symmetrical synergies dominated by primitive reactions **(reflexes)** to a child with a highly refined and integrated CNS. The limbs become skilled

23. www, brainconnection.com

Reflexes Present at Birth:

Basic Survival Reflexes – Seek nourishment and protection

Reflex	Stimulation	Response	Development Pattern
Babinski	Stroke sole of foot	Twist foot, toes extend upward	Disappears 9 month-1 year
Palmer Grasp	Stroke palm	Fingers curl, grasps tightly	Weakens after 3 months
Plantar Grasp	Stroke ball of foot	Toes curl, grasps tightly	Disappears after 1 year
Moro	Sudden head lowering	Arms, legs extend, clench fist	Disappears after 6 months
Startle	Loud noise, light change	Arms, legs extend, clench fist	Disappears after 3-4 months
Rooting	Cheek stroked	Turn in that direction, opens mouth begins sucking	Disappears after 3-4 months
Sucking	Touch mouth	Sucks	
Swimming	Lift prone position	Makes coordinated swimming movements, head up, leg up	Disappears after 6 - 7 months
Tonic Neck	Infant placed on back	Forms fist and makes fencer pose	Disappears after 2 - 4 months

Permanent Reflexes – Persist through adulthood

Reflex	Stimulation	Response	Development Pattern
Blinking	Flash of light puff of air	Close both eyes	Permanent
	Bright light	Close both eyes	Permanent
Cough	Airway stimulated		Permanent
Sneeze	Nasal passages irritated		Permanent
Gag	Throat or back of mouth stimulated		Permanent
Yawn	Needs additional oxygen		Permanent

Postural Reflexes – Provide maintenance of upright position

Parachute Reflex: occurs in a slightly older infant – if appearing to fall, infant will extend arms as if to break fall.

Step Reflex: stepping motions when foot touches hard surface

Crawling Reflex: crawling motions when placed on abdomen

Neck / Body Righting: The head will always attempt to right itself to nose vertical, eyes and mouth horizontal no matter what position the child's body is placed.

tools for manipulation of activities as they are released from their early functions of support.[24]

Early evaluation and development of these reflexes is important. Babies with compromised reflexive systems need every opportunity to achieve more normal sensory-motor skills before serious maladaptations occur.

An infant gains control over body and body movements as primitive reflexes are replaced with postural reflexes. The postural reflexes are regulated by the cerebellum, which acts as a tape recorder, recording every movement. Movements are then played back and adjusted to meet the demands of the task being performed. A child with cerebral palsy may never make the

24. Florentine, Mary R. Mus.B., O.T.R., F.A.O.T.A., *A Basis for Sensorimotor Development – Normal and Abnormal, The Influences of Primitive Postural Reflexes on the Development and Distribution of Tone.* (1981) Charles Thomas, IL

Four patterns of movement basic components:

- head control
- reaching (increased extensor tone)
- turning (rotate body on access)
- balance (equilibrium) reactions

transition from primitive to postural reflexes and movements remain random and uncontrolled. To this extent we are all born mildly cerebral palsied, but in the early months of life we rapidly gain control of the primitive reflexes, and lay the foundations for later voluntary movement.[25]

Preprogrammed into the brain stem, the Moro reflex is an involuntarty panic response to protect the newborn. It causes an immediate release of adrenaline and cortisol — the flight/fight hormones. When the startle reflex fails to develop into the adult response, the developing child will be on 'startle alert', easily distracted by sights, sounds, touches and movement. Trigger temper reactions and mood swings are common, change is very challenging. Once transformed into the adult startle reflex, the child uses eyes and ears to locate threats and make intellectual decisions chosing to be frightened or not. The adult startle reflex is a rapid intake of breath, blink, raise the shoulders and then locate the source. Liz remained locked in the infant startle reflex and melted down before she located the source of danger. Like a flick on a row of standing dominoes, her metabolic response wasn't the only siren that reacted. Her body prepared for danger, her pupils remained dilated and her chemical defense production of adrenaline and cortisol went to work. Friends nick-named her 'Indy 500 Race Car' from her noise as she revved up.

Liz's defense system remained stuck on alert, not progressing to the adult response. Her body struggled to build immunity to allergens, it was busy surviving. Sudden changes in outdoor lighting and fluorescent light vibration produced feelings of anxiety. She was sensitive and reacting to foods, lights and chemicals. After years of ignorance on our part it was time to remediate.

Retained primitive reflexes affect a child's sensory perceptions, causing the child to be **hypersensitive** (overly) in some areas and **hyposensitive** (under) in others. Conceptualization of certain movements may be impaired not just in the limbs, but in eye functioning, visual perception, balance and processing auditory information making it difficult to cope with stress and often overreact.[26]

25.-26. The Institute for Neuro-Physiological Psychology (www.inpp.org.uk)

It is currently believed that primary reflexes encourage movement to allow progress to the next stage. Primary reflexes have to emerge to do their job and then inhibit. If something stops this from happening the body adopts compensatory behaviors to cope.

Reflex remediation is accomplished by:

1) Normalizing tone
2) Changing abnormal patterns of
   movement by
      a) Integrating primitive responses
      b) Enhancing higher reactions
      c) Facilitating sequential development[27]

"Mom, I got pushed skating. I put my hands in front of myself. Is that bad?" Liz asked.
"No, Liz that's perfect. Your hands help protect you.
Way to go!"

Liz was 15 years old when she experienced her first parachute reflex (placing her hands in front of her to protect herself from falling).

A newborn's first developmental tasks are to attach, learn to self regulate and show interest in the surrounding environment. A calm, happy infant is a developing infant. The infant does this by showing interest in the caregiver and different sensations. For most infants, a caregiver can calm the baby out of distress within twenty minutes and the infant can remain calm and focused for up to two minutes.[28]

MEMORIES OF THE PAST

Liz's hair stood up like a little Einstein.
I pondered whimsically if her brains were contributing to the chaos of her hair or perhaps her hair was a picture of her brain wiring.

We were told to love her. With enough love Liz could overcome her traumatic beginning. In the first five months of life Liz was labeled a failure-to-thrive, unattached baby. She had already lived in four placements. Much of her critical early development was not established. Child development books, normal parenting and care giving strategies did not work. We didn't know we needed professional developmental support. We didn't know what was wrong.

27. Florentine, Mary R. Mus.B., O.T.R., F.A.O.T.A., *A Basis for Sensorimotor Development – Normal and Abnormal, The Influences of Primitive Postural Reflexes on the Development and Distribution of Tone.* (1981) Charles Thomas, IL
28. Greenspan, Stanley, *Building Healthy Minds, The Six Experiences that Create Intelligence and Emotional Growth in babies and Young Children* (1999)

Memories were burned into her **amalgyma** (a little almond shaped part in the brain pronounced 'uh mig duh luh') of hunger and abandonment as her immediate reference files. Even at seventeen, common everyday situations are acted upon without thinking. Her responses to food, relationships and security issue continue to cause trouble in social situations. In some cases her responses are more dangerous than the original danger.

We have separate systems for forming our unconscious and our conscious emotional memories. Whenever you experience something that is frightening it is registered as a conscious memory in the **hippocampus** (a little seahorse shaped part in the brain) and related cortex areas. At the same time it is registered as an unconscious memory in the **amygdala** and it's various parts, including the adrenal gland (which produces our adrenaline). These two memory systems work together.

The amygdala develops before the hippocampus which is not fully developed until about two years old. Children who experience trauma between birth and 34 months old usually have no conscious memory of the experience. That is why traumatic early life experiences can trigger fear and anxiety and be acted upon so intensely years later with no memory of the experience.

When a frightening event occurs again the conscious remembers and the unconscious will release adrenaline to prepare the body for danger. Adrenaline enters the body quickly and prepares all body parts for rapid flight or fight, producing feelings of anxiety or fear. In addition, cortisol is released to help the body build up its energy resources to deal with stressful situations. The hippocampus helps to regulate how cortisol is released. The amygdala asks for the cortisol delivery to 'speed up', the hippocampus asks for it to 'slow down.' This allows the stress hormone to be matched with the demands of a stressful situation. Abnormal levels of cortisol can cause changes in the hippocampus affecting memory and learning. If the stress lasts too long the hippocampus can be damaged.

It seems memory – however rudimentary precedes consciousness, and not the other way around. It can be argued that memories and the sense of continuity between them – are the necessary building blocks for any permanent sense of self.

Dennis O'Brien

LOVE DOESN'T CONQUER ALL

The best toy we can give to a child is an invested, caring adult. Someone to pay attention, play and engage the child with words, songs, touch, eye contact and smiles.

Liz floated from home-to-home during her first five months of life. It would be years of outpouring of love, attention and care before we plugged enough holes in Liz's leaky boat for her to hold love in her own heart. We beat down brick walls trying to help her. Until we got her diagnosis of brain injury, Liz lived traumatically. We could not break through until we began rebuilding early developmental pieces.

Our home atmosphere of love, patience, ordered activities and understanding were the elements we used to reach baby Liz, but it was the repetitive, consistent and predictable experiences day-after-day that allowed her to grow.

A baby cries to meet a need. It is the very basic form of communication. Babies learn other ways to communicate. They must learn sounds, facial gestures and eventually words. This kind of learning relies on people who know and understand the baby. It is their reaction to the baby that encourages the baby to try again and again. The caregiver provides a sense of calm, consistency and safety for the infant by being receptive, attentive, attuned, predictable and consistent in care. The child is safe, fed, protected and comforted. The infant responds by snuggling, babbling, smiling, sucking and clinging to the caregiver. Both the infant and the caregiver derive pleasure from these exchanges. The child thrives, plays and grows in this environment and this interplay between caregivers and a child causes them to 'fall in love'. Sensitive, responsive parenting

Liz's birth mother died when Liz was two-months-old. The day of her death she held baby Liz, told the foster mom that she knew a mother waited for 'her' baby and to keep her baby safe for the new family. She gave the foster mom a gift to give to Liz when she joined her new family. Six weeks after Liz moved into our home the gift was delivered – a hand crocheted baby blanket and a teddy bear that said Jesus Loves Me.

with unconditional positive regard for the infant is rewarded with an '**attunement**' of playful two-way communication. This connection is deeply tied to an infant's mind, body and emotions.

Most babies are born with the ability to encourage a communicating relationship from others. Our face is the human instrument of social communication. Infants and small children learn to communicate through voices and faces. Videos, cassettes and flashcards cannot replace our body language in child development. Smiles, soft caresses, tone of voice, sparkling eyes, facial gestures, and head movements communicate meaning to children who have no or limited vocabularies. Children learn to relate, be relational and rational through people experiences.

Children learn best when they are relaxed, rested, healthy, fed, not thirsty or overwhelmed. Liz was easily pushed over the edge into a state of distress. Childhood play was over stimulating and confusing to her. My husband struggled to reach hypersensitive who hated piggyback rides and bouncing in the air. Baby games like Peek-a-boo were overstimulating. It took twelve years before he received his first hug from Liz.

Sensory deprivation alters, delays or prevents learning. Stimulation and healthy touch are extremely important to help brain injured children. Liz tolerated neither. The child must establish meaningful input, active participation and repetitive experiences to establish learning and change within the central nervous system. Learning is delayed if the baby is faced with chaotic or multiple caregivers who do not intimately know – are attuned to – the baby's responses.

When babies are first separated from that special person, they protest to get their lost person back. Sooner or later the second stage of despair sets in. The child becomes apathetic and withdrawn. Eventually detachment develops

A newborn's sensitivity to touch is well developed at birth. The child's skin is so receptive that the brain registers it at the slightest pressure. The ability to calm is benefited from the comfort of a caregiver's touch, gentle motion, soothing voice, soft music, swaddling and being allowed to suck. When the child feels soothed, the brain produces substances to calm and reduce stress. The child should take less time to calm as it matures. Liz was still taking between 45 minutes and two hours to calm down even at age two, three and thirteen.

Liz, why are you sucking your thumb? You never sucked it as a baby. "I'm hungry and I can either talk and be obnoxious, jump around, fight or suck my thumb. I found out my thumb makes me calmer, so I use it."

when the special person returns, there may be complete absence of attachment behavior. Some call this a settling-in time and discourage parental visits
to avoid upsetting the child.

Humans thrive on intimacy beginning at conception. A baby needs to
be with someone special to best develop. Research shows in human and animal
studies that bonding between infants and caregivers changes the brain.
Experience will now play a heavy role in the parts of a baby's brain that grow
and the parts that don't. Poor treatment of a baby may lead to impairment of
intelligence, trust and compassion which can enable a child to survive and
overcome complex family circumstances and later life difficulties.

The time had come for us to add another child – David.

Play is Vital

Healthy play and exploration grow healthy brains. Play is the fuel. The
experiences, opportunities and environments we provide our children help
determine their strengths and vulnerabilities. They flourish in rich environments. On the other hand, an emotionally or cognitively impoverished, chaotic
or violent environment or series of experiences represses the child's potential.

David lived with us for ten wonderful baby months. Diagnosed with FAS at birth, he was placed in our foster home at eight-months-old. He was less emotionally fragmented than Liz. He cuddled. We could sooth him. He adored Karl. The two were inseparable. Then as foster children often do…David moved …

Liz's early beginnings in our home included
hours of riding under my oversized sweatshirt in a
snuggle sack to limit sensory overload, rocking, taking
warm baths on my tummy, gentle infant massage and
singing. Our second floor became a huge activity center where Liz could safely grow, explore and play.

My grandmother an early childhood development educator, watched Liz grow. She offered her
weathered college books. We discovered the work of
Friedrich Froebel and Mother Play – a lost art of gentle finger plays we used to reach, teach and talk to Liz.
Grandma's 1895 textbooks offered us a different
viewpoint from the fast paced 1990's.

One hundred years later we quietly and slowly
enraptured Liz into the world around her. Froebel's

gentle *19th Century Mother Plays* provided a backdrop of play Liz comprehended and enjoyed. This translation read by us almost 200 years later helped unlock Liz's mind. Our fingers became scampering squirrels, hopping bunnies and flying robins.

David joined our family as a foster child, at eight months. His cute facial features proclaimed FAS. A stroke as an infant paralyzed one side. He arrived with thrush, an ear infection and crossed eyes. Looking back, his paralysis, infections, crossed eyes and diagnosis were a gift to help his brain develop. Nurse Nancy, Karl, Liz and I doted on him with play therapy and laugher. We strengthened his weak side with swimming, crawling and climbing. We played eye rolling and listening games.

Unlike Liz, David was gleeful and cuddly. He laughed heartily encouraging laughter in Liz. At fifteen months, he stood up and ran as though he had never been paralyzed. Unknowingly we had remediated many of his early reflexes and developmental delays through play stimulation. At seventeen months, he assembled wooden puzzles with Liz with both hands and he spoke 25 discernable words. His world revolved around three large doggies, his wonderful sister he called Apple, a woolly-rough housing daddy and the only mommy he could remember.

Then, as foster children do, he moved on — into another home with a wonderful foster mother who would eventually adopt him. His development stopped. He quit speaking. He quit playing. It didn't matter how loving his new mother was. David was lost in the space of his mind.

Dr. Bruce Perry, M.D., PhD, a leading expert on violence prevention, brain development and children in crisis, has identified six core strengths that children need to be humane. A child who can form and maintain healthy emotional relationships; self-regulate; join and contribute to a group; be aware, tolerant and respectful of self and others will be more resourceful, socially successful and resilient. My two little warriors lacked the first step of attachment. How would they achieve a future of happiness, health and productivity as they thrashed through life?

DAY ONE: *"I have a daddy!" David announced to his foster mother at four. "Who, David?" she asked. "My daddy rubs oil on my body," replied David ending the conversation.*

DAY TWO: *"I have a daddy!" David, age four, announced to his foster mother. "Who, David?" she asked. "My daddy and I watch birds," replied David, ending the conversation.*

Biophyisicist Herman Epstein discovered that periods of brain growth occur during intensive spurts indicated by increased skull size and brain weight. Though each child's brain is different, the growth of the brain tends to follow a similar pattern in about 90 percent of human population. During these brain growth cycles, different areas of the brain connect and grow, bringing new levels of potential ability. These brain growth spurts result from increased neuron networking, development of blood vessels to bring more oxygen to the brain, the refinement of body to brain connections through spinal cord motor fibers, the growth of supportive glial cells, and the important production of myelin. Each growth spurt is followed by a plateau period of virtually no growth in the brain. These periods of brain growth follow development steps a child learns and masters.[28]

ANOTHER DAY: *"I have a daddy!" David again announced to his foster mother "Who, David?" she asked. "Karl who lives with Jodee," replied David.*

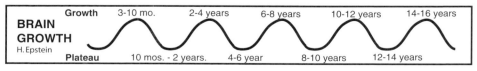

28. Brewer, Chris and Campbell, Don, *Rhythms of Learning, Creative Tools for Developing Lifelong Skills* (1991) Zephyr Press

Were Liz's and Dave's brain growth cycles altered due to early neglect and prenatal exposure? Had abandonment issues also affected their brain growth? If so, could we jump on a brain growth spurt and remediate lower connections? Could we ride smoothly on a plateau and reinforce previous learned materials preparing the way for future and further neural connections?

Brain injury is in the brain. Brain dysorganization is in the whole central nervous system. Treatment must either create function where none exists, or improve delayed or inhibited function. Normal functional activity — breathing, eating, walking, talking, playing, and academics — stimulates the brain. Somehow I would learn to teach functional activity. "Where there is a will, there is a way." Somewhere there was a path, a way to help these children. Yes, there was brain damage, but parts of each child's brain seemed to function better than a normal child. Perhaps somewhere between the damage and the operating pieces an area was set on idle, waiting to be turned on. I needed to find the ignition keys.

Karl, Nancy and I began with what we knew of Dave's and Liz's present metabolism and neurological issues. It was no use to dwell on the past. There would be no answers forthcoming regarding prenatal exposure, timing or dosages. We would never know what it was like to be the embryo, fetus or infant. We had limited genetic information or family history. We did have love, faith, creativity and energy. That would have to be enough.

For Liz it was thirteen years before she had the opportunity for her brain to have new beginnings. For David it was eight years.

We questioned?

1. Could the journey we were about to embark on prevent secondary disabilities (page 12) persons with FASD often face?

2. Could we avoid disrupted school experiences, trouble with the law or worse yet confinement?

3. Could Liz learn and remember skills for self-sufficiency to maintain medical care, plan meals and leisure time, use public transportation, make decisions, manage money and time as adults?

4. Could Liz become a good employee and manage frustration, anger and people skills at work?

It was worth a fight for attainment.

Frustration Balls and Holes in the Wall

David rejoined our family at eight-years-old to live with us and home-school to enable him to revisit his foster care past, grow emotionally and move forward in his loving new adoptive family. Together we carefully orchestrated a new healthy transfer for attachment repair. His incredible foster mother had adopted and loved him along with his four siblings. He could not reciprocate that love. School was difficult. Therapists were not making the progress hoped for. David's adoptive mom, called and asked if Karl and I would consider homeschooling David along with Liz. Dave would be our new exchange student. He was overjoyed. In his mind, he was coming home. In my mind, I wondered if homeschooling Liz who had her own behavior and academic problems along with David who had FASD **(fetal alcohol spectrum disorder)** was a crazy idea. It had been seven years since David had lived with our family.

He had control issues and rage along with academic and fetal alcohol related issues. Karl's eyes met mine and we knew the answer. We had rolled up our sleeves to love a lopsided baby boy; we would roll them up again to love the rage filled, eight-year-old.

> *"I love you too much, too, David."*
>
> *Jodee*

The popular term for Dave's behavior is **reactive attachment disorder** (RAD). Dave fluctuated between episodes of rage and sadness. Dave's brain, in it's ruptured emotional state, lost its ability for rational thinking, response flexibility and self-reflection. His behavior was bizarre and compounded with brain damage. When reacting to overwhelming arousal or stress (anxiety, worry, fear, sadness, anger and who knows what else) Dave was internally and interpersonally unable to function or reg-

The book Dave wrote to help him in his healing process.

ulate himself. At one end of the spectrum he was hyperactive – running, hitting, name-calling or screaming – at the other end of the spectrum he was reclusive and avoided overtures of human connection. His levels of dysregulation were high. His degree of rejection of his adoptive mom was alarming. Even the most patient and secure parent would suffer in trying to parent Dave. She is a super mom, but even 'Supermom' couldn't do it. It appeared to hopeless.

Out came the legos and construction sets as his baby room transformed again from our teen girl space into Dave's space. "Mom, you know what?" Dave asked. He immediately called me mom; I did not encourage or discourage how he addressed me. This was his healing time. Hopefully his soul could heal, he could learn to love again and return home.

"No, Dave, what?" I answered.

"My Thomas the Airplane used to live right there. Do I still have him? My bed used to be right there. I had puppy dog sheets. Remember mom?"

Dave and Liz are ten second kids in a one second world. Processing can take so long that by the time they know what is going on or what to do, the window of opportunity is closed.

"I hate you, you can't make me!" Dave sat on my lap as we worked on subtraction.

"No, I can't make you, Dave. Only you can make you. Let's go back and practice some addition and see how much you already know," I offered.

"Yes, Dave, I remember. How do you remember?" I asked.

"My baby dreams mom. My baby dreams!" Dave exclaimed.

"Dave, what are baby dreams?" I asked.

"Well every night I close my eyes, get out my baby dreams and remember everything. Mom, no one can take them away from me, no one," Dave proudly stated.

"How, often do you have your baby dreams, Dave?"

"Every night, mom, every night for seven years!" Dave beamed, as I opened the door to the linen closet to get bedding.

"Mom, mom! Here it is! My puppy sheet, just as I remember! My puppy sheet!" Dave jumped up and down as he wrapped himself around in his memories and for the next two months where ever he went the puppy sheet joined him.

Schooling Liz and Dave as a dynamic duo was more than I bargained for. The brother/sister relationship established as babies had remained. Liz and Dave felt free when they were together. Both children needed emotional and academic remediation. Hand-in-hand they pulled and pushed each other along their new bumpy road to healing. With Liz, we had always expe-

"My name's not Dave, mom. It's Joe. It's Joe Kulp," Dave said determinedly.

"That can be your nickname if you want, but your name is still Dave on your birth certificate," I answered. "I will still call you Dave because I like that name."

Tell me and I'll forget.
Show me and I'll be
more interested.
Involve me and I'll
remember

rienced growth in the essence of play – when her heart was free of anxiety and her mind was free to learn. I hoped to reach David the same way – through props he loved and enjoyed. With laughter and silliness, I would coax Dave wrapped in his puppy sheet out of his stupor and melancholy demeanor.

Young children learn best with their bodies **(kines-thetic)** in short bursts of energy with segments of calm. They learn by doing – moving, rolling, crawling, shaking, jumping, wiggling and running. That is why preschool and kindergarten programs are designed to allow learners to move around, stand while doing tasks and memorize materials while walking, talking and listening to music or rhythm. This was the strategy I used to reach Dave.

Writing was a painful for both children. Neither child could sit still. They struggled sitting straight and holding their posture for the duration of writing a word.

We used full body experience **(gross motor)** to access coordination **(fine motor)** skills with Dave's hands. We learned manuscript writing by engaging in box car races around tracks shaped like letters **(phonograms)**. We used finger play to develop fine motor and eye-hand coordination with lids, screwdrivers, nuts, bolts, erector sets and legos. Playing let Dave discover how his hands and fingers work without being stressed to write.

Play was essential in teaching Dave. We used our whole bodies to learn to make letters. We ran letter races on tape, in piles of leaves and in snow.

We worked with nuts, bolts, clothespins, screws and screwdrivers. We opened and closed our hands hundreds of times. Finally we grabbed the nasty pencil. We could read what Dave wrote.

Dave had trouble separating the two sides of the hand. There is a mobile side of the hand – thumb, index, middle finger – and a stationary side of the hand – pinky and ring finger. We discovered two rubber bands looped together with one around Dave's wrist and one loop around the pencil helped his pencil direction. We practiced playing Dr. Spock from StarTrek by separating our middle and ring finger to make a 'V', sending orders with "Aye, Aye, Captain Kirk." We made circles with our thumbs, We used golf scoring pencils and pencil adapters. We used a balance eagle to fly on the eraser as we drew lines. We drew and played before we wrote. (See additional information on writing on page 142.)

How could I reach them? *Dave and Liz were impossible to teach. I decided to video tape and let them watch themselves. No one would believe the reality of the behaviors I was experiencing. They were too bizarre to make up.*

Every word and letter was an accomplishment. Each day we began with three-dozen nicely sharpened pencils. There was plenty of opportunities to write, not all of it needed to be on paper. We wrote in the sand or snow with our hands and feet. We wrote on dusty furniture, mom's dirty car, frost on windows and condensation on mirrors. We wrote on white boards in a vertical position. We wrote lying down. We wrote in the air and played tic-tac-toe with Xs and Os. We wrote upside down with paper taped underneath the chair. We used lead pencils and colored pencils and water color pencils. Only a few pencils without broken tips remained at noon. I did not understand at that point retained reflexes – Palmer Grasp and Asymetrical Tonic Neck Reflex may hold them back.

We tried a clear ruler and magnifiers. Liz did not see the spaces between the words and tracking letters on a page. A page of letters looked like a pattern, no single word stood out. Then when she finally captured an individual word the space to the next word was an unjumpable chasm – erasing what she read. She put her finger at the end of the first word and made a little tick mark where she would start the first letter of the next word.

How do you teach a child with FASD? I devoured every book I could find. Dave's label pointed me in a direction to seek information and journey into the concept of his disability. I was interested however in his abilities. Treating the label instead of respecting the individual would only make matters worse and I could easily overlook his sense of humor, personal skills and gifts. I could lose his beauty in the quagmire referred to as prenatal exposure to alcohol brain damage diagnosed FASD.

Sonny, the bird sat perched on my shoulders. The phone rang. I ran to get it and slipped on water someone had spilled on the floor. The video camera was recording. Sonny squawked and flew toward the camera. It was a slow motion fall, as my head kerplunked on the kitchen tile. I closed my eyes and lay very still, wondering why I ever believed I could do this. Lying very still I heard a little voice, "Do you think we finally killed her Liz, she's not moving. Maybe we killed her." It was priceless, I had to giggle and open my eyes.

I felt inadequate to meet David's needs. I needed to discover his learning style, his interests and passions and respect them. I loved him as my own child. Love would have to be step one. I had danced with alcoholism as a child in my birth family. I understood inebriated behavior. Could I use my experience as an adult child of alcoholics to help Dave grow? His behavior often seemed intoxicated to me.

"Mom, can I snip this little piece of hair?" Liz asked holding a straggly bang I had been thinking about cutting.

The more I read, the more I questioned if Liz also had been exposed prenatally. Her behavior, her academics and her motor issues were red flags she may have brain damage like Dave. I could not accept that and determined we were dealing only with attachment issues and early neglect. Liz was fine! I was still sure we could love and teach her problems away. Meanwhile I had to learn how to teach Dave.

"Ok, Liz." What was I thinking? Liz turned the scissors the wrong direction and took off a two inch hunk of hair next to my scalp. I had always wondered what I would look like in short, really short hair. Now was my chance.

Dave reprocessed his toddler years and I reintroduced him to preschool. Liz and Dave spent hours playing, laughing and talking. Dave was growing. He was learning to love. Both children were dramatic. Dave loved cars. Liz loved Barbies. We made historic costumes for Barbies and GI Joes and reenacted history lessons. We flew airplanes into fractional hangars. We divided the hangar into two rooms and four bays — a full hanger equaled a 'whole' or 'one' hangar. It's four sections were quarters where four airplanes lived. Toy airplanes landed on math sheets and flew in and out of our airport.

I wanted to scream, "Don't you care about anything or anybody." Years later I understood that until a child has imagination they are unable to put themselves into the shoes of another.

Many brain systems must be in place in order to listen attentively. Children progress academically from body movement **(kinesthetic learning)** in kindergarten to hands-on **(tactile learning)** learning in first grade. By second or third grade children progress into visual academics **(visual learning)** as they process more information through pictures and reading. Finally, students move on in development of their auditory learning and enjoy listening and discussing issues. Liz's tactile defensiveness prevented her from beginning step one.

Liz and Dave appeared to use their auditory systems to learn, but not by listening and discussing. Neither of them carried on conversations with other people. They were 'own voice' learners and learned by hearing themselves talk. Their mental dialogues were often out of sync with the academics we were engaged in. 'Own voice' learning allowed me to know what they were thinking. I actively engaged and routed them to learn through their interests.

"Liz, what happened to the light switch?" I asked.

"It wouldn't turn on, so I hit it to make it go," Liz answered.

"Did it work?" I asked.

"No, that's how we got the hole in the wall," Liz replied. Nothing was sacred to my home improvement kids.

We visited Sea World. How did they train Shamu? No orca did a back flip in the ocean, and yet in every Sea World a different orca did. If orcas could learn to do back flips – Dave could learn to write and do math without raging. Liz could learn to read without throwing the books.

Some days it seemed like we had an animal show with the critters and kids in our home. Neither Liz nor Dave were bad children. Something inside of them just kept getting in the way of who they wanted to be – maybe I could teach them like Shamu. Both children were kind. They wanted to be good. Their combined bizarre behavior frustrated me. Their animal style reactions to life must have a reason.

KILLER TACTICS FOR LOVING RESULTS

SeaWorld's philosophy is there are no bad pupils, only bad trainers. When you pay up to half a million dollars for an animal, you learn to teach it. Period. Well Dave and Liz were worth millions to me.

Orcas learn by being rewarded for taking tiny, very tiny, steps toward a concrete goal **(operant conditioning)**. The trainer knows what goal is to be accomplished and breaks the task down to its most simplistic form (task analysis). A back flip out of the water begins with the whale swimming over a rope lying on the bottom of the pool.

Learning is accomplished when the orca is unstressed and well rested, when it is fed and in happy.

Orca training is accomplished by following a set of eight basic training rules enhanced with rewards, praise and enthusiasm:[30]

1. The trainer figures out what clear-cut goal is to be accomplished.
2. The trainer breaks the goal into miniature goals so the orca has a clear path to get to the goal.
3. The trainer is positive and happy when working with the whale.
4. The trainer rewards the whale each time it reaches or begins to perform the sequence of reaching the goal.
5. The trainer ignores mistakes and focuses on success.
6. The trainer slowly increases the expectations for performance and randomly rewards about a third of the time on material learned.
7. The trainer gives rewards immediately for approximations of the new next step.
8. The trainer repeats the process, adding step after step to each performance of miniature goals.

We wrote our learning goals and posted them in plain view. I would learn to teach, Dave learn to write letters and Liz learn to spell. I purchased small prizes. Tiny doll shoes and shirts were wrapped in hot pink paper. Lego and erector set parts wrapped in red. Their random rewards ranged from actively noticing their accomplishments with smiles and loud hurrahs to a wrapped present. Mom remained in control.

Dave's forlornly moaned, "Mom, I feel yucky."

"Come here Dave. Snuggle in my lap. Let's see what we can do about the yucky." Dave snuggled in, wrapped in his beloved puppy sheet. "I know what's wrong, Dave! You're 'love batteries' are low. Let's charge them up!" I smiled. Dave smiled back as I cuddled him and his sheet. "Dave, you and I have to sit really still. We'll put the love back into us by starting to suck it up with our tip-toes. Love batteries is a quieting, cuddle time. Sometimes mom need the recharge

"I got rid of my buts. I worked hard at noticing something each child was doing well, I quit finishing my sentence with but you... discounting the child's accomplishment."

"I designed planned successes. They would succeed no matter what they did. And I incorporated planned failures, so that I was in control of the outcome to help the behavior response."

30. Visit www.seaworld.org/AskShamu/training.html to learn more on operant conditioning.

One difference between reactive attachment disorder (RAD) and simply attachment disorder seemed to be when I finally felt so frustrated I blew up, David got a sneaky little smile like he had won a prize. I knew why they called it reactive. I was the one who reacted.

too."

We closed our eyes and snuggled in the puppy sheet. "Dave, do you have any love in those old stinky toes of yours?" I asked. He slowly shook his head yes. "Well, I can feel the love going up my feet, can you?" His head nodded again. We remained still as the love moved from our toes to our feet, up our ankles and shins and into our knees. Dave was feeling lighter. "Dave, you know what? When that love gets past our heart and pops out the top of our head, we can let go and share it with others. You want to try and get it to pop out of our heads." Dave shook his head with a smile and a quiet yes. The spark was returning to his eyes. He was ready to face the world.

"Mom!" Dave wailed on another day, tears streamed down his cheeks. "I can't love anyone ever. I can't mom. I can't!"

"Come and snuggle Dave. Why can't you love anyone?" I asked.

"I, I, I, can't because of the glump. The glump has my love. It won't let me love! Not even my mom!" Dave sobbed, finally thinking of his adoptive mom and family.

"What's a glump, Dave?" I asked

"It's black and yucky! It lives on my heart. It won't let me love anyone, not ever," Dave sobbed.

"Whoa, buddy, we better get that glump thing off there. I've got an idea," I offered, grabbing a box of crayons and a piece of white paper and drawing a big red heart. "Let's take out all the pink and red crayons and color your heart." Dave trembled as he shook his head. Together we carefully colored his beautiful heart

Children with reactive attachment disorder (RAD) need to maintain control of everyone and their environment. It's survival.

healthy hues of reds and pinks. "Well, the glump's not on your heart we just colored. Is it gone from your tummy yet?" I asked.

"NO! NO! It's not!" Dave wailed as I grabbed a sheet of tracing paper and laid it on top of his beautiful red heart.

"What color is this glump Dave?" I asked.

"Black!" Dave yelled.

"Well, here's the black crayon. You can color that glump right OUT of your heart." I gave Dave the crayon. Dave grunted and snarled and scribbled ugly black lines all over the tracing paper. He scribbled until he was exhausted. "Boy, that looks nasty. I'm glad it's off your heart, Dave," I pulled the glump up off his beautiful red heart, still fresh and clean and pretty on his white paper. "What should we do with this ugly glump thing?" I grimaced, pinching my nose and holding the glump high in the air.

Traditional holding therapy would not work with either Dave or Liz. They needed secure loving cuddling, not restraint. Restraint inflicted more stress, terror and bizarre behaviors. My imposed environmental structure was their safety net for growing and learning to love. My arms for Dave became his life preserver.

"I'm going to crumple him!" Dave said with a spark and proceeded to crush the glump into a ball.

"Do you want to burn him in the wood stove?" I asked.

"I can't, Mom! I might need him. We can't let him get out. What can we do?" Dave was perplexed holding the crumbled glump tightly.

I rushed down to my husband's workshop and grabbed some yellow electrical tape. "Wrap him up in sunshine Dave. We'll pray to Jesus to keep you safe from him. Keep him in that ball; not on your heart."

Dave fervently wrapped the whole roll of tape around the glump, transforming it into a bright yellow ball. "Mom, can I keep him in the freezer? Then if I get mad or feel him again I can take him out and stomp on him," Dave said determinedly.

"Sure, Dave," I said as he threw the glump into the freezer. For two months, Dave visited the ball, flung it to the floor, stomped on it, banged it and crushed it when he was frustrated. Then he'd put it back into the deep freeze. Finally, one day Dave threw the yellow ball into the wood stove. Like the witch on the *Wizard of Oz*, Dave screamed, "It's melting! It's melting!" **The glump was gone.**

Dave's heart opened. He began to think of "his adoptive family." He asked to call "HOME." He missed his brother and visited for an overnight. He discovered his princess mommy Jodee and airplane daddy Karl were simply pumpkins and not as precious as he had thought. Dave's homeschool student exchange experience lasted ten months. The brothers and sisters and mother he left behind were people who loved and wanted him too. Dave's healing had begun.

As a parent, you have to be able to continue to find inner peace — no matter how defiant the behavior or how huge the struggle.

Soon his rage and anger turned towards me — the person who 'threw' him away. In his baby memories I was the person who put him in his mind into the kidnapper's — his adoptive mom's — car. Handling his rage at eight-years-old was better than dealing with it during teen or adult years. I could still hold Dave. I was faster and stronger. Dave finally missed his family. He returned home. He finally left the glump and the memories behind. He had a new beginning.

If we can normalize early neural connections and turn on idling neurons — could we break through the barriers of attachment disorder.

Dave returned home knowing he had three 'real' mothers (a tummy birth mom, a heart mom and an adoptive mom) and one father Karl who would always love him, plus lots of brothers and sisters from both his homes. Dave returned to public school and though he still struggled, he was happy. Best of all he found his family and his 'home.'

CHANGING TIMES RAGING TIMES

Raising Liz was like raising a three-year-old in a woman's body. She reached puberty at eight, had the hormones of a teenager and the impulsivity of a preschooler. Life was lonely after Dave left. She'd grown used to a sibling. Liz began to spend more time with friends.

Sometimes there are risks in parenting. David's adoptive mother and our family determined we would let David return to the place 'he' called home, hoping he could heal, even though there was a chance it could cause adoption disruption.

We thought we kept our supervision tight. I was glad she had young people who enjoyed being with her. Little did I know why they enjoyed her so much. Liz was busy making friends regardless of the cost — alcohol, drugs, sex, theft. She was twelve and I had not prepared her for the dangers of the world. She rapidly spiraled downward. One moment she was her sweet, happy self

When the brain has faulty connections or holes, it is not a matter of will power to control impulsivity.

and the next moment a frustrated raging tiger growling and shaking on my floor. The best I could do was to not interfere until the rage was over. Her rages increased in intensity and duration. Karl and I began thinking we would be faced with institutional care. Whatever this was it was more than we understood.

Liz's rages scared me. She weighed almost as much as I did, even though she was just a bit over five feet. When a rage hit, her strength doubled. I learned to stand back and brace myself until her brain storm passed. I kept her safe and appeared strong but inside I felt like a wet dishrag when her rage subsided. Liz smiled and went on with her day. Perplexed from the sudden storm, I asked her, "Liz, doesn't a rage scare you? It scares me."

"It scares me too, mom," Liz replied.

"What does it feel like, sweetie?" I asked.

"It starts in my toes mom, like a tingling and then it goes up my legs. When it gets over my knees, it controls me," Liz revealed.

"Whoa, we need a fire drill. Let's keep the anger out of your toes. When you feel it again, get me and hold my shoulders. I will help hold you together. Perhaps together we can chase it away," I offered. From then on, Liz came to me. I'd look in her eyes, tell her I loved her and reinforce that she was a good person. She tried her best to say she was good and transport her thoughts to areas other than the rage. When I ignored her request for help, the rages came in a torrent. I felt awful. She questioned why I didn't help her. I determined in my heart to separate brat temper tantrums from rages and recognize the difference.

There was a difference between Liz's rages and being a brat. In brat behavior her mind remained engaged. In a rage her ability to think disappeared.

We knew little about the root cause to Liz's behavior? Karl and I sought a therapist as we saw her take a behavioral nose dive. In therapy, Liz worked on adoption, family and communication issues. Food seemed to cause behavior changes. Our next stop would be a clinical nutritionist and a qualified psychiatrist. We needed more professionals.

Dave had frustration balls and his loving adoptive home to move on to. Meanwhile, Liz still made holes in the wall.

4. BASIC FUEL

NUTRITION:
CREATING FERTILE GROUND

Two days before Christmas Eve we received Liz's diagnosis - permanent brain damage, Fetal Alcohol Effects. One day before the same Christmas Eve, blood tests red flagged cancer and ultrasound signaled a complex mass on my right ovary. On Christmas Eve I was handed the appointment notice to visit Dr. Savage, a top surgical oncologist. My brother exuberantly announced pregnancy and laughed that their doctors name was Dr. Miracle. So much for Happy Holidays.

When life hands me a bowl of lemons I can usually make lemonade. It seemed like a whole truck had just tipped its load in my front yard.

Liz's rage at her therapist after eating a fast food meal directed us to the psychiatrist which led to the FAE diagnosis. It also directed us to a clinical nutritionist because the rage appeared after she had eaten. I needed to know if Liz had food issues before we started medication. The little we knew of her family mental health history challenged me to make sure whatever medication prescribed it would be correct. If her family legacy of complex mental health issues were also hers, she needed to understand and regulate medication appropriately her whole life. There was no space to err at age twelve. Little did I know that day would be pivotal in my life as well as my family's.

Dr. Jeff Brist met with Liz and me to discuss Liz's prenatal brain damage and her nutritional needs. He had not knowingly worked with a child with FASD, but his experiences with alcoholism, schizophrenia and Downs offered him a beginning knowledge base. He suggested we do an elimination diet for the next thirty days to see how Liz reacted to various foods before beginning medication. This would help us discover if Liz was allergic or had sensitivities to frequently offending foods: wheat, milk, eggs, tree nuts, fish, shellfish, soy, peanuts (account for 90% food allergic reactions), plus sugar, corn, citrus, night shade vegetable, chocolate, yeast, malt, caffeine, food additives and grapes. This information would help to provide Liz the opportunity for a well-nourished body – a key to a well nourished mind. If our brain is starved for energy, then our memory is one of our first functions to falter. A full complement of nutrients is vital to provide the energy to power our brains.[31]

In addition to helping Liz, I asked if there was anything I could do to help me prepare for surgery and healing. Dr. Brist's calendar was open later in the day, I returned to develop a surgical training program. "Jodee, when a professional boxer goes into the ring, do you think he prepares to heal before he fights?" I had never thought about it. "Do you think an olympic athlete or professional sports person ignores the fact of potential injury and is not prepared? You're going into a boxing ring with surgery. You need to get yourself as strong as possible. The time to fight is now, not after the surgery." At that moment my life changed.

Nutritional healing is fascinating and there exists as much hype as truth. Wading through the myriad of information is senseless without some professional consultation. Being sick provided me a focused opportunity to pay attention to my body. I had never done that. My body was always there when I needed it, doing what I asked it to do. Prior to being sick I thought clearly. Now, whatever was happening was affecting my body, stamina and mind. I was in pain. By body had gotten my attention. My mind was foggy.

Each person has a different biochemistry. There is no perfect food consumption correct for everyone. Like an auto that requires unleaded gasoline, it won't run very well if you fill it up with diesel fuel.

I believed I fed my family healthy food. I baked bread, gardened and sprinkled our diet with some organic cooking. In reality our family diet had slipped a **SAD (Standard American Diet)** diet of hidden hydrogenated oils, overloading on dairy, wheat and corn products, preservatives, fast, and processed foods. Our life was too busy to always cook from 'scratch.'

Challenged with Liz's issues and my own fight

Our eloquent elder stammered at the pulpit. "This is hard, I have never done something like this …" he continued. "Jodee, I give you Luke 10:19 … I declare you healed." There was silence. Liz bounded down the aisle "Are you healed, Mom? Are you healed?"

"We will see Liz, we will see."

31. O'Brien, Dominic, *Learn to Remember: Transform Your Memory Skills* (2000)

for health I worked passionately. It felt good to do something to help myself while waiting for surgery. Better yet, I noticed the difference in my health and my daughter's behavior.

The diet change helped Liz calm down and focus. A month after my surgery Liz received a regime of nutritional supplements. These proved extremely beneficial and she exclaimed, "Mom, I can finally think! It is like someone just washed the dirt off my brain!"

Liz became healthier. She preferred natural foods to processed foods. She enjoyed water instead of soda. As she got healthier we reintroduced foods we had eliminated keeping four days between enjoying them. We kept our diet colorful and varied. Each fresh fruit and vegetable offered a different gift of nutrition. I choose from the rainbow of beautiful colors to keep my family's meals filled with a variety of vitamins and minerals. We incorporated foods rich in antioxidant Vitamins A, C and E found in colorful fruits and vegetables such as oranges, red peppers, spinach and bananas that are particularly beneficial to the health of the brain and memory. They help 'mop up' chemicals known as free radicals, which are naturally present in the body, but when we overproduce them (stress, pollution) can cause extensive cell damage in the brain as well as other parts of the body.[32] Raising a child with FASD was stressful.

Changing your shopping and cooking regime is difficult. We adapted our favorite foods first. We shopped the perimeter of the store, avoiding the processed foods in the aisles. We chose our favorite processed foods and made 'scratch' recipes to duplicate them. Each successful recipe simplified our life. I created homemade mixes from ingredients Liz could tolerate.

Even in the best of times your brain may be malnourished affecting your moods and emotions. The brain consumes 20% of your energy — consuming 50% of the bloodsugar circulating in your bloodstream, 25% of all your nutrients and 20%-25% of the oxygen you breathe - though it is only 2% of our total body weight. Fortunately, it is quick to respond to proper nutrition. Even a single meal will make a difference.

www.brain.com

Four interconnected nutritional components for proper brain functioning:

1. Fatty acids to build the brain
2. Antioxidants to safeguard it
3. Glucose to fuel it
4. Amino acids to interconnect it

32. O'Brien, Dominic, *Learn to Remember: Transform Your Memory Skills* (2000)

INTERNAL BRAIN ENVIRONMENT STEPS

1. Eat the right kind of foods to supply your body with healthy proteins, carbohydrates and fats and get the water, vitamins and minerals your body needs.
2. Eliminate or minimize foods sprayed with pesticides, contain food additives, dyes or are highly processed.
3. Learn about fats and oils. Replace bad fats (especially hydrogenated oils) for healthy fats and oils.
4. Drink plenty of 'filtered' water. Consider getting a filter on your shower head to eliminate the inhalation of chemicals.
5. Eliminate or minimize the use of chemical household cleaners.
6. Avoid aluminum cookware, utensils or foil. Avoid aluminum deodorants.
7. Avoid dental fillings that contain mercury (a known neuro-toxin). Currently the US Public Health Service and The American Academy of Pediatrics support the FDA's directive to eliminate mercury (Thimerosal) from vaccines.

We utilized the Health Coach® System designed by Dr. Mark Percival, D.C., N.D. working creatively with foods we processed well. When something seemed to cause trouble we substituted different products. Liz and I reacted to genetically engineered grains. Liz got headaches and foggy thinking. My stomach and joints hurt with gluten. I studied, researched and experimented. Liz tested, challenged, fed the dog and spat it out. The dog spat it out!

If balance is the essence in life, Liz and I were off balance. I added supplements to boost my immune system. Liz ate a healthy balanced diet as I worked to eliminate highly processed foods, hydrogenated oils, preservatives, dyes, additives and sugars. We increased our consumption of filtered water, vegetables, fruits, lean meats and natural grains. We replaced our bad oils with good oils. Grapeseed oil became the cooking oil of choice along side olive oil. Our white vinegar became a cleaning solution as we switched to apple cider vinegar. We purchased hormone free meats.

The brain needs glucose to function, but too much in Liz produced almost an intoxicated state. A sugar surge sent her into hysterics, an empty tummy into meltdown. If Liz ate too much sugar or high level refined carbohydrates (like grains), she felt euphoric followed by fatigue and fogginess. Natural fruits (fresh or dried) provided a more manageable energy burst.

We settled on three healthy meals with two to three small healthy snacks to stabilize her blood sugar and emotions. We tested products high on the glycemic scale and watched Liz's reactions. The glycemic scale ranks foods on a scale of 0-100 according to the extent they raise blood sugar levels after eating. Pure glucose is the highest. Corn syrup and products with corn syrup for whatever reason was the worst offender for Liz. We searched for substitutions and saved sweets for special ocassions loading up on healthy nutrition instead.

We located manufacturers and mills specializing in organic grain and natural oil products. Omega (www.spectrumnaturals.com) offered us a variety of healthy oils to replace vegetable oil. Ancient Harvest quinoa pasta (www.quinoa.net) products proved a wonderful substitute for wheat pasta, plus you could buy flours, flakes and grain. Quinoa a grain used by the Ancient Incas of South America was a great alternative, high in protein and calcium, containing all 10 amino acids and 50% more fiber than wheat. It was gluten free.

Substitution does not work for all children. Luckily it worked for Liz. We discovered using older strains of grain reduced reactions – we substituted organic spelt and kamut (grown from seeds found in the pyramids in Egypt) for wheat. We tried blue and red corn (Native American) chips, tortillas and blue popcorn! Sheep products were tolerated better than cow products. We tested recipes from South America, Africa, Asia and the Middle East.

I stared at the poster in the dental office. It stated the average US teenager gets 10% of the daily calories from soft drinks. I wouldn't dream of adding 'that' much sugar to anything I drank, yet a common soda contained over 10 tsp. (almost a quarter of a cup) of sugar in one 12 oz can in addition to the high acid content.

	Sugar (tsp)	Acid (ph)
Battery Acid	0	1.0
Pepsi	9.8	2.49
Coke Classic	9.3	2.53
MM Orange	11.2	2.80
Mountain Dew	11.0	3.22
Barqs RB	10.7	4.61
Water	0	7.0

3 tsp = 1 T   2 T = 1 oz.

All the calories were from sugar, there was no nutritional value. Both diet and regular soda replace more nutritious liquids including water.

www.mndental.org

We were on a food adventure. Fresh picked corn on the cob from a local grower produced no headaches. We preserved pickles with apple cider vinegar and less salt. We made tomato salsa, barbeque sauce and ketchup. We made baking flour with rice, potato and tapioca flours. We baked a wheat-free chocolate birthday cake, and brownies.

Liz loves very flavorful foods — very hot, very sour, very sweet and very salty. She tends to over-do flavors. If a little salt is needed it is poured on. If a bit of sugar is warranted it is scooped. I shudder at what she puts into her mouth.

I limited my coffee to weekend mornings and adapted to teas without caffeine. Caffeine pulls water out of the body and reduces the body's ability to absorb vital elements. It shrinks the blood vessels (is a powerful vasoconstrictor) that decreases the blood flow to the brain, especially to the temporal lobes. When caffeine is no longer in the system, the blood vessels expand and cause pain. Caffeine may make you feel energized in the short run, however, in the long run it will make matters worse especially if you increase your consumption or if you are already taking a stimulant (Adderall, Ritalin, Dexedrine, Desoxyn, Cylert) which together can over stimulate the nervous system. I needed restful sleep and caffeine wasn't helping me. *(Caffeine rich products: coffee, cola, chocolate and caffeinated citrus sodas — Generic soda's usually have less caffeine added than name brands, check labels)*

We read food labels — no longer assuming we knew what we were eating. Liz and her friends became food detectives finding hidden forms of wheat and corn syrup in everything from mustard to ketchup and soup to nuts. We discovered most frozen, canned or bottled fruit drinks are not 100% fruit and contain high amounts of corn syrup or other sugars. We looked for 100% juice on the label and diluted it with exta water. We replaced soy sauce (wheat based) with Braggs Aminos (soy based). We eliminated foods containing corn syrup and wheat which Liz had the most difficulty metabolizing. We avoided MSG, artificial dyes and aspartame. I substituted refined sugar with honey, maple syrup and stevia (South America).

We eliminated pesticides and utilized companion planting.

Highest levels of pesticides used in crop production:

FRUITS: apples, peaches, pears, strawberries, red raspberries, grapes from Chili.

VEGETABLES: spinach, potatoes, celery, greenbeans.

Foods least contaminated by pesticides include:

FRUITS: pineapple, bananas, watermelon, cherries from Chili.

VEGETABLES: corn, cauliflower, sweat peas, asparagus, brocolli, onions.

(Source 1999 from Environmental Working Group, Washington DC)

From the moment my friend spoke out Luke 10:19 my insides began to itch. The feeling drove me crazy.

We avoided produce picked early and forced to ripen with chemicals during or after shipping. Freshly grown and organic foods were less challenging. We chose the freshest, most colorful vegetables and fruits we could find. We bought organic when we could. We utilized our garden, co-op and the farmers' market during the summer. We sprouted seeds and used them in salads. Our favorite alfalfa sprouts are very mild and easy to grow. Sprouting increased the nutritional value of the seed itself — alfalfa is 35% protein, contains vitamins A, B, C, E, & K, calcium, magnesium, potassium, iron and zinc. It is rich in chlorophyll and contains as much carotene as carrots.

Restaurants accommodated our needs when we prewarned them. Upon entering a restaurant, we asked, "Can you please ask the chef what is on the menu that doesn't have wheat or corn syrup?" Local delis, cafes and sub shops turned sandwiches into salads. A Chinese grocery became a favored stop for rice noodles and flours made with rice, potato and tapioca.

We learned how to add enzymes to Liz's diet so she could join her teen friends to eat Pizza made with wheat and cheese. This avoided headaches, over-reactions and loud gas passing.

We built up Liz's metabolic systems.

As Liz became more capable she desired to find out how her body operated without the supplements. —it didn't. Within three days we had emotional outbursts, within a week living with her was unbeatble.

Food product by food product we upgraded or substituted to help me heal and Liz think. Improving mental function requires that we provide the proper nutrition and activities that stimulate the function of memory. Specific nutrients are needed in our bodies to make the biochemical process work properly. The nutrients act as co-factors in our biochemical reactions. For our body to proceed from point A to point B, certain nutrients must be available. When these nutrients are unavailable, abnormal behaviors may occur. [33]

To restore the function of someone who has problems with coordination or fine motor control, we must provide nutrition and stimulation of the body region in which we want to improve function. [34]

33. www.blockcenter.com. The Block Center is run by Dr. Mary Ann Block and works with ADHD and Autistic children. Address: The Block Center, 1721 Cimarron Trail, Suite 4, Hurst, Texas 76054. Telephone: 817-280-9933

I could not shield Liz from people who misunderstood her brain injury or obnoxious behavior. I could help her prepare for those instances so that her spirit would not be broken. I coached Liz to handle life's issues which gave her a head start in maintaining her composure.

New scientific research regarding the use of nutritional treatments of B vitamin choline to fetal alcohol exposed infants may offer triage damage control. In animal testing research has revealed the beneficial effects of choline were due not to immediate effects of the nutrient, but rather to long-term changes in the rat's brains.[35, 36]

A nutritional journey is not something you do on your own. You MUST consult the primary physician for your child or yourself before beginning any diet changes. Nutritional needs vary for each individual. Some vitamins and minerals may be toxic. Dosages are important. More can be dangerous. Body balance is the goal. Choose the highest quality supplements available. If they smell bad, ask why. Any supplement that makes you feel bad, STOP immediately. Do not use any supplements without clinical guidance as some supplements react adversely with certain medications. Give the supplements time to work and don't be afraid of getting a second opinion before proceeding. This is your child's body and you need to protect it. If your child is hospitalized or prescribed a new medication make sure to notify your health professionals of the contents of your child's supplements. See Appendix 6 (Page 274) for additional nutritional information.

Prior to getting sick I didn't take time to pay attention to the miniscule. I was too busy with my life. being sick taught me to lay my life down and refocus. Our nutritional program created the fertile groundwork we needed for the next steps. I had no idea what those next steps would be.

Current nutritional research in prenatally exposed infants is showing promising results for encouraging early brain growth.[37]

34. Schmidt, Michael A, Smart Fats: How Dietary Fats and Oils Affect Mental, Physical and Emotional Intelligence. (1997) North Atlantic Books

35. *"Neonatal choline supplementation ameliorates the effects of prenatal alcohol exposure on a discrimin. tion learning task in rates."* J.D. Thomas, M.H. La Fiette, V.R. Quinn, and E. P. Riley, Neurotoxicology and Teratology, Vol. 22, No. 5, September 2000, p703-711. Address: Jennifer Thomas, Center for Behavioral Teratology, San Diego State University, Suite 209, 6363 Alvarado Court, San Diego, CA 92120

36. *Choline: needed for normal development of memory"* S.H. Zeisel, Department of Nutrition, School of Public Health, University of North Carolina at Chapel Hill, Chapel Hill, NC 27599-7400.

37. *Choline: Help for Alcohol Damaged Newborns?* Crime Times, Vol 7, No. 2, 2001 Pages 1& 5

QUENCH THIRST FIRST

Our bodies are 2/3 water (55% of a woman's body weight and 65% of a man's). Water is a necessary conductor for all of our bodies electrical and chemical reactions. Water helps your brain's ability to remember and to focus. A 2% drop in body water can trigger difficulty with short term memory, trouble with basic math and diffculty focusing on the printed page or a computer screen. Water allows us to swallow and digest food. It carries the nutrients to the cells and transports wastes away from the cells. It allows us to eliminate our waste products from our system. No liquid dissolves molecules better than water - diluting, dissolving and disposing of body toxins. Water speeds up your metabolism. In addition it prevents the build up of internal heat and allows the body to cool down through perspiration. It provides our tears.

Mrs. Kulp, we found no cancer. We looked everywhere.We didn't need to do a hysterectomy, in fact we performed fertility surgery. If you like, you can have a baby. The 17 staples in my stomach weren't interested in thinking about a baby at that moment. God took me this far, if there was to be another child added to our family, I am sure it too would be arranged.

We added a water filter to our kitchen sink for drinking water and carried a portable water bottle while on the go.

Manageable Water Consumption

- 1 cup of water when you wake up after brushing your teeth
- 1 cup of water at each of three meals (3 cups)
- 1 cup between meals (2 cups)
- 1 cup before you go to bed after you brush your teeth

Fruit as a general rule is rich in water and is excellent for between meal snacks.

Neurologists who specialize in ADHD warn if the fluid intake is not adequate, the viscosity of the blood increases, which irritates the brain and can be reflected in irritable behavior. There is a delay from the time your blood becomes overly concentrated, to the time your brain detects this change and feels thirsty. Once you are thirsty you have already been dehydrated for a period of time. If your urine is light yellow color you are doing great, if it is deep orange you need more fluid. Some people confuse being thirsty with being hungry.

Liz takes an intensive care multi-vitamin, an antioxidant, brain supplement combinations, DHA, additional C and enzymes when needed. She drinks filtered water and tries to maintain a brain healthy diet.

You Are a Big Fat Head

Fats are essential to our health. Sixty percent of the brain's structure is fatty material. The brain tissue and nerve cells have a protective outer layer of fat. The membranes around every cell in our body require essential fatty acids to control the intake and output of materials.

Any new growth in nerve cells requires the raw materials of which the nerves are made. This includes fatty acids. Whenever we wish to improve brain function we must provide both the raw materials and the stimulation. This means providing the proper balance of fatty acids needed to foster brain repair and allows the body to perform activities.

The fats we put into our mouth have a profound affect on the fats in our brains. Fats and oils affect our learning, memory and mental intelligence; moods, behavior and emotional intelligence; and our movement, sensation and physical intelligence. An excellent book *Smart Fats* by Michael A. Schmidt can provide you additional insight.

There are good fats and bad fats — a balance of fats is essential. Fats fall into three categories.

1. Saturated fats come from animal food (meat, cheese, eggs, dairy) and a few oils like palm kernel oil. If consumed in excess they can be difficult to metabolize and lead to heart disease.

2. Unsaturated fats come in two forms

a. Mono-unsaturated found in olive oil, canola oil, nuts and seeds. This oil helps to reduce the harmful low density lipoproteins (LDL) which can cause blocked arteries.

b. Poly-unsaturated fats also contain essential fatty acids (EFA) vital for regulating mental health, growth and vitality. They are believed to assist in transporting oxygen through out our bodies. These include Omega 3 and Omega 6 oils.

3. Trans-fat or hyrdrogenated fat is a manmade found mainly in margerine and shortenings. These are especially unhealthy.

Common foods with hyrdogenated oil include:

- Salad Dressings
- Most Margarine
- Boxed Cakes
- Candies

- French Fries
- Microwave Popcorn
- TV dinners
- Potato Products

- Doughnuts
- Mayonnaise
- Cookies
- Many Processed Foods

- Snack Products (potato chips, corn chips, tortilla chips, puffed cheese snacks)

Check labels for partially hydrogenated when you buy oils
(minimize or eliminate these products if partially hydrogenated)

- Soybean oil
- Corn oil

- Sunflower oil
- Safflower oil

1. DECREASE BAD (TRANS FATTY ACIDS) FATS

You want to avoid trans fat. When you see 'partially hydrogenated' look for an alternative product. You will be surprised how many partially hydrogenated products there are. Read the labels. If products say "baked" on the label they are probably not deep fried in oil and a better choice.

Hydrogen is added to liquid oil to make it a solid and creates unnatural fatty acids known as trans fatty acids, which block the formation of the body chemical to prevent blood clots. This allows manufacturers to turn cheap, low quality oils into butter substitutes and prevent rancidity. It also makes it harder for you to use the good oils you eat. Manufacturers of fat free foods may compensate for the fat removal by adding sugar or salt. Hydrogenated vegetable oils can set up a chronic inflammatory response in brain tissue and foster blood damage. They interfere with the brain blood barrier and exchange of nutrition for waste. They are harmful to blood vessels and ultimately blood circulation. This deprives the brain of necessary nutrients and oxygen.

We increased our good fats and decreased our bad fats without increasing our salt and surgar. This took time. We again had to find substitute products we all enjoyed.

2. INCREASE GOOD FATS

Both Omega 6 Fatty Acids (alpha-linolenic acid) and Omega 3 Fatty Acids (linoleic acid) are vital to our health. The optimum balance is considered to be three Omega 6 to one Omega 3 (3:1). The current average western diet is 10-20 Omega 6's to 1 Omega 3 (20:1 or 10:1). We increased our Omega 3 foods. It was important that essential fatty acids are refrigertated can turn rancid quicky by exposure to light, heat and air. They were too expensive to spoil.

*The good fats are the essential fatty acids found in olive oil, grapeseed oil, sesame seeds and sunflower seeds (Omega 6), pumpkin seeds and flaxseeds (Omega 3), fish oils (DHA, EPA) and evening primrose and borage (GLA). These are the oils our body uses for lubrica*tion.

OMEGA 3 helps improve general brain functioning and restore memory. They are believed to create new communication centers in neurons which help brain functioning and mood. Supplements are available. **OILY FISH** contains folic acid and several essential fatty acids – all are vital in the functioning and development of the brain and central nervous system. **FLAX OIL** has the highest level of Omega 3. We used flax oil in homemade salad dressings or lightly tossing pasta or vegetables. We ground flaxseeds.

Best OMEGA 3 Resources

• Salmon	• Sardines	• Flax Oil	• Walnuts
• Mackerel	• Herring	• Pumpkin Seed	• Soybean Oil
• Tuna	• Oysters	• Hemp Oil	

• Eggs from pastured vs factory hens contain 20 times more omega-3s

OMEGA 6 is an essential fatty acid in ample supply in the Western diet. Intake of Omega 6 has doubled since 1940 and our intake of Omega 3 has shrunk to one sixth since 1850. We focused on ways to increase our Omega 3s and decrease our usage of Omega 6.

Best OMEGA 6 Resources

- Olive Oil
- Sesame Seeds
- Canola Oil
- Sunflower Seeds
- GapeseedOil (raises HRL, lowers LDL)

DHA/EPA Ensures the fluidity of the brain cell membranes and is essential for proper transmission of cerebral nerve signals. It lowers the bad chloresterol (LDL) and raises the good cholesterol (HDL) It also affects an infants ability to utilize glucose. Alcohol decreases levels of DHA in the brain, a specialized fatty acid essential for healthy brain cell manufacturing.

Best DHA/EPA Resources

- Fish oils from cold water fish (salmon, trout, herring, bluefin, mackerel, sardines, anchovies, albacore tuna, caviar, eel)
- Some forms of algae (plankton)
- Fresh water fish (lake trout, walleye, haddock, northern pike, carp)
- Chicken and egg products when organic and poultry is fed on a high Omega-3 fatty acid feed.

SWEET DREAMS

Dr. Brist asked how much sleep I've been getting since Liz joined our home. "Oh," I answered "I don't need much sleep. Liz never has been able to fall asleep before midnight and she is always awake before five or six."

"Mom I remember my night terrors. My eyes couldn't see when I woke up. Everything was white. I screamed my way out of the whiteness."

"Is she a restless sleeper?" he asked

"She sleeps soundly for the first ninety minutes, then wakes up screaming and walks with our dog to our room. Her eyes are open. The doctor said it is no problem. They are normal night terrors." It didn't feel normal to me.

"I asked about you. You fall asleep after working with this child all day at midnight, wake in the middle of the night to care for her and get up at the break of dawn. Jodee, you need to sleep to get well. Sleep is the time your body cells have the opportunity to repair themselves and remove body waste. Sleep refreshes the body and the mind. Make sure you are relaxed before you go to bed. Make sure you sleep enough to dream, it generally takes 90 minutes

Nap Power *A 90 minute nap or a 10 minute power nap can help produce improvement to memory and learning.*

to pass through all the stages of sleep. You should work up to at least four full 90 minute sleep cycles. A chronic lack of sleep will keep your adrenaline levels high which will add to your sleep disruption." If Liz turned my life upside down twelve years earlier. Dr. Brist and my illness turned my life upside down again. "If you want to heal and be able to help your child, you need to take care of yourself," he smiled. "You are strong, determined and positively passionate. Those skills got you this far. They have also masked the messages your body sent you as you were getting sick. A sleep deprived person cannot perform mental tasks as well as a well rested person. You need to learn to listen to your body."

Years of limited sleep had taken their toll. I gave myself permission to sleep and let go of some of the Liz worry. Liz was required to go in her room after 9:00 pm and only leave for the bathroom. Mom slept until 7:00 am. We added a humidifier to Liz's room with jasmine, chamomile, lavender, or ylang-ylang. When Liz had a cold we added eucalyptus. The humidifier made it easier for her to breathe. It also added a soft white noise. The white noise seemed to make a difference. The temperature was cool with big snuggly blankets and a scented sleep pillow. The dog joined her. Still she had trouble falling to sleep, but I didn't. I found sweet dreams.

Late afternoon sugar cravings disappeared once I was rested, I no longer needed that late day energy boost. I switched my highest carb meal to the evenings and built in time to destress, (a hot bath or sauna and curling up in bed to read alone in my room). I wrote a worry note to myself at my desk before heading off to relax. My worries were always waiting for me in the morning.

Sleep ideas:

- Hot herbal tea like chamomile or warm milk
- Hot bath, sauna
- Soothing sounds aquarium, rain, light music
- Sleep pillow filled with lavender, hops, mint, chamomile, thyme, rose petals and/or lemon balm
- Deep breaths
- Good mattress (some families use sleep foam or magnetic mattresses with good results)
- Herbal supplements (see your doctor beforre trying)
- Bedtime routine
- Write a worry note and let it go
- Eliminate caffeine.

A Breath of Fresh Air
Was Right Under Our Nose

"What do you do on the bus for all those hours of traveling?" I wondered.

"I study. I have thousands of miles of peace and quiet to think and learn new things. It is my time alone to become a better neurodevelopmentalist. Perhaps someday we will have clinics and fly, for right now this works for the people I care about — the families."

Toni Hager

Liz and I worked on nutrition noticing results in both our bodies and minds. The internet offered online support groups for families working with special needs children including homeschooling families and families living and loving children with FASD. I continued to gain ideas, courage, patience and understanding through morning email. Liz and our family were not alone. Liz's behaviors and challenges were shared by other children.

Reading through morning messages the ideas shared by Toni Hager, NDS impressed me. Each time I tried one of her practical ideas it worked. I wrote her privately. Liz had completed her portion of her new book, *"The Best I Can Be: Living with Fetal Alcohol Syndrome or Effects"*. I sent Toni the manuscript and a copy of *Families at Risk*. We read each other's materials. Toni sent me her professional articles. She would be riding the Greyhound through Minneapolis in two months and we could meet then. She promised to bring audiotapes so I could learn more about neurodevelopment. What kind of professional would ride a bus from Washington state to Virginia? I was curious.

One year to the day after my surgery I met Toni Hager. Was I a crazy person going downtown to a bus depot at 5:30 am, in freezing Minnesota January weather carrying a thermos of hot chocolate, to meet a stranger passing through town? Recognition was instant — two mothers of special needs children — two professionals working to help families. Toni traveled by bus so her client families could afford her. She stayed in their homes so she could understand the realities of living with the children she

You can live without food for a while.
You can live without water for hours.
Try living without oxygen for five minutes.

was evaluating and for whom she was setting up neurodevelopment programs. She offered to show me a couple of exercises to help Liz. Liz's manuscript provided Toni enough information to begin to help Liz without evalution. I could try a couple of neuro exercises for two weeks and see if I noticed any difference. If I did, Liz and I would return and meet Toni on her way back.

Toni demonstrated tactile sequences on me showing me how to begin to normalize Liz's hypersensitive sensory system. It felt wonderful and when I opened my eyes I was refreshed. She advised me to start slowly, with only the tips of Liz's fingers, the ends of her toes and to try touching her face. I was shocked that Liz liked the sequences and asked each morning before we began school to have me "plug in her brain." When Toni returned through town our tactile sequences had progressed up to Liz's elbows and knees and I could gently rub her face. Liz was sitting closer to family members. She had come to me 'for a hug' — a new experience for all of us. I had listened to Toni's audiotapes. My friends listened too. We agreed trying neuro couldn't hurt.

Liz joined me to meet Toni. I was worried about having thirteen-year-old Liz in the depot at midnight. Luckily there was a small corralled area for child play. I ordered Liz to stay within its fence, as Toni and I sat on the fence rail talking. Toni watched Liz interact with her girlfriend.

"Does Liz breathe through her mouth or hold her breath while doing activities?" Toni asked.

"I don't know. I never thought about it. She had trouble breathing when she was a baby, so once it got smoother, I just never paid any attention," I answered.

"We've got to get her to nose breath. Liz needs more oxygen to her brain. She won't be getting enough with the way she is breathing. Let me give you some ideas to help her learn to breath correctly," and off Toni rambled regarding the details of the why, where, when and how we breathe. I

Observe yourself breathing. Do you breathe through your mouth or nose? When? Does your breathing change if your are physically, emotionally or mentally stressed? If so, remind yourself to breathe; to stop holding your breath.

"Liz is the first client who provided her own history. With this information I can give you some ideas to help her. Bring her to the depot on my way back so I can meet her."

Toni Hager

never knew it was so important or had so many pieces. After all, isn't it the first thing we do if we are going to live out of the womb? All this was new to me. Toni had words and language and parts of the body in her vocabulary I didn't know existed. I felt inadequate. Could I really learn to understand what she was saying enough to help my daughter?

I was so glad when baby Liz breathed quietly, I never realized she didn't nose breathe.

"Except for emergencies, our breathing was designed to take place through our nose," she continued. "The hairs that line our nostrils filter out dust and dirt. The mucus membranes that divide our noses into two cavities warm and humidify the air we breathe before it enters our lungs. Breathing through the nose helps us maintain the correct balance of oxygen and carbon dioxide in our blood. Lack of sufficient oxygen going to the cells in our brain can activate our 'fight or flight' mechanism. We become tense, irritable, anxious, depressed.

"I remember listening to Liz breathe as a baby," Liz's social worker said. "It was gaspy."

Discover the difference in nose and mouth breathing yourself. Slouch deeply in a chair. Slouch your shoulders and open your mouth. Breathe shallowly. Think about how you are feeling and pay attention to your body as you breathe in your upper chest. Now sit up straight, shoulders back and breathe deeply through your nose so that the air goes into your lower lungs.

Do you feel the difference?

"Breathing is a body function you can do consciously or unconsciously. It is controlled by two different sets of muscles — voluntary and involuntary. Breath is the connection between the conscious and unconscious mind, it can be trained and learned. Liz is a shallow chest breather. She barely takes in enough oxygen to keep her functioning. The brain uses 20% of all the oxygen we breathe, even though it is only 2% of the body. Ten minutes without oxygen can cause neural damage. You need oxygen to survive. Few people other than athletes or musicians are aware that the abdomen should expand during inhalation to provide optimum amounts of oxygen needed to nourish all the cells of the body. Deep breathing nourishes the brain, strengthens the lungs, improves circulation, oxygenates the blood and minimizes respiratory ailments," Toni concluded. "Step one is nose breathing for Liz."

We said goodbye. My head spun as my second neuro lesson ended. Did we want a complete evaluation when

Toni returned in March and start a program?

How many things didn't I know about my daughter? How blind had I been believing that if I loved her enough I could make a difference? I looked at all Liz's childhood pictures to see if she closed her mouth. The photo albums answered Toni's question. In every picture Liz's mouth was opened.

Make a fist and squeeze. What happens to your breathing? When we get anxious we tend to hold our breath or take shallow breaths.

Teaching a thirteen-year-old mouth breather to breathe through her nose was not a simple task. Liz was afraid she would suffocate. Because of our nutrition program, Liz no longer had a stuffy nose, her nasal passages were clear. She did not have a cold. There appeared to be no physical reason she could not learn to breathe through her nose. We practiced nose breathing one nostril at a time so it wasn't frightening. Liz soon had confidence her nose worked and she snuck a few snorts of air in once in a while and practiced while I wasn't looking. Liz loves looking beautiful. We practiced nose breathing in front of the mirror. The difference in appearance was startling. She looked more alert and aware. Nose breathing was definitely an improvement.

We made up breathing games to see who could hold a breath the longest. She was allowed to beat me if she cheated by breathing through her nose. We used a stopwatch and charted our progress. I watched Liz's times climb. It wasn't long before she was winning. We practiced in the car, riding through tunnels was a favorite. Doing chores together also offered us opportunities. We went on walks. How many steps could we take before we had to breathe through our mouth?

Toni sent an arsenal of tools to help Liz — Krazystraws, bubbles, horns, kazoos, and whistles. Toni understood from being the mother of two special needs children that if it wasn't fun, it wouldn't get done.

Once Liz no longer feared nose breathing we got creative. We inhaled with our noses and exhaled into a bubble blower, horn or whistle. We inhaled deep breaths through our noses and exhaled as though we were gently blowing out a candle. We pushed our exhaling to last longer than our inhaling. This longer exhalation triggers a relaxation response in our body.

Liz had more on-task time for school work with nose breathing. Deep breathing allowed her to regain composure, focus and try again instead of fighting me or running from learning. It was a key to access attention.

We played with airflow. We made strange shapes with our mouths and listened to the different sounds we could make. We copied noises each other were making. We learned to breathe deeply, but gently and effortlessly when we felt frustration to nourish the brain, stop the fight or flight response **(limbic)** and encourage the reaction response **(cerebrum).**

We lay on our backs, inhaled through our noses and blew out letter sounds. We started with vowel sounds. We paid attention to where in our mouths and bodies the sounds came from and how they were made. We giggled and laughed.

- Could we make exhaled sounds louder, softer, higher or lower?
- Could we connect them with each other aaaaaaaeeeeeeiiiiii on an exhale?
- What happened if you made the sounds underwater?
- Could Liz breathe through her nose and continue to go pppppppp or bbbbbbb or pbpbpbpbpbp?
- Could we mix consonants?
- How did sounds come out of our mouths?

Liz did not have automaticity in walking, so each step was thought out in her subconsciousness. She couldn't walk and chew gum at the same time. If she were moving she held the gum between her teeth, then she stopped walking and chewed the gum or in frustration threw it out of her mouth for someone to step on later.

Each developmental accomplishment Liz made opened a new set of problems. There was no parenting book to teach me normal three or four-year-old behaviors expressed by a teen. Excessive makeup and jewelry were part of the new package — at least she decided to wear clothes!

Watch a healthy baby breathe. A baby is a natural belly breather — the little belly goes up and the little belly comes down. Using breath to quiet the body can be powerful. Liz and I lay on the floor with toys on our stomachs and watched them rise and fall. I placed my hand on Liz's belly and asked her to make her belly soft as she exhaled air into my hand. I gently encouraged her to slow down and relax as she breathed through her nose and into her belly. She learned to relax, breathe calmly and become aware of her breathing. During inhalation I told Liz to feel the air go into the tip of her nose, through her nasal passages, down her throat and trachea and into her lungs (deep into her belly). As she exhaled I narrated the reverse, letting the air go out of her belly and lungs, up her trachea and throat, through her nostrils and out her nose. This encouraged deeper breathing and allowed more oxygen to reach Liz's brain. To teach Liz the physical sensation of breathing from her belly (diaphragm breathing), she stood straight up with her arms at her sides. Then she raised her hands above her head as she stood on her tip toes. Staying on her tip toes, she lowered her arms, as she exhaled, feeling the change in her belly. We tried toe breathing, pretending to suck air through our fingers and toes and up to our brain.

Toni introduced us to Nancy Thomas 'strong sitting' instead of time out. Strong sitting allows the brain to shift gears. It is a time to dream, plan, pray or think. It allows children the opportunity to pull life back together, when things go out of control. We found a spot in our living room with few distractions. Liz sat cross legged with her back straight, her hands folded in a comfortable spot, her arms relaxed and her head and neck facing forward. She then breathed deeply into her chest cavity through her nose, taking a break and refocusing so she could start over in a positve way. This made Liz responsible for figuring out the right behavior.

Research is being done with **Hyperbaric Oxygen Therapy** *(100% oxygen under pressure) for a wide range of conditions including neurological issues. There are promising results for children with cerebral palsy, perhaps our children could also benefit.*
www.perlhealth.com
Perlmutter Hyperbaric Center

Liz no longer feared suffocation if she closed her mouth. She began to learn to chew with her mouth closed. She gets less winded and she "nose" how to get more oxygen to her brain when she needs it. We also noticed physical changes. Liz's cheeks filled out, her lower lip protruded less, her tongue rested behind her teeth and she seldom caught a cold.

Even as a young adult if Liz is stressed or tired she shuts down further by mouth breathing. The correct breath of fresh air made a huge difference. It was free and it was right under her nose the whole time. We would find out what neurodevelopment therapy was. We would give it a try.

"We only come alive when we invent our future and then live into it.
If we do not invent the future, it is determined by our past."
www.innovationcentral.org

NEURO WHAT TONI? I CAN'T EVEN SAY IT!

By Toni Hager, NDS
www.kidscanlearn.net

I had not worked knowingly with a child who was prenatally exposed to alcohol. Liz was full of life. She was going to be a challenge, fun and interesting to work with. She was beautiful inside and out. Very few people would know she faced mountains of challenges each day. So many simple things were difficult for her. How often had her spirit been crushed? She seemed so resilient.

Neurologically, 'labels' are symptoms of neurological dysorganization, which, in most cases, can be improved. For whatever reason developmental stages have been skipped, halted or interrupted (sometimes in the womb). Neurodevelopment provided drug-free sequential enrichment for the central nervous system (CNS) to reorganize or move through the needed developmental stages.

Humans begin with the merging of egg and sperm. From that point on cells are duplicated and moved into their various job functions. If damage is done to a developing cell, all cells that are duplicated from that cell may be damaged.

To analyze a child's neurodevelopment needs, the first step is to examine the child's health. Problems in this area include metabolic, sensory, muscular and neurological problems. In

First steps to assure the brain/body machine will be able to take advantage of life's learning opportunities.

- Thyroid test
- Glucose tolerance test
- Alimentary track assessment (intestinal flora testing, parasites, etc.)
- Consider an elimination challenge diet (remove dairy, corn, wheat, soy and eggs for one month, then rechallenge one food at a time every five days)
- Consider comprehensive digestive stool analysis
- Hair analysis for heavy metals
- Food allergy/sensitivity testing
- EFA assessment (what children actually learn)
- Consider organic acid test

A Chance to Grow   www.actg.org

Wellness strategies to consider:

- Whole foods diet, no additives or colors.
- Avoid any allergies/ sensitivities found
- High quality multi- nutrient
- Probiotics (good intestinal bacteria)
- Introduce digestive enzymes when indicated
- Normalize any findings on lab tests
- EFA - mix Evening Primrose Oil, Flax Seed Oil, Cod Liver Oil 1:1:1 Take 1-2 tsp a day
- Reduce or eliminate hydrogenated oil
- Eat three meals and two snacks daily (macro and micro nutrient balanced)
- 8.5 to 10 hours of sleep including weekends (cool, dark and quiet place)
- Participate in physical exercises – 20 minutes of vigorous cardiovascular activities – three times a week minimum.
- Keep a food and drink diary and note how you feel/ perform relative to food drink consumption.

A Chance to Grow www.actg.org

addition, food or chemical intolerances can make it hard for a child to learn despite being provided remediation and the best therapy. When a child's general health and wellness are compromised, the brain/body is not able to take advantage of learning opportunities.

Step one accesses baseline information at the metabolic level. This includes a complete physical, review of medical and prenatal history, a work up by a qualified clinical nutritionist to determine nutritional issues or if modification of the family diet can help your child and assessment of the accuracy of the information received by the child through the senses: eyes, ears, muscles, balance and touch.

As you will learn in *Our FAScinating Journey* not all specialists are trained in diagnosing the accuracy of the information received or the ability to process the information by the child, even though they are excellent in determining that the information is received.

For example: *A child may have sight capabilities of 20/20. These high sight scores mask the underlying problem in visual processing. Liz and other children also have acute hearing. This acute hearing masks auditory processing difficulties.*

Step two is to determine which areas of the child's development are immature.

You can use the information in Appendix 5 as a beginning guide. You will find the most help in working with a professional trained in neurodevelopment as they have activities and ideas to help you and your child.

A Neurodevelopmentalist will assess these developmental issues:

Academic/Emotional: Where on the developmental scale is the child?

Auditory Perception: Does the child make sense of what she hears?

Spatial Awareness: Can the child make sense of what is outside herself?
Is she aware of her body?

Body Integration: Can the child move in many directions?
Can she wave her hands from one side of the body to
the other **(midline crossing - horizontal & vertical)**?

Language: What it the listening level **(receptive language)**?
How can the child communicate **(expressive language)**?
What is the quality of the child's sounds **(articulation)**?
Does the child have an inner voice dialogue or is all
communication still external?

Memory: What level of short-term memory does the child have
hearing **(auditory short term memory)** or seeing
(visual short term memory)?
What happens if you mix auditory and visual together?

Reflexive: What reflexes does the child have?
Are the early infant reflexes still engaged?

Time, Sequence, Organization: (These skills are needed for classroom work.)
What is the level of development of the child?

Visual Perception: Can the child look and understand what she sees,
rather than just being able to see?

Visualization: Can the child make mental pictures?

Deficits in these areas can often be remediated. Many times it will take sessions with a number of different professionals at different times as integrated services are not always readily available. Families with brain injured children may collect an entourage of professionals — in different locations, with varying schedules — who are often not covered on insurance. Physical therapists evaluating and treating components of movement; occupational therapists evaluat-

"Neurotherapy must be fun to avoid active refusal by either the child or the parent, who believes it is futile to even try. I continuously search for play, silliness and enjoyment." Toni Hager, NDS

Oh Liz, for twelve years you have avoided touch. My heart broke for you and your father. The healthy child play that daddies do with infants, toddlers and preschoolers was denied both of you. Your dad's dreams and desires for you were stripped away one piece at a time. FASD is a long cycle of grief.

Was thirteen too late to develop a close father / daughter relationship.

ing and treating problems interfering with functional performance; speech and language therapists evaluating and treating oral motor, speech and voice issues; behavioral optometrists remediating visual processing; behavioral audiologist remediating auditory processing; clinical nutritionists overseeing digestion and nutrition . . . and on and exhaustingly on.

The integration of information received through the senses (eyes, ears, skin, muscles, balance, smell, taste, touch) and the integration of the whole brain prepares a child for learning. When a brain reaches the right developmental level you no longer have to push the child to do something. It just happens. We utilize a process we call sequential enrichment to help create new neural connections.

New or strengthened connections can form with a specific frequency, intensity and duration of neurodevelopment sequences. It takes a team of concerned family members, friends, teachers and professionals to reach the child's highest potential. It takes smiles, love, humor and play. It can be done.

Thankfully neuroscience is moving from working with a diagnosis to working with an individual. Brains are very adaptable. An individualized therapeutic program can be designed to stimulate the brain.

Hopefully, someday schools like the Minnesota charter school 'A Chance to Grow' (www.acgt.org) and centers like CanLearn will be commonplace around the world. Hopefully other professional disciplines will utilize the strengths of neurodevelopment and incorporate its methods within their own training. As we join hands we will all learn more

Parents of a special needs child are in for the ride of their lives. The emotions are intense, burning — love, desire, pride, elation — on the flip side — frustration, anger, fear, disappointment. Normalcy becomes what is typical for the family as they let go of dreams.

Carol (FASD mom)

ways to help these special children. It will take more than a village. It will take the world.

    I reviewed the curriculum the Kulp family had been using to homeschool Liz. It was solid. Jodee appeared qualified to teach Liz, yet Liz's initial testing scores showed reading at 3.1 decoding, 3.3 comprehension, less than 1.0 spelling with my southern accent and 4.1 in math. She was definitely hyper- and hypo-sensitive. We would see what we could do, at the starting gate – remediating life in the womb. She was already thirteen. What could be done?

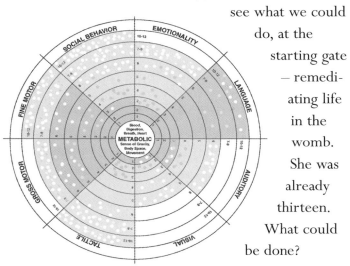
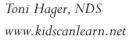

This is Liz's brain map. The darker grey area is where we begin in January 2000 and the lighter grey area is as of August 2001.

Toni Hager, NDS
www.kidscanlearn.net

Liz at thirteen.

Liz Kulp at fifteen

Life doesn't have to be 'normal' to be complete. Love doesn't have to be sophisticated to be the reason the heart beats. Seeing the tender love story of John and Sheena (both FAS) made me realize there will be moments of magic for them, moments of achievement. There will be love and communion of hearts for them. Sometimes our minds get trapped into what is accepted as 'normal' and you know I think the slow road to love, friendship and struggles is more romantic. Life is a process not a result. I am raising my two boys to be the best they can be.

    Anne (FASD mom)

LIZ'S PROGRAM OUTLINE

We utilized all the developmental work we could get our hands on in helping Liz grow.

We discovered when Liz mastered 75% of a lower level of development it was time to slowly introduce the next level.

Here is our strategy. We offer this information in hopes we can provide you clues to help your child. Remember each child who has been prenatally exposed is different.

1. Unconditional love

2. Metabolic processing
- nutritional deficiencies
- chemical sensitivities
- allergies
- immune system functioning
- inflammation/infections

3. Reflexes
- muscle tone
- security in gravity
- sucking
- eye movement
- tactile defensiveness

4. Basic senses – Sensory input neurological
(each of the basic senses has its own development sequence)
- touch
- auditory
- visual
- balance (**vestibular**)
- kinesthetic
- body in space (**proprioception**)

5. Sensory-Integration
- touch
- auditory
- visual

6. Gross motor
- balance
- right from left
- motor planning
- visual motor integration
- knowing body's position
- use both sides of body
- dominance (**favor one side**)

7. Fine Motor
- use and control of mouth, tongue (**oral motor**)
- speech and language
- use and control of eyes (**ocular motor**)
- eye and hand coordination (**fingers**)

8. Body awareness
- attention
- concentration
- organization
- self-counsel
- visual perception
- visual motor planning
- visual motor integration
- concentration
- auditory perception

9. Detailing
- silent thinking
- writing
- reading
- math
- spelling
- imagination
- visualization
- interjection
- body language

HAGER NEURODEVELOPMENT VORTEX

EACH CHILD is very different and will require a different set of exercises,
play and academics to help the child achieve new developmental levels.
Not all children can reach all levels, but improvements
in abilities can be achieved thereby allowing the child an opportunity to
become more self sufficient through learning, laughter and play.

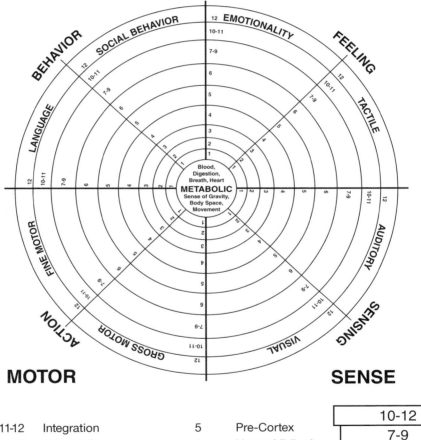

11-12	Integration	5	Pre-Cortex
9-10	Frontal Cortex	4	Upper Midbrain
8	Cortex	3	Lower Midbrain
7	Cortex	2	Pons
6	Lower Cortex	1	Medula

For more information regarding the Hager Neurodevelopment
Vortex visit www.kidscanlearn.net

Building Bridges Between Isolated Islands?

We discovered no single health practitioner knew our daughter better than we did. But each specialist offered tools, knowledge and experience we didn't have. Each of these incredible professionals made a difference in Liz's and our family's life discovering where on the developmental scale Liz was and providing information and tools to help her. There were no magic pills or silver bullets. It was hard work.

An appropriate intervention plan was designed based on Liz's developmental profile. We became the cog in the wheel of communication between the people who interacted with Liz. We live with her. We love her. We had the most experience with Liz. Karl and I needed more tools.

We partnered with professionals, family, neighbors, friends and the community. Everyone interacting with Liz provided opportunity for her growth. The more knowledge people had regarding FASD the better outcome for Liz. We read everything we could about the brain, it's development and how it works. As we learned how Liz's brain operated we shared this information with her. Liz became a partner in finding exercises and solutions to help her reach her goals. Her ability to communicate her needs and express how she felt provided insight for understanding other individuals with FASD.

Whether a brain is damaged by trauma, compromised by blood supply (stroke) or prenatal

Liz's Learning Sequence

1. Nutritional - Metabolic
2. Sensory to Motor
3. Sensory to Visual
4. Sensory to Auditory
5. Short Term Memory
6. Visual to Motor
7. Auditory to Motor
8. Motor to Auditory
9. Motor to Visual
10. Visual to Executive Functions
11. Auditory to Executive Functions
12. Auditory/Visual to Motor
13. Motor to Auditory/Visual
14. Motor to Visual/Auditory
15. Visual to Motor, Timing and Sequencing
16. Auditory to Motor, Timing and Sequencing
17. Repeat, reteach, repeat, reinforce previous teaching with different strategies to lay the information into the brain. We accessed positive emotional academic experiences using Gardner's eight intelligences - musical/ rhythmic, mathematical/ logical, body/ kinesthetic, spatial/visual, linguistic/ verbal, natural, interpersonal, intrapersonal.

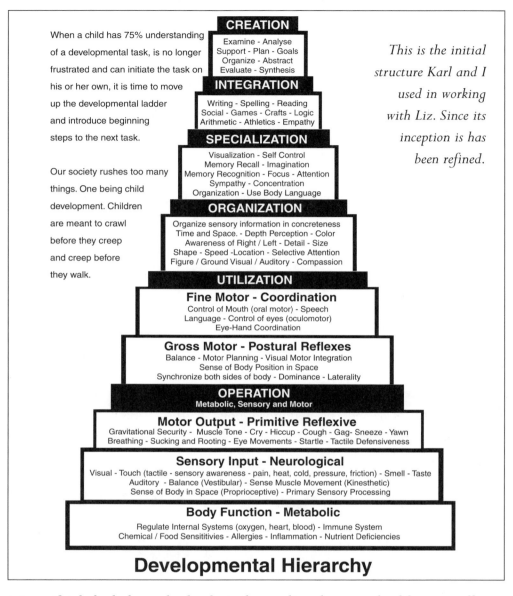

When a child has 75% understanding of a developmental task, is no longer frustrated and can initiate the task on his or her own, it is time to move up the developmental ladder and introduce beginning steps to the next task.

Our society rushes too many things. One being child development. Children are meant to crawl before they creep and creep before they walk.

This is the initial structure Karl and I used in working with Liz. Since its inception is has been refined.

CREATION
Examine - Analyse
Support - Plan - Goals
Organize - Abstract
Evaluate - Synthesis

INTEGRATION
Writing - Spelling - Reading
Social - Games - Crafts - Logic
Arithmetic - Athletics - Empathy

SPECIALIZATION
Visualization - Self Control
Memory Recall - Imagination
Memory Recognition - Focus - Attention
Sympathy - Concentration
Organization - Use Body Language

ORGANIZATION
Organize sensory information in concreteness
Time and Space. - Depth Perception - Color
Awareness of Right / Left - Detail - Size
Shape - Speed -Location - Selective Attention
Figure / Ground Visual / Auditory - Compassion

UTILIZATION
Fine Motor - Coordination
Control of Mouth (oral motor) - Speech
Language - Control of eyes (oculomotor)
Eye-Hand Coordination

Gross Motor - Postural Reflexes
Balance - Motor Planning - Visual Motor Integration
Sense of Body Position in Space
Synchronize both sides of body - Dominance - Laterality

OPERATION
Metabolic, Sensory and Motor

Motor Output - Primitive Reflexive
Gravitational Security - Muscle Tone - Cry - Hiccup - Cough - Gag- Sneeze - Yawn
Breathing - Sucking and Rooting - Eye Movements - Startle - Tactile Defensiveness

Sensory Input - Neurological
Visual - Touch (tactile - sensory awareness - pain, heat, cold, pressure, friction) - Smell - Taste
Auditory - Balance (Vestibular) - Sense Muscle Movement (Kinesthetic)
Sense of Body in Space (Proprioceptive) - Primary Sensory Processing

Body Function - Metabolic
Regulate Internal Systems (oxygen, heart, blood) - Immune System
Chemical / Food Sensititivies - Allergies - Inflammation - Nutrient Deficiencies

Developmental Hierarchy

injury (fetal alcohol, cerebral palsy), the gradient between healthy normally functioning brain tissues and areas of completely dysfunctional neurons is indistinct. It is in the intermediate zones between healthy and severely damaged tissue where a population of cells exist that, although damaged, are still able to be brought back on line with appropriate therapy. These neurons have been termed idling neurons – an appropriate title for cells functional but not functioning.[38]

38. Perlmutter, David, M.D., *BrainRecovery.com: Powerful Therapy for Challenging Brain Disorders.* (2000) Perlmutter Health Center, 800 Goodlette Road North, Suite 270, Naples, Florida 34102   (941) 649-7400

When teaching Liz we discovered that her emotional state at the time of learning was directly connected to the amount of information she remembered the next day or the next week. I taught to her interests with drama, humor and enthusiasm.

We followed developmental sequences to help Liz develop brain connections. We introduced new material in miniature steps and guided Liz to the edge of frustration. She was capable and not falling apart. Then we repeated the material slowly adding more substance and reintroducing it in a variety of ways to build retention. Liz grew; her eyes sparkled. We empowered her as we empowered ourselves with more understanding of human development. We strengthened Liz's central nervous system before growing her connectors just as a plant grows builds a stronger root system before growing new shoots.

We utilized the same process that worked with teaching Liz to play the harp – one note at a time – and introduced a behavior repertoire – one step at a time – beginning with senses and reflexes, basic action sequences, instincts and integrated action sequences, learned and experiential action sequences, play, exploratory behavior and goal directed behaviors. We built a solid foundation at each base to stabilize later developmental piece.

We brainstormed to discover ways to access and normalize her senses – smell **(olfactory)**, sight **(vision)**, touch **(tactile)**, hearing **(auditory)**, movement **(vestibular)**, taste **(oral)**, and body position **(proprioception)** hoping to remove the storms in the brain.

- We strengthened her visual area **(occipital lobe)**
- We strengthened her auditory area **(temporal lobe)**
- We strengthened her sensory area **(parietal lobe)**
- We strengthened her executive functioning **(frontal lobe)**

We investigated her reactions and responses:
- How did she act when she was hungry?
- How did she respond to loving feelings?
    Did these get confused with lust or sex?
- What was her response to fear or anger?
- When did she feel hate? What made her irritable?

When teaching Liz a new concept, I introduce it gently. If I know Liz is going to get frustrated learning, I forewarn her, "Liz, this will probably get you frustrated. Tell me when you feel a little frustrated." I can teach longer and provide more information when Liz monitors her own frustration.

Our genetics may establish our potential but our experiences determine how this potential is expressed. Early experiences have a decisive impact on the architecture of the brain. Early interactions don't just create a context; they directly affect the way the brain is wired. Children must be loved, held, talked to, read to and allowed to explore in order to thrive and survive.

- Was she territorial or possessive? With what? When? Why?
- Did she tend to be dominating or submissive? Did it switch in different situations?
- What made her vulnerable? When was she serene?
- Was she attached to her family or friends? Was each relationship healthy?
- Was her emotional growth following a logical developmental pattern or was it stuck?
- Could she learn to respond instead of react?

Toni Hager *(www.kidscanlearn.net)* designed an in-home therapy program that included a combination of occupational therapy (OT), physical therapy (PT), sensory integration (SI), and therapies to stimulate reflex, oral motor, speech and language, auditory processing, vision and academic achievement. We organized her medulla (level 1), pons (level 2) and midbrain (level 3) before we moved on to working

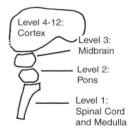

Level 4-12: Cortex
Level 3: Midbrain
Level 2: Pons
Level 1: Spinal Cord and Medulla

with the cortex (level 4-7) of her brain and the frontal and prefrontal cortex (level 8-12). (See Appendix 8) We worked with her cortex in developmental sequences at the most primitive level working towards sophistication.

Could Liz learn to think and feel at the same time? Without these two systems working together Liz's life would continue to be complicated by her primitive and simple responses. Her emotions overrunning her judgment, her life a continual soap opera with relationships of – but – he said, she said, we did, you did, they did. Liz's behavior miring her in an emotional madness sabatoging a successful and independent future.

What most children learn naturally we had to teach Liz. We worked with Liz's available toolbox –

The therapies and strategies in this book are complementary to traditional medical, psychological and educational protocol. The path we took is not traditional. We tried to create supportive environment for remediation, restoration and renewal.

her mouth, eyes, ears, skin and motor skills. After we completed initial sensory issues we focused on building capacity in her **motor cortex** - controlling speaking and writing, **auditory area** - increasing her processing and listening capacity, and her **visual area** - training her to process what she was seeing and utilize her eyes. We exercised her neurons to make connections, hoping that the connections would make more connections. A small change was a major victory.

The lower levels of Liz's central nervous system began to harmonize. We slowly merged motor and sensory experiences hoping to make smoother, faster, less impulsive and frustrating connections between vision, auditory and motor areas.

We progressed. Dr. Jeff Brist helped us with nutrition and supplements. Toni Hager, N.D.S. helped us organize Liz's central nervous system. We added a body-training program to help Liz with posture, strength and walking. Dr. Don Sealock's team of eye therapists worked to strengthen Liz's visual system. Dr. John Nash opened the window to Liz's working brain. We watched it work and she trained to manage her emotions, frustrations, impulsivity, attention and focus. Karl and I provided unconditional love, structure and belief in Liz's abilities. Liz provided the perseverance to keep trying.

Liz has always been able to learn. She now learned sequentially to enhance her capabilities. We mixed modalities — she was walking and chewing chew gum at the same time. She skipped and laughed. We talked on walks. She remained unable to coordinate dance using her hands and feet. She upped the anty and found a producer to manage her hip-hop rap group. Performances and group interaction was a new endeavor.

We understood the truth in Toni's statement, *"a person can't do what a brain isn't ready to do. When we get her brain to the next level you'll be surprised at what Liz can accomplish and enjoy."*

I am grieving. My son plead guilty to grand theft. He did not steal the car. There are actual witnesses who testified he did not steal the car. My son says it will be easier to be in jail. He won't fail school there. He won't disappoint his family there. Jail is more cool than trying to live life with FASD.

Sue (FASD mom)

I sometimes wondered if Liz picked a fight or riled herself up just to get her brain waves moving. She would hit herself on the head and say "I wish I could turn this damn thing on."

Liz stormed into the bathroom. "I am taking ten Advil to get rid of this headache." Oh no you are not!

Liz was doing new things. Best of all she was enjoying them. Her head was not filled with air – her brain was slowly being interconnected with tiny important pieces. We slowly built new bridges. Our professionals provided us a blueprint.

MEGABYTES AND MEGA BITES

Karl and I had to change our 'software,' as Liz's 'hardware' was upgraded. No longer could we speak to her in two to three word statements. As she profoundly stated "I am not a dog, don't speak to me like one." Her working memory had expanded and language patterns that had worked for thirteen years were no longer effective. Liz now processed what she heard.

Liz, life is not a soap opera. It does not need to be one dramatic event layered upon another. Let's see if each day we can move forward, instead of spin out.

"Mom, remember the report I wrote in 2nd grade? I did my best writing it, but I couldn't read it. I worked so hard and I typed it all myself. The teacher got mad at me for not being able to read it and made my friend read it for me. Everyone laughed at me. They thought I was stupid. I had tried so hard. They were wrong Mom, weren't they?"

I remember thinking years earlier, if I can teach Liz to write, maybe I can also teach her to think!

A child with brain damage may wear a smile and appear to submit willingly to education that he is developmentally incapable of learning. He may be compliant to correction that will inevitably come his way even though he is not being disobedient – he is simply unable to respond and incapable of retaining the information. This cannot be disciplined away – the child who has been prenatally exposed lives with the scars of another person's poor choices.

We would not put a child with FAS (fetal alcohol syndrome) – who has fetal alcohol facial features – through the paces a child with FAE (fetal alcohol effects) faces – whose affliction is not visible. We would not feed a diabetic child improperly, yet for years we fed Liz food her body could not process. We would not expect a deaf child to hear; yet we went thirteen years before we met Liz's auditory needs. We would not expect a blind child to read without feeling; yet we expected Liz to struggle day after day with visual processing issues and written words. We would not expect a child in a wheelchair to stand up and do jumping jacks. In our ignorance we failed to see the innocent child behind the appearance of acting out and disobedience, the child whose only voice and advocates may be the parents loving and caring for them. Our world does not feel, sound or look to them as it does to most people and our ignorance is not bliss for these kids.

Children with FAE look normal and society expects them to act normal. As a result they experience failure and frustration. They know inside they are different but don't know why. Their self-esteem nosedives. Gradually they go from a happy, achieving preschooler to a depressed, struggling teen. They don't understand the behavior they are blamed for. While we look at the big picture, they process a tiny corner. They perceive themselves as innocent while we interpret actions and expressions as dangerous, lying or manipulating. Life happens 'to' them. It's someone else's fault, "they made me do it," or "I didn't do it."

Some days Liz does well and other days she performs poorly. Inadequate sleep, poor nutrition, change, stress and poor peer choices compromise her capabilities. Days of excess wind, rain, temperature extremes or seasonal change are difficult. The inconsistency of her ability to hold things together is frustrating. It is the inconsistency that confounds people's expectations. The good days cause teachers and extended family (or us) to shake a finger at the child and sternly warn, "You aren't trying hard enough. I

Your working memory stores ideas just long enough for you to understand them. Liz's working memory was that of a three-year-old. We built auditory sequential (short term) memory throughout the day. I would say two to four word instructions without visual cues (ie "right hand on left shoulder"). We played repeat back in the car. I said silly words, vocabulary or words within a pattern and Liz repeated them to me. We used humor and praise. We began simply with two to three bits of information and moved on to more complexity. Soon Liz was beating the electronic Simon game she had previously thrown across the room.

We built connections between Liz's right and left sides of her brain. Liz suppressed the vision in her right eye and the hearing in her left ear. Perhaps this helped her cope with her confusing world. It meant her visual information went into one side of her brain while her auditory information went into the other. I gave her auditory only directions without visual clues. I whispered in her non-favored ear. I silently showed her how to do what I had just told her by drawing or writing. This decreased her frustration and opened a door for understanding.

know you can do better."

Our words beat the child down emotionally and contribute to the chronic frustration they feel with themselves, leading to the secondary disabilities in adolescence. Karl and I reminded ourselves this was a teen in an adult body with the IQ of a grade school student and the EQ of a preschooler.

GARBAGE IN GARBAGE OUT

Liz's fetal brain development was altered by prenatal substance exposure. Her early infant development had been stymied by four out-of-home placements in less than four months. These initial fourteen months — from conception to her arrival in our home at five months — would jeopardize her opportunity for a successful, independent adult life.

Prenatal and early infant care are significant in the future development of a human being. Liz lacked early infant stimulation. Much of a child's early development of vision is done while feeding. Liz fed herself as her bottles were propped up in an infant seat. For children fortunate enough to be breastfed the rotation between breasts allows the child the opportunity to utilize both eyes and ears while suckling, learn to breathe through their nose, engage in skin-to-skin contact and look at mother from different directions.

Karl, Nancy and I had introduced Liz to all the normal child developmental milestones thinking we were doing the best for her. We unknowingly built connections upon weak and missing synaptic connections and Liz appeared to progress well for a while.

Liz desired to do things right, yet often felt she had failed miserably. Her senses felt bombarded by information we experienced as mundane. She was incapable of

If you've told the child a thousand times and she still doesn't get it, who is the slow learner?

Input and Output

1. NORMAL INPUT
2. ABNORMAL PROCESSING and ABNORMAL OUTPUT
3. ABNORMAL FEEDBACK

FASE PERSON

Abnormal patterns of response establish abnormal feedback and more abnormal responses. This cycle is difficult to break as the responses become habits even when no longer necessary.

Different receptor neurons in Liz's sensory system to delt with different kinds of energy.

• We rehabilitated her eye response to the spectrum of visible light.

• We exercised the hair bundles in the clochea of her ears to sense sounds, movement, and vibration.

• We normalized her responses to chemical substances entering her nose and mouth.

• We dealt with her touch, balance and motor issues.

accessing complete data or filtering out noise. She could not organize the input in a meaningful way, and so her output was abnormal. This meant the feedback she received was abnormal. Like reflexes, the organization of our senses begins to function in the womb. We were still untangling both for Liz.

Hundreds of millions of cells act in precision to change stimulation into electrical impulses. These impulses flow through the central nervous system to the brain where they can be understood and acted upon. Everything we know about our world comes to us through our sensory system. **Sensory Integration (SI)** is our ability to take in, sort out, and connect information from the world around us harmoniously. Integration of our senses nourishes the brain by helping the brain properly digest the sensory information it receives. For most people, a sweater against the skin is soon ignored, unchanging objects become part of the scenery and no longer seen, and customary sounds become background noise. What draws our attention is change, to alert us to potential danger. Any degree of change caused whirlwinds of random reflexes without thought for Liz.

Unlike Helen Keller who became blind and deaf at 19 months, Liz's issues began before she was born. The damage was far subtler and remained misunderstood as "bad" behavior or attachment disorder. Liz saw, but she could not process what she saw. Liz heard, but she could not process the sounds accurately. Liz felt, but she could not understand sensation.

Our nervous system reacts to a selected range of **wavelengths** (vision), **vibrations** (hearing) and **chemicals** (taste, smell). Liz's neuro knobs needed fine tuning.

Neurodevelopment utilizes the brain's neural plasticity, redundancy and branch effect to remediate and progress through missed developmental stages. We began at Liz's lowest attained developmental levels and worked upward through the whole central nervous system. Karl and I were team players in therapy, observing, reporting, and documenting. Toni was our home-based coach taking into account our lifestyle and parenting. She taught us in language we understood to help Liz.

> *Telling a child with a biological problem to control himself or try harder is useless unless the core problem is addressed and remediated.*

Brain cells are different from many other cells in that they can grow by sending out neurons far beyond their own nuclear masses. Neurons have specialized extensions called **dendrites** and **axons**. Dendrites bring information to the cell body and axons take information away from the cell body. Neurons communicate through electrochemical processes called neurotransmission. If the particular neuron exists, gentle enhancement of weak functions and proper nourishment to strengthen the weak area may allow it to wire and fire. As long as we are able to learn, we can 're-wire' our brains. For individuals with brain damage, this requires many repetitions, but it can often be done. We cannot reverse the damage but reroute the neural pathways. We can use existing idling brain cells in new ways. We do not yet know how to replace them, and few areas of the brain regenerate.

The work of researchers of cell biology and neuroscience at Rutgers, The State University of New Jersey have discovered a protein known as cypin. Cypin is found throughout the body, but in the brain it regulates nerve cell or neuron branching, it appears that increasing the Cypin increases the dendrite growth. Cypin also appears to act like a glue that cements other molecules together in long chain structures that extend throught the branching of a dendrite as a skeleton. This is promising for the development of new drugs to help persons with learning disabilities or Alzheimer's disease.[39]

Simple Brain Nerve (Neuron) Pathway

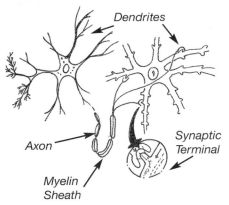

Dendrites

Axon

Synaptic Terminal

Myelin Sheath

39. *Rutgers Scientist Discover Protein in Brain Affects Learning and Memory,* Jan 18, 2004- Press Release, Rutgers, the State University of New Jersey

The brain works through networks and systems. The basic structural unit in brain function is the neuron. Each of our billion neurons branch out from its center, called the nucleus. Each branch, or dendrite (from dendron, meaning tree), is covered with little nodes called dendrite spines. Information jumps across the tiny gaps between the spines. This junction is called a **synapse**.

Practice made permanent. Through many repetitive small steps she built new usable neural pathways.

Synapse is another word for the connection between two neurons. A person's thinking is a vast network of synaptic patterns. Actions become automatic. Practice makes permanent. The more often a synaptic connection occurs, the stronger it becomes. That is why a 'professional' typist can type error-free so quickly, a cellist can play a complicated piece so beautifully, and Tiger Woods can master the Master's.

Nerves are the pathways moving information and instruction – at speeds of up to 200 mph or across a football field in one second – between the brain or spinal cord and the rest of the body. If all the nerves in the body were stretched out they would be around 75 miles long.

Our developmental goal for Liz was to alter the biology of her brain, one tiny developmental step at a time.

Myelin is the fatty insulation covering the axons of nerve cells. Myelin wraps around the axon and helps electric current flow down the axon. It facilitates faster transmission and insulates the axon from other cells. It keeps electrical impulses from randomly jumping. When myelination is delayed, many motor and sensory developmental milestones are also delayed. The spread of signals around the central nervous system is not as efficient as it should be. Medical research indicates that some people have thinner fibers than others, and that thinner fibers process more slowly than fatter ones.[40] Myelination begins prenatally and continues throughout life. Myelination increases as neuronal connections stabilize.[41]

It is projected there are over 100 billion neurons in the brain. To illustrate this imagine a stack of 100 billion sheets of typing paper 5,000 miles long reaching from San Francisco to London (www.brainconnection.com). In addition there are ten to fifty times that number of **glial** cells in the brain. Glial

40. The Handle Institute (www.handle.com)
41. Geake, Dr. John, *The Gifted Brain*, University of Melbourne, Australia.

comes from the Greek word meaning glue. They have processes, but do not have axons or dendrites. They aid in connecting and providing communication circuits to and from different areas of the cerebral cortex. They insulate the axons and support the brain structurally, clean up the debris and regulate the chemical composition surrounding the neurons.

Research by Gary Lynch of University of California at Irvine, shows that the glial become very active in the fetus before there is any neuron axon sprouting. They divide and move through the intact tissue of the brain. They migrate through large sections to get to active glial sites. They send out branches and become very large — before there is any axonal growth from the neuron.

Finally, we understood why sweeping was so stressful to her — Liz could not cross her midline.

ACTION AND REACTIONS

By age ten, we knew something was wrong. Day-to-day life and tasks for Liz triggered rage attacks. We didn't understand her brain couldn't perform like other children's. We thought it was a *won't* issue, not an incapability. We thought it was misbehavior.

There are two categories of nerves: **motor nerves and sensory nerves**. When you want to touch something, a signal is passed from your brain or brainstem to your spinal column and then to your **motor nerves**, which tell your muscles to move. The motor pathways can control posture, reflexes, muscle tone and voluntary movements. **Sensory nerves** work in the other direction. Messages from your senses are sent through your sensory nerves and the spinal nerves to the brain to be understood. In case of danger your spinal nerves red flag the signal and send out an immediate reflex message to protect your body as the signal continues to propagate up to the brain. When your brain decides what to do with this sensory information it sends another signal back along another set of nerves forming a closed circuit. Liz's neural highways were in desperate need of road repair — neuro development helped us stimulate her nerve receptors and teaching

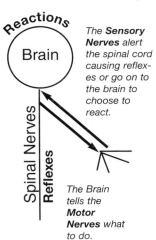

The **Sensory Nerves** alert the spinal cord causing reflexes or go on to the brain to choose to react.

The Brain tells the **Motor Nerves** what to do.

us to rebuild roadways to her brain.

      There was so much Karl and I needed to learn to help Liz. We were determined to help Liz integrate her senses and make more synaptic patterns with the exercises we were provided in neurodevelopment. Each morning we 'plugged in her brain' as Liz referred to our neuro exercises. We did a series of **tactile sequences** (healthy touching exercises) to wake up the nerves in her skin triggering as many neurons as possible. We started at her fingertips and toes and soon progressed to complete tactile sequences of deep pressure, vibration, pain, hot, cold, wind, light touch and texture. Within a short time we could touch Liz from her toes to her knees, fingers to shoulders, along her neck, spine and trigeminals pathways in her face. She began liking her back scratched and looked forward to lighting up her neurons and brainwaves in the morning and shutting them down at bedtime. A year later the child who avoided healthy touch was able to visualize words written with a feather on her soles, palms, cheeks and back. Her lack of **internal sensation** (pons area - receptive sensory) contributed to her lack of bonding and attaching. Liz's **expressive** (motor - pons/medulla) delays contributed to fidgeting, constant moving, poor balance, lack of an internal clock and sudden outbursts when physically touched by another.

      We built auditory and visual sequential (short term or working) memory – the number of pieces of information a person can hold together at one time – in day-to-day life. Liz held only three pieces of information (digit span of 3) together when we began. Limited short-term memory simultaneously stores and manipulates information to accomplish a task. It helps the prefrontal lobe understand. This includes the executive functioning and how it integrates planning and preplanning information. This affected her ability to function, learn, understand instructions and sequence.

The trigeminal nerve carries signals from the face, nose and teeth to the brainstem. Sensory input from the face does not enter the spinal cord.

Several nerves connect the ear area to the brain.

• The cochlear nerve conveys sounds. Liz heard things differently – a group of children coloring, mom's fingers on the keyboard, the drip of a faucet drove her crazy.

• The vestibular nerve signals for balance and head movements. Liz avoided sudden or subtle movements like boats, planes, car, playground play and amusement park.

Our emotional feelings ultimately mature into values — how we make choices, perceive and feel about things — looping through the arousal system entering into the cingulate and limbic systems. Many times what appeared to be attention difficulties was when Liz used all her brain power to keep the jumbled pieces together, remain composed and organize the pieces in her 'right' order.

Five factors for brain plasticity:

- Environmental stimuli
- Frequent stimulation
- Proper duration of stimulation
- Motivation
- Consistency

www.crossroadsinstitute.org

OUR DIGIT SPAN AFFECTS OUR EMOTIONALITY.

Liz's **working memory** (digit span) of three pieces of information had become ingrained in our family culture. We asked short questions. We made short statements. We received answers from her but not reciprocal conversation. We were used to Liz responding back to us like we had spoken into a tape recorder. Karl and I worked hard to camouflage exercises to raise Liz's digit spans. We gave a series of three, four and five directions. We played repeat back games in the car with number, letters, words and nonsense words. We played *Simon Says* and *I Am Going To Grandma's and in my suitcase I will bring a . . .*

Liz learns best in play and pleasure. **We develop through play – words (wit, humor), bodies (running, jumping, swinging), minds (imagination), things (toys, games) and nature (exploring, climbing, hiking).**

We separated visual and auditory exercises to strengthen each independent of the other. We practiced in the car when we were stopped at a red light. We practiced in school, in waiting rooms and while we did the dishes.

My digit span increased as I worked with Liz. Life was easier. I retain nine pieces of information in the correct sequence. Liz's therapy was helping my brain!

The results were less confusion, clearer and quicker thinking, and better communication, for both Liz and mom!

A **digit span of two** is basically equivalent to the amount of information a two-year-old can handle. When a person with a digit span of two throws a temper tantrum he/she is not out to get a parent or trying to drive you crazy today. The child's communication is far simpler — "I'm tired, hungry or stressed out," "I know what I want, but I don't know how to explain it," "I can't stand this noise or these lights anymore," "I feel crowded, I need space," "I'm scared, I need you to hold me and comfort me," or "I am so frustrated, I can't stand it."

If this young person is responding to everything as "no," the child is not trying frustrate you. The person may simply mean "I don't understand what you are saying, so I will just say no," "I wonder how much I can test the limits," or "I'm me and not you and I can feel differently." Listen to the thoughts and feelings the person is trying to convey. If you are able to reflect these back to her, you can help the child understand herself.

If a person's **digit span is three** you can expect her emotionality to be that of a three-year-old. She may just be beginning to think of consequences. Her temper tantrums will be less spontaneous than a two-year-old, but just as glorious.

The person's ability to retain information, manage emotions and participate in daily life also grows as the **digit span increases up to four**. The world is more balanced and the person can see the bigger picture.

When a person has a **digit span of five** it may be harder for them emotionally and it may take longer to mature, but they can catch up. The world opens up, questioning and understanding begins.

The average adult American has **a digit span of seven** plus or minus two, which is why the original phone numbering system was composed of seven digits. In some cases the short term auditory memory differs from the short term visual memory. When this happens the child is often drawn to the dominant sense, paying attention to the auditory if the visual is lower or vise versa to the visual if the auditory is lower. Saying you're not listening to me may be absolutely true, since they are busy watching what you are saying.

Test Your Digit Span.

Make a set of cards with the following:

6 9 2

cat goat cow

4 6 3 1

car pen truck house

4 5 2 7 0

grape orange lemon lime fruit

7 9 4 8 2 0

six words

seven number

seven words, etc.

Auditory: have a friend read with a monotone voice. Making the letters into chunks like 4,631 or 46 & 31 is cheating!

Visual: have a friend show them to you like flash cards.

See how high you can go!

MAKING SENSE OF
THE LESSER-KNOWN SENSES

A. Jean Ayres, Ph.D. believes the primary building blocks of the central nervous system are the senses, particularly the special senses —

1. **vestibular** (the sense of movement),

2. **tactile** (the sense of touch) and

3. **proprioception** (the sense of body position).

These sensory processes take place within the brain at an unconscious level. Cells within the skin send information to the brain regarding light touch, vibration, texture, pressure, pain and temperature. Structures in the inner ear detect movements and changes in position of the head. Components of muscles, joints and tendons provide an awareness of the body. The basic senses (taste, smell, sight and sound) are all interconnected with these lesser-known senses. Their interplay is necessary for a person to interpret a situation accurately and make an appropriate response. Dr. Ayres believes all other skills are complex processes based on a strong foundation of the senses working together **(sensory integration).**

We retain and lose information all day. We gather information, reassemble it and keep only a gist of what we take in. If we are not interested in it, goes in one ear and out the other, if we are interested it is filed. I watched in awe. Liz remembered each hand-clap rhyme she tried to learn with classmates at eight-years-old. Not only did she remember every word, but at 14 she performed the action flawless.

1. The Vestibular System *(the sense of movement)*

• Affects our ability to balance and our muscle tone.

• Processes information for our sense of taste, smell, for joint and muscle sense.

• Allows coordination of two sides of our body at one time and cross our midline.

• Helps the brain process what is heard.

• Helps with visual focusing.

• Helps with our emotionality.

The receptors for the vestibular system are located in the inner ear and are stimulated by movement of the head and input from the other senses. It

A gentle breeze felt like a gale to Liz. To help normalize wind sensation we introduced small battery operated fans and blow dryers. Gentle rocking in a boat caused nausea. We spent time reading in the hammock.

tells our brain whether our movement is fast or slow, up or down and if we are moving or our environment is moving. Astronauts deprived of gravity in space often experience vestibular issues including mirror writing when they return to earth. Children with vestibular issues may have balance problems, disorientation, disorganization and clumsiness. They may have trouble with right and left discrimination, directionality in team sports (heading to the opponent's goal post), difficulty in spatial accuracy, spacing, reversals and staying within the lines while writing. The child may crave movement or be intolerant of movement depending on a hypoactive or hyperactive vestibular system. They may rely on their visual system for balance.

2. The Tactile System (*the sense of touch*) originates with touch receptor cells in the skin. These receptors have two tasks:

Liz desired to wrestle, roll and tumble much like preschoolers do as her vestibular and tactile systems grew. This proved a great sport for urban boys and another worry for mothers. Karl snowplowed a bigger mound of snow and bought Liz the thickest parka and snowpants he could find. I went looking for a Twister® game.

a. **to alert a person to danger** - protective (pain, temperature, itch, tickle)
b. **to provide information** about objects and the environment - discriminatory (touch, pressure, vibration).

Sensory seeker ideas:

- Five minutes of physical activity before learning
- Fiddle with stress squeeze toy
- Drink water from bottle
- Weighted vest blanket or neck wrap

Children who are tactile defensive (hypersensitive) like Liz are overly sensitive to being touched by objects and/or people, especially when the touch is unplanned. Their reactions are not due to problems in interpersonal relationships, but have their root within the CNS, brain and skin. Other children who are hyposensitive may get hurt and not realize it, or they may know they were touched but not know what part of the body. With eyes closed they may not know body parts.

The skin is our body's largest organ and just under its surface lay five types of nerve endings. Each of these serves a very important function for normal daily living. They provide acknowledgement of the body to pressure, touch, pain, heat and cold temperature, and movement of the skin hairs. Liz's receptors have communication trouble. Her deep pressure receptors fail to make contact, so when she is badly injured she doesn't know it. Her touch receptors are highly sensitive – mild wind feels assaulting, color book paper hurts her hands, texture and temperature changes can trigger meltdowns. Bumps and bruises most people ignore create foghorn screams.

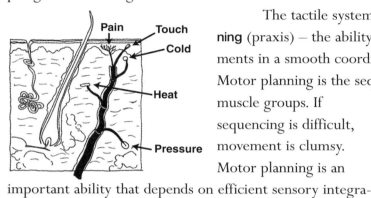

The tactile system affects **motor planning** (praxis) – the ability to perform movements in a smooth coordinated fashion. Motor planning is the sequenced order of muscle groups. If sequencing is difficult, movement is clumsy. Motor planning is an

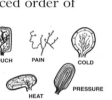

Different types of nerve receptors in your skin.

important ability that depends on efficient sensory integration. Motor planning involves having an idea about what to do, using knowledge of past experiences and the sensations that accompany them. This capacity to plan and sequence actions relates directly to a child's ability to attend; follow directions; carry out, plan actions and solve problems; as well as read, write, do math and think. When motor planning occurs, a person is able to deal with a new task by organizing a new action. Motor planning relies on conscious attention to the task, while relying on stored information regarding unconscious body sensations.

Each new task or experience was a frustrating blank slate for Liz distorted by limited sensory integration. In addition some of the reflexes she should have outgrown as a baby still engaged and other reflexes were nowhere to be seen.

Motor planning is not easy. A child has to learn to remember things. The more simple and clear the directions the less fuss, tears and confusion for the child. Association helps. A child can associate toothbrush, toothpaste, brush teeth with a goodnight kiss or the school bell with homework, lunchbox, jacket.

3. The Proprioceptive System *(the sense of body position)* receptors are located in the muscles and joints. These microscopic spindle-shaped stretch sensors detect whether a muscle is pulled tight or is hanging loose. They sense if a tendon tension is tight. They provide information to the brain about where the body parts are and what they are doing. That is how you know your arm is bent. A child with poor proprioception may crash into objects in the environment, have trouble climbing or descending stairs, slap feet when walking or hold a pencil so hard while writing that the

A child first performs movement with both sides of the body. Then the child is able to use reciprocal movements — each side of his body doing the same thing at different times. Finally he is able to do a different movement with each side of the body at the same time.

lead breaks. Liz had trouble copying information from a standardized test booklet to the testing sheet, from the chalkboard onto a paper and from a recipe card onto the original manuscript of her book. Each page she copied in *The Best I Can Be: Living with Fetal Alcohol Syndrome or Effects* took her 20-30 minutes. Each letter was arduously made. Each word over three letters challenged her to remember what letter to write next.

The vertical midline goes down the center of the body. The horizontal midline crosses at about the waist. Liz was unable to cross either midline.

I watched my 14-year-old skip happily through the parking lot. I remember longing for that sight when she was in preschool. Side-to-side she danced happily in the sunshine toward the green car. She opened the door singing, got in and sat down — however, it wasn't my car!

Prior to neurodevelopment we had tried to work with **Brain Gym**® with little success. Brain Gym designed by Paul E. Dennison, Ph.D. and Gail E. Dennison *(www.braingym.com)* is based on Edu-Kinesthetic and helps many children. It includes many midline movements and brain building activities. Liz hated the program that most children enjoy. What looked easy to me was impossible for her.

If Liz did something requiring her to cross her arm over her midline, she turned to avoid the perilous crossing. If she was doing something that required simply reaching over, she moved her whole body. Sweeping, raking and snow shoveling were frustrating. If Liz was writing she turned her body toward the

I noticed that Liz had a bruise on her leg while doing tactile sequences. Just one . . . I always thought she bruised easily because she always had bruises on most parts of her body. She never knew where how they came. I now realized she was running into things her whole life, not feeling the pain of injury and not even noticing what happened. "Liz, where did you get that, bruise?" I asked.

"On the car door. Don't do tactile there mom, it hurts." She had come so far.

paper. She turned her chair while she was eating. Liz was not developmentally ready to cross her midline. To work with Brain Gym® we remediated rolling over and cross pattern crawling. In a few months of neurodevelopment training Liz was able to cross tap, cross skip and cross crawl without major outbursts. The hated Brain Gym program became part of our daily routine.

The neuro development results were promising. Liz's senses began connecting, no longer ignoring or assaulting her. She hoped on one foot without thinking. She skipped. She began to filter out unnecessary noise and lights – she was learning to concentrate. She cuddled and came to her family for healthy affection. She wrote reports, understood rhymes **(receptive prosody)** and wrote rap lyrics **(expressive prosody)**.

At 15, Liz said, "Mom, I like doing jumping jacks. You know once my phys ed teacher had me show off my jumping jacks. Everyone laughed at me. They talked all day about how stupid I did them. I never wanted to go to a gym again. I am glad we are rewiring my brain." Simply impossible mountains a short time ago became naturally integrated into her teen with a twist life. She was able to play her harp with both hands, dance with midline cross-ing, make balloon animals, draw with an Etch-a-Sketch and help rake the neighbor's yard.

With mini bites of information we were devel-oping mega 'brain' bytes.

I KNOW. THANK YOU.

Toni arrived for our third neuro development evaluation – eight months on the program. We had witnessed and enjoyed significant progress. Liz was happier and more confident of her abilities. She out-

Liz and I joined Step Aerobic Class. Her step work was perfect. Her hand work was perfect. She could not use her hands and feet at the same time. We designed exercises to slowly build up her horizontal midline connections.

grew many of her 'friends' and developed a few 'real' friendships. She wore clothing that was no longer street corner attire! We still hovered 24/7 but she was gaining small pieces of independence and freedom.

On the way to visual therapy, Liz noticed the 'door open' light on in my car. At 40 mph, she promptly opened and closed her door to check. Shocked I turned back and asked, "Liz, why did you open the door?" "I didn't open it, Mom, I closed it." Toni's neuro files and a book were missing, probably strewn along the road. Faced with being late for therapy and an ensuing FAS attack, we opted to have a good session and backtrack when the session was over. Liz believed nothing fell out. She 'only' closed the door and never opened it. The proof lay in the autumn leaves – a wide radius of tire tracked papers and a much thinner learning strategy book. Liz retrieved the papers. One person's file had fallen out of the car – hers!

Running down a set of steps, I solidly placed my foot on the last step – that wasn't there. I landed face down in what appeared to be a slide into home plate in front of Liz's feet. I discovered what it felt like to have proprioception problems.

We climbed developmental ladder rungs. She gained a year in mathematics and over three years in reading decoding and comprehension in four months. Her digit spans settled at a constant five with access to digits of six and seven – at times she was processing auditory information better than many American adults. She conversed with us. We rarely heard her babbling with random thoughts popping out of her head. Her walk was softer, her balance more controlled. She cuddled and remained briefly still. A pepperoni pizza was no longer forbidden food. She relaxed her diet regime by adding correct enzymes for digestion. She was breathing through her nose. Her sinuses were clearer and she had avoided having a cold. Clearing her throat and spitting had subsided, instead she was drooling.

Simple things in raising a child with FASD can make such a difference. Liz may have learned to eat more properly if I had fed her with the spoon going into her mouth sideways as a baby, like we eat. Instead I had made airplane noises and put the spoon directly into the little mouth hangar. The exact way she still ate at fourteen, sometimes with noises included.

We were now able to give Liz more than one instruction at a time. We made a game of it and used two instructions. Soon she managed three actions in a row.

Table manners continued to be an issue. "Liz is now a nose breather," Toni explained, "It is time to retrain her to eat." Liz chewed with her mouth open mashing her food on her teeth with her tongue. She feared suffocation if she ate with her mouth closed. Toni provided exercises with horns and straws and bubbles. We played air hockey on our dining room table with cotton balls and straws. We lifted weights with our lips to stop drooling.

Now that Liz crossed her vertical midline, she was able to learn to eat more appropriately with utensils. She was capable of holding a fork and knife and crossing her midline to cut her food.

We worked on oral sensitivity and Liz's food choices broadened. Hot sauce was no longer a major food group next to olives and pickles. Salt was heavily sprinkled, but not poured. Her father no longer needed to wear a raincoat to dinner.

My beautiful daughter with FASD was now only spitting in a bag in my car, instead of leaving the remains of her throat clearing on my car seat, window, her pants or as a new gel for her hair.

Raising teens is never easy. Raising a teen who has grown developmental years quickly was mind boggling…we struggled. We had a different child.

When Liz is alert and attentive I push for new learning while she is capable of tolerating frustration. When frustration hits, I reinforce materials already mastered and heap reinforcement.

As I dropped Toni off at the terminal, she said "I went in and said goodnight to Liz after you went to bed. I wanted her to know that her behavior wasn't the only reason for the migraine I got last night, and I didn't retaliate by giving her a nasty program. I told her she was doing great and was a super star. Do you know what she did? She reached out to hug me and said a very quiet "I know, thank you." I checked on her later, Liz was asleep and her mouth was closed.

"Many will be brave in your courage"
Alexander Graham Bell to Helen Keller

IS IT THE CHILD CAN'T? OR IS IT THE CHILD WON'T.

Diane Malbin, M.S.W., *is a clinical social worker, program developer, and consultant who provides information and services for individuals, families, and agencies. Preliminary findings of improved outcomes for people with FAS/ARND based on her work have been presented nationally and internationally. She teaches and consults with parents, educators, health and social service providers, treatment professionals and others across the US and Canada. She is a published author and parent of a child with FAE. FASCET website is located at: www.fascets.org*

Primary Characteristics: Neuropathology	Standard Interpretation: May Lead to Punishment	Secondary Defenses or Characteristics
Memory problems	Could remember if he/she tried	Fear, self protection
Inconsistent performance	Not trying on "off" days	Anxiety
Forgetful	Willful	Frustration
Poor short term (auditory) memory	Not listening, paying attention	Anger, avoidance
Remembers some things, not others	Seen as lazy	Confusion, depression
"Gaps": Talks the talk, doesn't Walk the walk: disconnections	Willfully disobedient	More defensiveness
Can't link words with feelings	Seen as uncaring	Shut down, confusion
Forgets words, ideas	Doesn't try, could do it	FRUSTRATION!!!!
Decodes, doesn't comprehend	Manipulative	Inferiority, fear, masking
Difficulty forming associations	Does it 'on purpose'	Internalizes negatives
Doesn't see similarities differences	"Should" know better!	Isolated, fearful
May not generalize or apply rules in new settings	"Trying to make me mad"	Masks mistakes, lies
Difficulty with abstractions: money, math, time	Has to know times tables!	Avoids homework
Poor planning, sequencing initiating, following through	Punished for not doing tasks	Feels blindsided, may not understand
Difficulty understanding danger	Psychopathology	May shut down
Impulsive, suggestible	Daredevil, sociopath	Behaves accordingly
Can't see consequences	No conscience, punished	Blames others
Fatigue	Passive resistive	Irritability to rage
Long response time	Trying to be controlling	Gives up or acts out
Acts young for age	Too dependent, irresponsible	Overwhelmed
Socially "inappropriate"	Poor values, insensitive	Gravitates to "comfort" friends
Perseverative	Controlling, wants own way	Rigid, resistive
Oversensitive	Hypochondriac	Discomfort, distress, whiny
No response, flat affect	Doesn't care	Lacks language to clearly communicate

BUILDING A HEALTHY SENSORY DIET

A professional skilled in sensory integration (SI) can recommend a sensory diet specific a child's needs after carefully observing what mix of calming and energizing experiences the child needs to remain attentive and unstressed during the day. Children with hypersensitivity may have difficulty concentrating or interacting in the environment if they are trying to protect themselves from common everyday elements

TOUCH (Tactile)

Touch Issues –

- **Clothing on self –** Stiff tags, stiff fabrics (jeans), seams in socks, clothes, jean seams, appliqué on clothes, waistbands/wristbands, belts, ties under chin, jewelry, synthetic fibers, pant legs rub against each other, stripes or polka dots, material that does not breathe, too hot / cold, new shoes, wool, sweaters
- **Touch –** Rough or cheap paper (telephone book, newsprint, manila paper, color crayon paper), people touch them by accident, teeth cleaned or brushed
- **Hair –** Hair bands, barrettes, hair brushed or combed, hair shampooed, haircuts
- **Touch behaviors –** Avoid bare feet, shorts, finger-play activities, dislike texture of objects or clothing cause or compounds hyperactivity, distractibility or withdrawal, aggressive behavior, cannot stand in line; excessive pushing and shoving, easily frustrated or upset, picky eater, avoids certain foods (rice, celery, carrots, chunky peanut butter, lettuce) due to texture, always touch people or objects, insensitive to temperature, chews on inedible objects (hair, fingernails, pencils, shirt cuffs), trouble holding or using tools (scissors, forks, pencils)
- **Other issues –** Sweat on body, rain, wind, temperature or weather change, feel too hot or too cold, entering water, fabric rubbing, toothbrushes

Family Ideas

- **Toy play –** Build with blocks, play with Legos, dominoes and jigsaw puzzles, color on rough paper
- **Kitchen play –** Stir cookie and cake dough, eat snacks with different textures, (cheese, pretzels, fruit), play with pots, pans, rhythm
- **Water play –** Baths, bubbles, soap and toy play in the sink or bathtub, wash hands with soap and drying hands with towels, wash toys in sink
- **Touch experience –** Make believe dress up, draw letters on face or back, healthy snuggling, hug and roughhouse gently with friends, pillows or beanbag cushions, curl up in "secret hideaway"
- **Outside –** Make mud pies and sand cakes, draw with wet or dry chalk, painting with water, run in sprinkler or hose play, stomp in puddles, tricycles, wagons, bicycles, walk barefoot, garden play, forest adventures, care and love of animals, examine natural objects, (sticks, pinecones, feathers, rocks).
- **Art play –** Finger-paint with paint, shaving cream, or pudding, glue art projects, play dough, crayons, scissors, and brushes, collages

SEEING (Visual)

Visual Issues – Fluorescent, halogen , strobe lights, LCD signage, car lights (at night, in rain, tiled tunnels), lighted mirrors, reflective materials (metallic look, shiny sequins, watches, jewelry glossy white paper), flickering sunlight (through leaves, off water, blinds, snow), severe contrast (red/black, blue/orange, black/white, cinema/plays), intricate patterns stripes, polka dots, loud colors, black and white linoleum tiles, bright yellow signage)

Visual Behaviors –

Difficulty with

- Discriminating one object within many, building blocks, puzzles, letter/number spacing, steps/curbs, stay focused on deskwork, moves head while reading, uses finger, pencil to track words

Inability to

- Follow moving objects; sports, teacher in classroom, cross midline, reading, writing, recognize the similarities/ differences in pattern/design, copy from chalkboard/books

Family Ideas

- Play flashlight tag
- Play balloon volleyball
- Dance with scarves
- Toss small beanbags
- Dot to dot, maze, hidden picture books, puzzles
- Trace letters/numbers on a person's back
- Take photos with a camera
- Blow bubbles, horns, whistles
- Suck through straw
- Make snow angels
- Draw chalkboard circles, using both hands
- Play board games, tangrams and pattern blocks, bead work, sew or other crafts, jumprope, jacks

SOUND (Auditory)

Sound Issues – High pitched sounds, deep resonating sounds, background conversation, discord, unexpected loud sounds, instrumental music mixes, intercoms, fluorescent lights, noise makers on others (jangle bracelets, watch alarms, cell phone ring, fabric rubbing)

Sound Behaviors – Unable to discriminate sounds; reading, speaking, verbal instructions, filter out sounds; distractibility; disruptive behaviors, remember verbal information, poor concentration, always talking, hypersensitive to sound

Family Ideas

- Sing "drop-in" songs (ex- Old MacDonald had a ---)
- Play a kazoo or harmonica.
- Jump rope and chant
- Sing vowels while moving (ex- eeeeeeee, oooooooo), hum
- Dance, move, draw to music.
- Beat rhythm instruments
- Move hands, feet, or body up/down to slide whistle sound.
- Make up rhymes
- Play non-competitive musical chairs

BALANCE (Vestibular)

Balance Issues – Fear playground equipment, cautious, slow moving and sedentary, fear any risk, decreased rhythm patterns, direction and speed problems, balance and equilibrium, follow directional instructions (over/under, on top of), falls frequently, movement activities cause nausea (spinning, carsick, fair rides), misunderstand words in relation to movement or position, constant movement, inability to stand or sit still, poor safety awareness, craves intense, fast, spinning movement does not get dizzy, rocking or swivel in chairs, riding on roller-coasters, career around

corners, bumps into objects and furniture, apparently on purpose, low muscle tone and seem to be loose and floppy, tire easy in physical activity, confused what is moving (like a train, ball, car) is moving

Family Ideas

- **Forward and backward –** Swing back and forth
- **Spin or circles –** Swing in circles on a tire swing, ride merry-go-round, somersaults
- **Walking and running –** On uneven surfaces, grass or sand, balance beam, railroad tie, or low wall, crawl through tunnels or large cartons
- **Up and down** – Ride, walk, balancing a seesaw, jump (trampoline, mattress, from step, playground equipment, climb a jungle gym, slide down a slide, ascend and descend stairs, roll and sled down the hill

MOVEMENT (Proprioceptive)

Body in Space Issues – Swivel chairs, being seated when others are moving, tipped chair or surface, light contact with ground or seat, open area behind child's back, close quarters (lines of people, tents, elevators)

Moving Behaviors – Slaps feet when walking, sit on feet, pokes cheeks, pull fingers, cracks knuckles, trouble managing small objects (buttons, snaps, eat sloppy), inability to perform smooth and coordinated movements, poor or odd body posture (melt into desk, leans, bumps, or crashes against objects and people. Invades other's body space, can not perform motor tasks at an automatic level, must show to tie shoes, fold clothes, set-up math problems), stiff, uncoordinated or clumsy, pull or twist clothes or other materials.(stretches tee

shirt over knees, chews collars.), play with hair clips, crayons, pencils, so hard they break

Family Ideas

Pressing, pushing and pulling – Push and pull wagons, push palms together, hold up the wall, press pegs into pegboards, hammer nails into tree stumps or golf tees into Styrofoam, open doors without help, rip paper, get in and out of seat belts, jackets, boots, shoes and socks, knead dough or meatloaf, balance book on head, roll a big snowball

Walk, dance, run, jump – In boxes or dishpan with rice beans, stretch up to sky, walk like animals, wheelbarrow walking.

Playground / Outdoors – Obstacle course, play swing "bumpety-bump", hang from monkey bars, pour from one container to another, sand, beans, rice, water, juice, tumble on the ground, go up slide and slide down, swing, hammock, swim, hopscotch, jumprope, hose the car, sprinkler play, sports, games, outdoor activities

Throwing – Play catch with a ball, throw snowballs at trees, pillow fight, ball up newspaper and throw at each other

SMELL (Olfactory)

Smell Issues – Unexpected body odor, vomit, gas, burp, animal or human feces, paints, varnish, glue, hair spray, gel, dry cleaned clothes, fabric softener, gasoline, oil, fatty foods deep fried, orange, banana peels, very sweet smells, cologne, perfume, aftershave, smell of plastic. clinics, hospitals, antiseptics, medicine or alcohol

Smelling Behaviors – Overly sensitive to odor, smells, smells food before eating, lacks awareness of odors

6 . SELF-CARE

CARE FULL

Caring for children with FASD is at times exhausting and overwhelming. To be effective for your child you have to be effective for yourself. In my training sessions I tell parents to free themselves from thinking they are a 'bad' parent living with a 'bad' child. A child with FASD may feel powerless, scared and out-of-control; they may be relentless in pushing the limits of tolerable. Think of yourself as the glue gun that holds your child together.

Get some fresh air and sunshine. Place a chair by the window, take five minutes to sit on the steps with a glass of cold water or hot cocoa.

When your child is first diagnosed, you may feel relief that you can now arm yourself with support and services, only to discover there are many misleading paths, professionals who misunderstand FASD and a child who is noncompliant. In addition, it is normal to grieve the dreams you had for your child's future. This grief may repeat itself at life junctions — transition to school, first love, adult life, independence. Give yourself permission to cry. I discovered sad movies provide release of tears necessary to purge my heart.

I ask parents to make a 'To Do' list of 50 things you enjoy or encourage happiness for you. Some can be as small as enjoying a new flavor of tea, others as far fetched as a trip to China. After you come up with 50 ideas, post this list where you can find it. This list provides ready relief when life becomes stressful.

In Australia they chose not to own the worry. Statements such as "It's a worry" or "That's a worry" makes it clear it is something to ponder, but you needn't get upset or increase your own personal stress level because of it.

Laughter is good medicine and a sense of humor makes a huge difference in daily living. Rent a comedy movie, visit a humor site on the internet, call a friend who shares your sense of humor and find joy in the little things. Laugh when your child polishes all your wood furniture with 'Goo Off', it is not the end of the world, after all the furniture polish was orange

Our FAScinating Journey ©2004 Kulp

too! When you are down, take a deep breath and put a smile on your face. Our facial muscles contain direct linkages to our emotions. Play with your body language and face by practicing the six basic emotions: happiness, sadness, anger, fear, surprise and disgust. You will be surprised at the difference a smile makes inside your heart.

Understand the challenges your child faces. FASD is an information processing disorder and hard for persons not affected to understand. Regard your child with love and respect. Model how you want people to treat your child as they grow with increasing challenges due to permanent brain injury:

1.   **Feeling and Reacting Challenges** — these include sensory and reflex issues and are most noticeable in early childhood years as the child learns to cope and adapt.

2.   **Think About It Challenges** — these include central nervous system and memory problems and become apparent as the child struggle to learn basic academic skills

3.   **Think Ahead Challenges** — these include executive functioning skills and abstract reasoning. Grade four is the beginning of abstract reasoning, the child now begins to struggle with making choices, peer influence and being different.

Discover your child's treasures. Make a list of the traits your child has that you value and post them in a prominent place. Think about the traits your child has that are most difficult for you, now think of how these traits can be used to enhance your child's life. Liz's obsessive behavior is an asset when she has homework to do, her repetitive behaviors are great when a task has to be repeated, and her assertiveness gets her needs met. In addition, she is loyal, friendly, fair, concerned and sensitive. Share the list of positive traits with school, friends and family. Build on them.

Seek emotional support for yourself from friends, family and organizations. Online support and training workshops are places to meet others with children similar to yours. Take time and be CARE FULL to keep your own love tank filled.

Accept
- FASD will change your life in ways you cannot control.
- FASD does not go ever away.
- Your child as perfect and the FASD as the obstacle.
- Your child's and his or her limitations

UNITED WE STAND,
DIVIDED WE FALL.

I jumped passionately into working with Liz. Karl gravitated toward his business, hobbies and clients. Work and friends became his safety net. Isolation became my refuge as I developed environmental controls and strategies to stretch Liz. While we longed for togetherness, Karl and I aimlessly drifted apart. Liz sensed our differences and played against us. **We drew a line between our partnering and our parenting.** Twenty-five years of a happy marriage was not going to dissolve because of a child's neurological issues. We were not going to join the statistics of marriages torn apart while learning to deal with the complexities of special needs children. We became co-coaches on a unified team. Liz was going to be a player. We humbled ourselves to each other by sharing our hidden feelings. It no longer was us against FASD. We added FASD to our team. We were going to play to win. Saturday breakfast dates, while Liz was asleep allowed time alone together.

Liz medical diagnosis of FASD was fact. Our responses to her diagnosis was ours to choose. When she didn't understand what we said, she watched. She saw our every behavior. We had to change too.

We searched for islands of intimacy in the ocean of FASD. We found the intimacy in tiny details — a special look, a warm comment, holding hands. We

The real news is parents of children with FASD who have had to deal with children suffering from fetal alcohol syndrome. The real news is how much pain and sadness this condition brings. The real news is about the unsung heroes who live a daily battle with FASD. The real news is how many victims there are …

Calgary Herald Article -
Sept. 4,2000

"Disability shatters the dreams, fantasies, illusions, and projections into the future that parents generate as part of their struggle to accomplish basic life missions. Recovering from such a loss depends on one's ability to separate from the lost dream, and to generate new more attainable, dreams."

Ken Moses, Ph.D.

kissed and hugged. We smiled with our lips. We smiled with our eyes. We encouraged each other finding solutions in our differences. His logical engineer side blended with my compassionate artistic side. We traded approaches and intensity. We stopped viewing behavior as good or bad.

We questioned behaviors:

- Where did her behavior come from?
- Why was it there?
- Were there slow triggers that built up to the expolsion or behavior?
- Were the slow triggers adaptable or changeable?

Parenting strategies that may have worked in a more normal family blew up in our face. Liz brought out the best and the worst in us. Living daily with FASD forced Karl and me to seek out and abandon unhealthy family of origin programming we brought to our marriage. Liz had a ravenous appetite for my kindness, time and energy. Her concrete logic triggered Karl's high level abstact logic.

Karl and I needed to learn to speak out our personal desires and needs. Our independent natures were not healthy to our relationship, especially while raising a child like Liz. We needed each other, we swallowed our pride, stripped our emotions bare and lay new foundations of true feelings, then we rebuilt our united front.

I was overprotective and anxious. Karl was frustrated and aloof. We feared letting Liz interact with others who were out of our sight. We feared letting go. We hindered everyone's development. I sacrificed my whole self to help her and abandoned my own needs. My gift of giving devoured me to the point of having nothing left to give. I was sucked dry. I needed Karl to fulfill me emotionally and nurture me. I needed to learn to ask for help and let go.

A little gratitude goes a long way. Tell your significant other:

- what you love about him or her.
- what you are grateful for being with him or her.
- why you are proud of him or her.
- what you appreciate that he or she does for you.
- what you are thankful for. For example: fresh laundry, a telephone call, dinner, time with the kids, patience, strength, etc.

We adopt these children with love. All the love and patience in the world did not fix them. Solid appearing marriages break apart and crumbled in this difficult lifestyle — 85% of them. If we could survive, could we help others?

Each of us has our own Achilles heel. Our children with their complicated developmental challenges seem to know how to kick them and add pressure. Some days are worse than others. My husband's and my feelings are real. They cannot be denied. We realized when we started blaming Liz for the things she could not achieve or understand we were burning out.

Feeling a certain way does not mean behaving a certain way. Karl and I consciously reach out daily to each other as Liz exposes FASD to the community. It is not easy. You learn the most of what family means when the family is stretched. Life with a prenatally brain injured child is like living on a rubber band.

How can we do any kind of parenting, stand for unexpected outbursts, and yet find a way to reach a permanently damaged brain that is hard to reason with? How can we not internalize, take it as a personal affront? How do we come back to the inner calm and peace of the soul after an FASD episode when we have quelled the inner storm, to remain calm on the outside after having an explosion we wish we could erase? And then just when we think we can relax and rest, another storm breaks!

There are no easy answers. We cannot view the life of an individual with FASD in a snap shot. We must gaze longingly at the slow but steady climb over a lifetime. We must not stare in horror at the moment, but find progressive patterns of hope.

Just as we openly talked about adoption we now spoke about brain injury. Liz's needs, ideas and opinions are important. Our family unit is more important. FASD behavior can be acknowledged and understood with honor as long as it is not bratty, spoiled or manipulative. Karl and I must be astute enough to recognize the difference in guiding Liz in the development of responsible and self-directed behavior. It is a delicate balance

Tears streamed down my face. Parenting a child with brain damage was so hard. "I'm not strong enough. I'm not good enough. I don't know enough. I feel like a bad mother and I don't know how to make it better." The logical side of my brain seemed to watch as the pent-up emotional side finally broke loose. I dissolved into my own FASattack pity party. "Mom, you're acting childish," Liz exclaimed. She was right, but the depths of my humannity needed expression. Longingly I gazed at Liz, "Liz this FASD stuff is hard, really hard. Neither of us is going to be perfect. We just have to be the best we can be and forgive each other when we fall."

between control and freedom. Our goal for her is to be a sensitive and spirited individual who understands her abilities and her challenges.

- How much independence and freedom could we allow her without putting her in grave danger?
- Could she learn to keep herself safe? Each step of independence created new problems and surprises.
- How much care could we give her without creating a spoiled monster? Where was the balance?
- Could we develop a toolbox for her to cope with adult realities?
- Could we help her sense the social cues people emit?
- Could Karl and I continue to hold onto our precious relationship and remain united?

It remains to be seen.

POWER TOOLS FOR PARENTING

Telling Liz she did wrong focused on the wrong and encouraged more wrong. We had to teach her to do right. Liz learned appropriate behavior by being taught appropriate behavior. Karl and I needed to focus on her positives and our positive comments needed to be just as spontaneous, sincere and expressive as our negativity could be. We had to believe in Liz so she could believe in herself. We pulled Howard Glasser's, book *Transforming the Difficult Child: The Nurtured Heart Approach* (*www.difficultchild.com*) from our parenting toolbox.

The **Nurtured Heart Approach** was designed to create a transformation in the lives of difficult children and their families. It is based on energizing a child's successes while refusing to energize failures—yet still provide accounta-bility. It builds a child's internal strengths and helps the child shift his or her intense energies into positive behav-ior. It is geared toward reversing a child's negative impres-sion and helps them trust they can access internal and external energy for success. The model strategically cre-ates a new scenario supporting the occurrence of this transformation. Dr. Glasser's mantra is **"Create successes**

Liz asks why I am worried about something that was forever ago even if it was just this morning or yesterday.

and then stand on your head and let them know you noticed!"

Karl and I adjusted our parenting with Dr. Glasser's tools, adapting it to Liz's special needs.

1. We began telling Liz "I need you to....." not "would you", "could you", or "please" since they provided options for no. If there was not an option and I needed Liz to do something we said what we meant… "I need you to take out the trash. Now. Please."

2. We no longer picked or chose our battles. We gave Liz a short 10-30 second time out to reframe her behavior. This allowed her an opportunity to recognize inappropriate behavior and pull herself together. It also provided us the opportunity to compliment her on paying attention, gaining self-control and not escalating. Liz and I named this STAR time….Stop Think Air* Review. *(See excerpt on next page.)*

3. We took "positive" verbal snapshots called **Kodak Moments** (active recognition) of Liz "all day long." These statements offered proof to Liz that she was capable and successful and we acknowledged her hard work.

- *"I noticed you are frustrated and really working on controlling yourself, good job."*
- *"You have been using more self control lately. It's nice to see."*
- *"Even though you were upset, you handled your feelings well."*

Children instinctively download positive recognition as a success. Liz developed a new perception that she was making progress and could continue. Being noticed has a powerful effect.

4. Karl and I discussed the qualities we wanted Liz to grow. We selected two at a time and used Glasser's **Canons** (experiential recognitions). We focused on any tiny attribute of what she was did right, instead of focusing on what

You don't raise FASD kids on the side. It's a full-life commitment. They don't accompany us on our life's journey; they sweep us off the path and down their own rocky roads with a flash flood. Only the best survive these rapids. We grasp at sandbars along the way; find temporary high ground only to be swept away again by the tidal wave of FASD. Our consolation is that, together, this child might survive those rapids. Alone, they drown. Can we teach them to swim? Can we keep them alive? Maybe. Can we let go and watch them drown alone? Impossible.

Vicki, (FASD Mom)

she did wrong. Whenever Liz showed respect for us or acted responsibly, we tried to acknowledge it.

- *"I love that you are so responsible in cleaning the kitchen."*
- *"Your room is much neater. Good effort, good attitude and good responsibility."*
- *"I love that you do your chores without being told. That is so responsible."*
- *"You've been using much better self-control when you're mad. I appreciate that."*
- *"Yes, you can have your friend over because I noticed how respectful you were with me today, even when you were frustrated."*

We tried to avoid reactions rewarding disrespect and irresponsibility. If she was disrespectful I asked her to reverse her reaction and try again. "Put that statement in reverse" gave me the opportunity to compliment the effort, or encourage her to back up. For children with FASD our intense negative reactions to their behavior can be very confusing. This technique is a way of energizing and teaching important values and embedding them in an actual successful experience for the child.

5. When Liz obeyed our family's rules we took **Canons of Unbroken Rules** (proactive recognition). We amplified her good choices and provided a snapshot of the feeling or skill used to get there.

   - *"I noticed you have not yelled all day. Wow! That must have taken some will power."*
   - *"I appreciate you didn't answer that question with a 'no'. That showed me you have fortitude. Good job."*
   - *"I noticed you thought about my feelings too. I appreciate that. You showed patience and maturity."*

Be a STAR
- **S**top
- **T**hink
- **A**ir*
- **R**eview

* Air was the most important part of this. Liz's was responsible to take a deep nose breath, make her belly expand and then exhale through her mouth. This provided increased oxygen to her brain allowing her a moment before she reacted.

When Liz drove out-of-control into the FASlane I set her up for success. I gently whisper *"Be a STAR"* or *"FAS Attack, watch yourself. Think about what you're doing now."* Then complimented her on listening to me and working on getting herself under control. We found Glasser's techniques repeatable and win-win! They created successes that would not otherwise exist using normal parenting reactions.

The Nurtured Heart Approach proactively creates more experiences of success for children by using actual experiences of valued actions, relationships and acknowledged moments in time. Children like Liz, who cannot make the connection on what to do about a problem action or behavior, are much more receptive to the intended lesson when they are not confused by our negative reactions.

We are what we energize. If I make a big deal over my disdain of bad manners, a child will decode my statements as "I love bad manners," unless I find a way to make a bigger deal over instances of good manners.

Howard Glasser, Ph.D.
www.difficult child.com

I whispered fortified breakfast wee-tees (affirmations) in Liz's ears when she was a small child. Karl and I began doing it to each other. "I love you." "I really appreciate how hard you work." "Thank you for . . ."

Karl and I discovered when things were going right, it was the perfect time for the most intense, fun and outrageous spontaneous reaction on our part — Glasser's ideas provided us our best power parenting tools.

PROVIDING BEGINNINGS AND OFFERING ENDINGS

With each task Liz was taught or each chore she was asked to do, Karl and I realized she needed provision of the initial steps to start and a finality of completion. We provided short explicit directions, wrote short lists and added small pictures. Liz's need for clear direction "This is what you do. You are finished when you . . ." could prove fatal in the employment market. I often proved voice and hair raising in our home.

Examples:

- Put the towels on this shelf, when you are done come and see me.
- Stack this row of firewood, when you are done come and see me.
- Take this medicine first, then you can eat your dinner.
- Finish your homework, then you can be with friends.

"Your child is more normal than different and different does not mean defective. Find opportunity in the differences and enjoy your child with a little twist."

8. EMOTIONAL BEHAVIOR

ANGER

I wonder if I will have any hair by the time Liz emancipates? I have changed my expectations in teaching and parenting. I understand life is not fair. I cannot change the world nor can Liz. Liz's brain damage will not disappear. I can help guide Liz through life experiences to become the best she can be, but I cannot be there for her forever. I will not always be there to plan successes so it is impossible for her to fail or plan safe failures so she will eventually learn to succeed. I am not able to untangle so many confused brain wires or rebuild all the neural pathways she is missing? I feel like I turn my cheek so many times it has turned inside out. I know it takes distance and time to act appropriately . . . to disengage and redirect. But in some cases physically moving away from a volatile situation is impossible or dangerous. And sometimes I wonder by disengaging emotionally to redirect her behavior, to help her understand the problem and to move on in another direction, if I do not handicap her since the world will be cruel.

As Liz got older and wiser she challenged our parenting almost to the breaking point. We had to decide that our partnership was the more important than our parenting.

"Bang!" My handmade German coffee mug shattered into a hundred pieces as I assertively planted it on my desk. It was the millionth little thing that crossed the line to anger. Liz's mouth opened and she looked surprised, "Are you mad Mom?" she asked confused. She hadn't noticed we had been debating about not riding the bus to an unattainable location for 45 minutes. I made no headway and was frustrated. She had just declared she was going, knew what she was doing, and had turned to go to the bus stop. Not only was her idea dangerous, it was impossible. The teenage years have stubborn stages but this manifestation is far stronger than simply stubborn. There is no logical way to penetrate. The noise of the cup shattering grounded her thinking. She smiled and innocently said, "I am sorry I made you mad, Mom. I love you. Why did you break the cup?" Cleaning up my mess, I asked Liz to give me ten minutes in the bathroom (my retreat) then meet me at the Truth Table.

Cognitive perseverative behavior manifests itself in young children with repetitive behaviors — spinning, twirling, banging, repeating, tapping toes, drumming fingers, knocking, pacing — like a skipping record. For an adolescent or adult it manifests as a particularly rigid way of looking at things, a refusal to let go of an idea (rigid tenacity which can border on fanaticism) and/or a certain way of feeling or interpreting a feeling and refusal to consider any other explanation. It may be a narrow interest in something excluding everything else. It was the one thing Liz did that could push all my buttons and send me into a tailspin. She seemed to 'lock in' to her behavior and was unable - not unwilling - to change. To 'talk sense,' 'rationalize' or intervene verbally usually made the situation worse. It didn't matter what negative consequences she faced or what positive reinforcement I offered. The strongbox remained locked.

How does one maintain a sense of calm and maturity amid chaos?

I understood Liz's first choice as her familiar and safe choice. She had not thought of any other choices yet and so she did not own them. She had trouble holding her own thoughts let alone listening to new thoughts, processing new thoughts, comparing new thoughts and determining which of the new thoughts could benefit her. According to FASCETS, (www.fascets.com) adults who perseverate usually have great difficulty in seeing similarities and differences in behaviors and situations. They have problems in sorting and classifying sub-sets of their behaviors. The first choice is seen as the only choice, once a plan is made, whether agreed upon or not, whether approved by authorities or not, it must be carried through. Liz will self destruct trying to carry out a plan, going from one disaster to another, until she crashes.

How could we help Liz not be the victim of abuse at the hands of a future lover? How could we help Liz not abuse another individual — most importantly her own future children?

Liz and I met at our Truth Table, a place of safety to express our opinions without anger or loudness. We discussed the bus incident. We set up signals. I would watch for 'lock-in' perseverative behaviors and advise her when they were happening. We would work together to find safe options.

"So Simon, what's the big deal about sex? You like it?" The boy nodded. "Well," Liz continued, "at our age you get two options. First, you have a good chance of getting HIV/AIDS. Then you die. Do you think sex for 10 minutes is worth dying for? You get so sick you are in a hospital and never come home. Arhhggg! Then you're dead. Second option, you get a baby. You know what a baby is! Poopie diapers, crying. Eighteen years you take care of 'em. Eighteen years, that's older than you are. You want new jeans. Nope! Your kid gets the jeans! You ready to pay all the bills, talk to teachers, visit doctors for a kid. So you get a choice — death or a baby. You're pretty stupid if you want either of those." Was that my daughter talking? I hope she can walk the walk. The kitty litter seemed to be working.

KITTEN KABOODLES

"Mom, look at my totally free kitten," Liz showed me a tiny orange ball of fur with a crooked tail. "Can I keep it?" Karl the dad, Jodee the mom, Becky the dog and Sonny the bird were in agreement, we didn't need a cat.

"Mom, she can't bring it back. We have to keep it." Dave pleaded snuggling LaKiesha.

"It will be my kitten. I will take care of it. You won't have to do anything," Liz added. Karl's twinkling eyes met mine — a totally free kitten was far better to learn to take care of than a baby. We decided Liz could be a "totally" responsible parent for her new baby.

"Do you have money for the food for your kitten?" Dad asked.

"I can't buy food with my own money. Can't you help?" Liz tried to debate.

"It's your baby to care for — food, litter and veterinarian," Dad added.

"Can't you help me at all?" Liz begged.

"You can have the litter box in the garage, the rabbit hutch for a kennel and some feeding dishes. I can supply the gas to the pet store," I offered. "You can buy the rest of the things your kitten needs."

We headed to the Pet Superstore where an excited Liz picked out food, toys, litter and treats, while I held the tiny ball of fur. "Liz, that's about $30 worth of things. Do you have everything you need and the money?" I asked.

Liz was livid. "Thirty dollars, you've got to be crazy! That kitten is not worth $30! All that dumb

"I did just what you said. I waited to be in love. We will get married later." Teen Girl FASD

cat needs is litter and food." She threw the toys, treats and book on the store floor. Liz appears to be the master of the task as long as every-thing is on her agenda. If something happens beyond her expectations, her world falls apart. Life's tiny curve balls trigger immense emotions and a preschool reaction — a stuck zipper, a broken egg yolk, a missing CD, an unresponsive light switch. People say she makes mountains out of molehills. But in her under-standing of the moment, the molehill is a mountain. Well, it was her kitten and I wasn't going to intervene.

David, wasn't about to give up chimed in "Fine Liz, it will be my kitten too. I'm buying the treats. How will we train it with the litter box with-out treats?" At $11.59 it was no longer a free kitten.

A 24-year-old adult with FASD told me. "I just had my tubes tied. You know why?"

"No" I answered.

"Because I am still a baby and babies can't parent. I don't want to hurt a baby when I get mad or confused. What do you think, Jodee?"

I was silent. It was a very mature decision for this delightful young woman and I wanted to find the right words to honor her.

Kitten babies like human babies wake in the middle of the night and cry. Kittens bite. Kittens scratch. And unlike dogs, kittens are very independent. This was going to be an object les-son in life — Karl and I needed to stand back and let it happen. It didn't take long for the reality to hit. "Let's get rid of it. That cat is a pain."

"Liz, you made a commitment to LaKiesha when you chose to take her home. We don't break our commitments to animals or people. We didn't send you back because you're a pain sometimes"

Early pregnancy is a common occurrence for adolescence with FASD. Their impulsivity, limited cause-and-effect thinking combined with a normal human sex drive that is not limited by boundaries or conscience makes them very vulnerable. A person

How does one select a proper birth control for this vulnerable population with limited restraint in sensual issues? Can they remember to take pills, or properly use a condom? Will their already compromised bodies react to IUD, NorPlant or DeproVera? Will the patch be an effective concrete method of birth control or will they come to rely on the morning after pill? Without respectful sup-ports in place will they be able to parent children? Will they die early from an untreated STD?

"She can't be pregnant I never fell asleep. You said a girl could get pregnant if I slept with her!"

Teen Boy FASD

with FASD is often very slow to learn, intolerant of change, and does not fit into normal growth patterns. A child's role in life is to learn, change and grow. A mother or father with FASD who is easily frustrated and impulsive and who doesn't understand consequences provides a very volatile combination. It is not uncommon to have social services intervene. Our child protection files are filled with undiagnosed mothers with FASD who have terminated rights.

Even more abstract than a pregnancy is the possibility of HIV or STD's. Liz innocently bought a copy of the movie '*Kids*.'[42] It is a hard-hitting movie designed for urban teens regarding sex and HIV. It

"I need a man now to marry so I don't have to have sex with everyone."

touched Liz in a way Karl and I had not been able to reach her. She 'locked-in' to avoid sex for her whole life. Her thinking is always all or nothing. "Mom! Help! The kitten fell into the toilet and I can't get her out. She went down the hole!" Liz shrieked. I rushed to the motor home bathroom, expecting a fiasco that would take hours to solve. "Where is the kitten?" I asked as calmly as I could. "Down there!" Liz shouted pointing down the toilet bowl. A tiny puff of orange fluff pranced out from behind the toilet.

"Don't worry Mom, we didn't do it in public or at our house, we used the dumpster." *Teen Girl FASD*

Knowledge of neurological brain disorders and methods to work with this special population are crucial. Sexuality is not an issue of morality or values for a person with FASD, sex is a concrete basic mammalian instinct, regulated by impulsivity and inhibition is an abstract rule of a soceity. Professionals in the medical, educational, child protection, juvenile justice and chemical treatment fields of work may overlook the glaring reality of FASD. Excellent techniques and systems may fail miserably or cause additional harm to an already traumatized population.

Karl and I signed up for the ride of our life when we adopted Liz, and if we've calculated right, it will be a long time before we get off. Luckily we have LaKiesha the totally free cat Karl and I can love.

It had been two weeks since Liz had abandoned LaKeisha, refusing to feed it, touch it or care for it. It was too much work and a pain. She didn't like it.

42. *Kids* (1995) VDMark Entertainment. Critically acclaimed film for mature audiences. Parental discretion advised. Unrated.

The Whole Back End Fell Out

Liz started having two-way short, logical conversations with us. She still lacked the ability to see nuances of meaning (it didn't matter what reality was, it was what she thought at the moment), to weigh contradictory viewpoints (only hers was allowed) or read between the lines (social cues appeared as bridges instead of boundaries). She often was caught up in the moment or thrown into experiences because of her strange reactions.

"Mom! Come and get me. I can't ride the bus home!" Liz screamed into my cell phone. "Mom! Help! I jumped a fence. You can see my buns! The whole back end fell out of my pants!" She was hysterical. "Tie your jacket around your waist and stay next to your friend's mom," I offered. There was little I could do to help her. I was in a meeting and thought she was safe and chaperoned. Her friend's mother assured me she could handle Liz. I offered to come in thirty minutes to save her from riding the city bus. Liz, seeing my car, rushed over to show me the huge rip — a one-inch slit above the back pocket.

He said, "Promise you won't get mad?" I said, "OK." "I was supposed to go bowling after school. I was swearing, so I didn't get to go bowling on Thursday." I asked him if he'd learned anything from that. He said, "Yeah, I shouldn't swear on Thursdays!"

Patty (FASD Mom)

To deal effectively with life you must be able to conceptualize and abstract at a fairly sophisticated level of accomplishment. You must be able to respond instead of react spontaneously in a helter skelter unpredictable way. Persons like Liz often cannot understand why they keep running amok of our expectations for their performance, never mind predicting how they should behave in the future or how we might react to their behavior. Liz's range of emotions was narrow. She was unable to sustain an idea, a conversation or a feeling for more than a few minutes. She could not journey into concepts or abstractions. No wonder her whole back end fell out.

"What do you mean I broke the window? I didn't break the window. The ball broke it."

PLAYING WITH EMOTIONALITY

I told Liz she couldn't rent an R rated movie. So she bought it thinking purchasing, not renting, would not be disobeying me.

We discovered the work of Dr. Stanley Greenspan and his book, *The Child with Special Needs: Encouraging Intellectual and Emotional Growth.* Our eyes were opened to the possibility of developing her abilities in logic, abstract reasoning and imagination. Each gain Liz made improved her quality of life. Dr. Greenspan's recommendations were non-invasive and written for younger children. We decided to adapt it to a teen.

Dr. Greenspan believes there are six developmental milestones in intellectual and emotional growth (Appendix 5) Liz hadn't completely mastered **Level I – self regulation and interest** in the world. We began on Level I filling in the missing blanks and little by little

"You told me I couldn't be with him. I wasn't with him. We weren't having sex."

Level II – intimacy emerged. The relationship we had never been able to achieve was evolving. The neuro work with sensory integration brought on the enjoyment of healthy touch. Vision work allowed sustained eye contact. We encouraged curiosity in academics and play. We negotiated taking turns and experimented with different approaches. We joined in behaviors we didn't like and helped Liz become aware of them.

We pushed for **Level III – two-way communication**. Liz's new skills in auditory processing enhanced her communication and we continued to work on increasing the depth of our conversations. We started asking abstract questions − why, who, where, what, when and how. We playfully stretched Liz for answers. We verbally pushed her into abstraction. We provided emotional and visual support. We exaggerated our facial expressions, body postures and hand gestures to get a point across. We asked her what she understood in a situation. What better place to negotiate the understanding of abstracts at a basic level than within a crazy and loving family.

Children with sensory, processing or motor difficulties may miss the millions of unencumbered experiences that provide a palette for new and creative ideas. Our ideas grow from experiences with all of our senses as well as

"Why?" I asked. One would think that little three letter word was a four letter epithet. Crack. Another pencil was broken in two and developed wings as it sailed through the air, landing against my forehead. "How come?" I again tried. Grabbing a new pencil I began to draw a mind map. "Let's see what we already know. Maybe we can find the answer there."

our motor system. Liz's difficulties in holding words or pictures in her mind, processing information and controlling and organizing her motor sequences limited her experiences. We worked on visualization and seeing patterns, seeing the hidden pictures within a picture and seeing the whole picture. We jumped into hypothetical and imaginative play – an unchartered territory for a mind that mixed up reality.

Attunement to Liz's emotional state was crucial – fear, anger, confusion, frustration, boredom or preoccupation created learning deafness. Play created an oasis to deal with academics and life. Within three to five minutes of sustained activity, neurons become less responsive and need a rest. Liz remained engaged longer within a playful atmosphere. I mixed dry, boring facts with humor and discovery, compassion and drama.

We used mind mapping to build elaborate stories about teens with pink Mohawks and peacock tails and children who turned into flying colorful parrots who helped others. We played with teens who became mermaids and swam under the ocean to find lost secret treasures. We encouraged her fantasy characters to have feelings, conflicts and issues just like normal teens. We developed dialogue and drama and acted out the parts we created – the more intricate and outrageous the better. We laughed until we cried. Fantasy emerged.

Mind Mapping Example

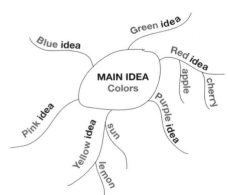

Mind Mapping invented by Tony Buzan, author of *How to Use Radiant Thinking to Maximize Your Brains Untapped Potential* utilizes both sides of the brain (rational and artistic) which allows more effective thinking.

"Imagination is the beginning of abstract thought."

ABSTRACT THINKING IS PLAY.

We merged the work of Dr. Stanley Greenspan with that of Dr. Bruce Duncan Perry, M.D., Ph.D. Dr. Perry's work emphasizes the importance of play. When a child fantasizes, she is playing. Children create by taking images, concepts and ideas in their own minds and sort, reorganize and reconnect them. If a child is able to visualize and fantasize unstructured free time provides a backdrop for creative play – a tree becomes a fort, a rock is a mountain to climb. The child becomes the hero. Electronics – television, computers, electronic games – and structured play – scouts, sports, organizations – often provide little in creative abstract development.

On a clear day, I tried getting inside John's head. "Why do you do it when you know the consequences?" I asked. "Well, I think that maybe this time I won't get caught," he answered. John cannot adequately weigh the risk of taking the action.

Teresa (FASD Mom)

Play is the element in life that allows a child to develop interpersonal and social skills. Play teaches problem solving and frustration tolerance. Play is more than just social; it teaches self-control, strategizing and planning. At each stage of development it is play and repetitive elements of play that help organize neural systems which will ultimately support more complex motor, social, emotional and cognitive skills. Patterned repetitive activity results in patterned neural activity that changes the brain.

A child cannot ask a question if a child cannot formulate a question.

Learning to think logically and abstractly, like most learning, is often a process of two steps forward and one step back. Emotions drive behavior. Liz's developmental ladder becomes a slide when frustration hits. I viewed the mud puddle at the bottom as an opportunity to reinforce

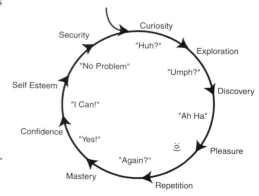

Adapted from the work of Dr. Bruce Perry, M.D., Ph.D.

already learned steps. We dry ourselves off, knowing we've progressed and try again.

- Could we develop inquisitiveness and curiosity?
- Could Liz become a self-learner instead of being force fed instruction?
- Could we capture Liz into a learning circle that was self-perpetuating?

Only four to eight minutes of factual data can be listened to before the brain of a child fatigues and seeks other stimulation — daydreaming (internal) or looking out a window (external). Liz's brain was closer to two minutes on her best days.

While Greenspan's young children have tea parties and play with vehicles, we adapted our fantasy floor time to creative writing and drama using mind maps. Liz enjoyed the freedom of imagination – the beginning of abstract thinking as her sensory issues knit together. Within the land of imagination Liz answered the dreaded who, where, what, when, why and how questions without fear of failure. Humor, silliness, and joy were the keys. During our creative floor time all her ideas were honored no matter how strange. My entrepreneurial spirit soared.

My business success had been built on my ability to ask tough questions, find the answers and then move those answers to solutions.

Strategies we used to elaborate stories and brainstorm:

We magnified: stronger, higher, longer, thicker, add an ingredient, multiply, exaggerate, more often, more time, embellish.

We minimized: take away, smaller, lower, shorter, lighter, remove, split.

We modified: shapes, colors, sounds, odor, form. We added a new twist.

We substituted: who else? what else? Was there another place, approach, time, style, material or tone of voice we could try?

We rearranged: what if another character solved the problem, what if it was a different time, what if this happened first?

We reversed: backwards, inside out, upside down, opposites, negatives and positives, what if they went down the "other" path?

We combined: who was alike, why, when, how?

We discovered other solutions and other uses.

Play develops skills:

Creativity

Teamwork

Cooperation

Communication

Negotiation

Compromise

Developmental
   Skills

Goal Setting

Following Rules
   and Directions

Self Reliance

Empathy

Social Interaction

Problem Solving

Self-expression

Self-confidence

Bruce D. Perry, M.D., Ph.D.

In the freedom of imagination, Liz the parrot, skittered through a plumbing pipe, and confiscated a nurse's uniform. Then she used a pair of crutches as stilts to save her hospitalized friend Nick.

Liz grew through her preschool years not realizing she was different. She was happy, secure and interested in life. Her eyes sparkled and though her play was not imaginative it was filled with joy, she felt safe and approved. She enjoyed life.

Children become motivated through pleasurable play. Playfulness is the door to gain entrance into new areas of learning. In elementary school, Liz watched children play. By the time she was ready to participate, they had gone on to other activities. Her slower processing left her in the wake of their laughter while she attempted to become a part of the group. Her pleasure was strangled by teasing she did not understand. Her "I can" statements were replaced with "I'm stupid" and "I hate myself." Anxiety kills curiosity. **When fear of failure encroaches onto a child's curiosity, they no longer risk enthusiastic exploration.**

Greenspan uses relaxing and fun time together to build skills. Through play, I developed a safe atmosphere to help Liz deal with complex and difficult concepts. Liz – who I nicknamed the Drama Queen – and I dramatized reactions and relationships. If we were lucky we practiced actions instead of getting caught up in reactions. It was her reactions that continued to cost her so much.

Mom, I need to sit here for a while away from all these people and put myself back together.

Role Playing (or rehearsing) is concrete and we continued to use it to build skills, however if Liz was going to survive independently as an adult we needed a beginning understanding of abstraction.

Liz could not hold a picture in her brain (**visualize**). Peter Riddle of Empowered Learning Resources provided us clues to teach Liz this important developmental step. Mr. Riddle uses visualization to develop better spelling and geography retention. We used flash cards of two to three random numbers, shapes or letters. I flashed cards toward Liz and she repeated back what she saw. Soon she remembered dreams in color as she gained visual attention. We talked of memories we shared and tried to remember tiny details — smells, colors, sounds and sights. We recreated happy places in our minds, snuggled on the beanbag chair.

I asked Liz to spell 'gnat' with Riddle's method. Liz placed her eyes in an upper

UPPER RIGHT	UPPER 10% CENTER	UPPER LEFT
Visual Construction	Memory of Smell	Visual Memory Recall
CENTER RIGHT	CENTER FOCUS	CENTER LEFT
Auditory Construction	Sensory Synthesis	Auditory Memory Recall
LOWER RIGHT	LOWER 10% CENTER	LOWER LEFT
Body Sensation Recall	Memory of Taste	Memory of Emotion

EYE PLACEMENT When the eyes move to certain positions, consciously or subconsciously, they send a signal to wake up certain parts of the brain. Neurolinguistic programming is based on these theories. We have used this information to help Liz recall information. (Left handed people are sometimes opposite.)

right position and say "g-n-a-t, 'gnat', t-a-n-g" spelling it both forward and backward and rolling the picture of the word and it's letters in her mind. Liz said it and she wrote it. I wrote on her skin. If the word was longer like 'perspiration' we broke the word into syllables 'per-spir-a-tion, perspiration, noit-a-rips-rep'. If we studied multiplication and division we put the sequence of numbers in our mind — like a circle $7 \times 8 = 56 \div 7 = 8$ $x \, 7 = 56 \div 8 = 7$ or triangle sequence of the numbers 7, 8, 56. Liz said and wrote it. We broke continents into regions, colored the regions (northern region in yellow) and put the picture of the country's outline in our mind. We began by saying "Africa - Northern Region - Yellow; Morocco, Algeria, Tunisia, Libya, Egypt" then we looked in our mind at our picture and repeated the sequence backwards 'Egypt, Libya, Tunisa, Algeria, Morocco - Yellow, Northern Region, Africa.' She drew what she was memorizing to build visualization.

Once visualization began to emerge, Liz and I imagined social situations and reactions. Lying on the

Four letter explitives resounded through the halls of our home. It is remarkable to me that the 'f' word can be an adjective, noun and verb all in the same sentence. Something major had just happened.

*"Liz what happened?" I asked as I saw blood flying off her hand and onto the refrigerator. "I put my hand through the window. #***@! It's bad, Mom. I think it is bad. I was mad so I punched the window. He stole my money. He stole my birthday money." Pointing to the boy standing smugly behind her friend.*

beanbag chair Liz imagined simply walking into her room. What was her room like? Where was the bed? What did the carpet feel like? Then Liz added herself to the picture. The phone rang. What did she do? Who was it? What did she talk about? Next Liz added another person into the picture — mom joined her. What did mom say? Where was mom? How was mom standing? What was mom wearing? We complicated the visualization. Liz imagined a friend talking in a mean way about her. Where was she standing? What was the friend saying? How did her body feel? What did she feel like doing? What things could she do differently? Since it was not real, she had freedom to try new and different ideas in her mind without the fear of failure.

We had learned to help Liz's sensory issues; we were now helping her emotional issues and then hopefully, move on to intellectual levels, not just programmed fundamentals. We kept our sleeves rolled up and plunged on. No one was going to take as much interest in her as we did.

Children take their emotions with them and use these emotions to determine what to do and say in different situations. According to Greenspan's clinical observations the capacity for abstract thinking develops when a child is able to connect different ideas and behaviors to underlying emotions. Could we reach and solidify the final **three milestones? Level III: Complex Communication, Level IV: Emotional Ideas and Level V: Emotional Thinking** are usually mastered by young children. We had a long way to go. Game playing simulated these experiences.

We could not expect Liz to find help for herself. We had to learn to understand her and reach her. This required adjustments to our parenting style and

Liz let me wash her hand as I examined the injuries that were more than I could deal with at home. We rushed to the clinic. By the time we returned the boy was gone, the money was gone and Liz was left with a bandaged hand, stitches and the very tip of her thumb missing. "Mom, I didn't know that I could get cut if I punched the window." Liz called the police.

Liz fixates on special events. She repeats questions. She talks incessantly about what will happen. I realized that in order for her to hold an important thought in her mind, she had to repeat the information.

marriage. We took Greenspan's approach and discussed issues with Liz. She could argue if she was reasoning and not locked-in. We asked her about her feelings. We acknowledged her feelings and pointed them out to her. We let her solve her problems with limited guidance. We let her succeed. We let her fail. We picked her up. We asked for her ideas. We didn't talk down to her. And as her sensory defensive issues subsided we reintroduced experiences we had abandoned — museums, theme parks, concerts, and movies. We began to use the dreaded word — why?

We videotaped interactions and watched the videos discussing social cues and behavior alternatives. I dramatically demonstrated behaviors back to her and we acted out different ways of acting and reacting.

When Liz is frustrated, angry or worried she paces at the same pace as a caged tiger. When she is excited her hands involuntary flap at the side of her head like a butterfly. She arches her back and raises her upper lip in a contorted smile. "Mom I don't like how I look when I am really happy. Do I always do that?"

"Your motor overflows and you don't even know you are doing it." I agreed to smile and give a 'high five' each time I caught her flapping. This encouraged her involuntary reaction to reach awareness and not bring

We must not choose over-protection or under-protection to keep our teens with FASD safe. We must choose different protection.

attention when out in the public. Hopefully it would become intentional. When Liz overreacted I whispered in her ear — *"FASattack. Watch yourself. Think about what you're doing now."* Later in private I dramatized the reaction and we thought of new ways to respond.

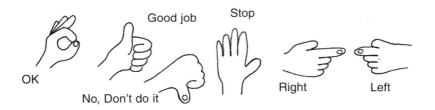

OK   No, Don't do it   Good job   Stop   Right   Left

AMBI GOOEY TEA

Giving John cues and reminders helps him to control his impulses, because it interrupts the process between impulses and actions long enough for the information to get where it needs to go.

Teresa (FASD mom)

"I want a turkey salad, with pepperoni, white pepper cheese, and a lot of black olives," Liz told the sub shop employee.

"Can't mix turkey and pepperoni anymore," he answered "We don't have a key on our cash register and we can only enter products we have keys for." I could see Liz ready to pounce. This did not make sense to her. In her mind there was no pattern to NOT mix pepperoni and turkey. The gentleman was in trouble and he didn't have a clue. The program had changed. Her only fast food restaurant had betrayed her and she wasn't going to stand for it – the turkey was in front of her face, behind the glass next to the pepperoni. "Yes, you can! You always put pepperoni with my turkey."

A person with FASD knows stealing is wrong, but the end justifies the means. The moment of taking something overrides the person's thinking.

"Well, I can't any longer. The boss said so."

"Yes, you can! It is right there. I see it. There is the turkey and there is the pepperoni. Are you blind?" The debate escalated while the line lengthened.

Realizing he wasn't going to win, the employee sighed, grabbed double turkey and slapped it unto the counter. "I'll give you extra turkey!" he snarled as he wielded his knife and chopped it into squares. The eight other teens I had brought for sandwiches stood silently watching the action. The other customers watched with anticipation. My position at the end of the line held little opportunity for intervention except paying for the order.

To think beyond the moment is difficult for individuals like Liz. Life is one cataclysmic experience after another.

Liz had come so far and yet still had so far to go. She had no confusion endurance. In a world that continued to change faster and faster, how could my child gain tolerance for adult life? If a change in a salad throws her into the FASlane, how would she ever navigate the tension of opposites and learn to embrace uncertainty or ambiguity? If every paradox she traversed sent her into a tailspin, could she ever fly like an eagle?

My mind wandered and the days passed as I wondered how many individuals with FASD were in confinement gulag (jail or hospitals) due to their outbursts from not getting their unwavering expectations met.

Crash! Liz's impulsively stacked her breakfast plates on the other side of the booth Dave and I were sitting in. Heads in the restaurant turned to see the commotion. "I didn't get my hashbrowns. I can't eat my breakfast without hash browns. I ordered hash browns and they aren't here. Well I guess I'll just starve," Liz roared. Dave and I rolled our eyes.

"Easy Liz, all they have to do is make you hash browns and bring them to you. It's simple," I said.

"Then my bacon will be cold and I can't eat breakfast with cold bacon," She was obviously locked in, a new brain burp. She seldom eats bacon, eggs and hash browns. They are a treat. Liz did not understand that if they were not there NOW (concrete), they could be there in a short time (abstract). Dave, who understands FASD from the inside out, smiled and said, "Hey, Liz you can have mine. I will get the new order."

"Thanks, Dave," Liz smiled and traded her plate like nothing strange had happened.

The discernment between 'brat' behavior and 'brain injury' behavior is muddy. I have watched other children with FASD react with the same steadfastness - the inability to think the next step when the world rearranges.

I discovered a safe haven in most public areas that I can retreat to with urgency when I feel my own anxiety escalating. I simply say, "I have to go to the bathroom." It is often just the break for peace and distraction I need to settle my thoughts, rub my brow, regain composure and get a cup of ambiGOOEYtea.

The problems with labels are they don't tell us the skipped or unmet milestones in the development of a person. Labels don't consider biological, processing, family, or cultural differences. They don't tell us how to adapt, manage or institute positive change. They don't encourage healthy growth or enhance a family's stability.

9.1.1.

If normal appearing Liz was an adult without caring support the results could have been much different. She could have escalated to the point of being physically removed from the restaurant. And if someone tried to physically remove her, she would have hit him or her for touching her. Misunderstanding her behavior (loud, obnoxious and potentially violent) the police may have been called. Their physical force being met with more physical force from Liz.

The next person who tells me how to care for my child can take her home and fix her!
FASD Mom

Gentle, funny and kind Liz with her neurological barriers could be charged with assault of an officer, her independence lost, her new residence in the public housing system — jail — all over a plate of hash browns.

"9.1.1. May I help you."

"This is an emergency, I've been attacked by a dog and my arm is going to fall off," Liz hysterically screamed into the phone. Two minutes earlier I had asked her to go next door and check if her sister wanted to join us grocery shopping. The neighbor's dog had barked and jumped on her. His claws dug into her skin and she was bruised, but no blood was flowing. I took the phone.

"She is ok, just a bit overwhelmed," I offered calmly as I placed a cold compress on her arm.

Liz screamed, "Ow! You're hurting me. Quit hurting me!" Three squad cars and an ambulance headed to our house to save her. Two hours of discussion and reports later we left for the store.

Liz struggles while on her own even for a short duration. Without the supervision provided by her family and the understanding and support of her school, friends and their families she easily finds herself in situations she can not handle. The unsuspecting public is unsure what to do.

"I'm going to kill her. I am going to rip her face off and kill her," Liz screamed. Another teen had tried to hit Liz in the back of her head. "I am not taking any vitamins all week so I will be really mean and beat her up when I see her next weekend." We spent the week foiling her plans.

Do we make better choices when our brains work right? Of course we do. Liz's brain works best when she is well nourished, rested, not stressed and on a routine. Proper medication allows many persons with FASD higher levels of function.

Hidden potholes sink us on this slippery road. Some we cannot detour. We struggle to build bridges and avoid emotional traffic jams. When Liz gets stuck or obsesses we try to stop our own thoughts, take a breath and listen. We model attentiveness to her words by mirroring back her statements. Once we are in the loop of her fixation, we tie a verbal safety line on her by slowly and carefully interjecting our ideas within her statements. We tactfully increase her range of thinking.

Timeouts with Nancy Thomas' Strong Sitting allow gearshifting in her brain. We sit on the floor or pillow – straight, still and quiet – with our legs crossed and breathing deeply through our nose with no muscle movement. This exercise shifts our brain focus from limbic (emotional/love) to neo-cortex (reasoning/logic). It stimulates both of these parts of our brains. Each minute we spend doing this correctly exercises the logic and/or love parts of our mind and providing increased brain power and focus. Other times we use a 'time-in' approach when Liz is glued to us for a short period of time to regain composure.

"Mom you have to come and get me, I can't get home, no one will drive, I am not in a safe place."
Through snow and accidents I drove to save Liz. "Liz you can't go outside in a snowstorm." Liz was frantic, "You mean I can't go anywhere all winter." Thinking quickly I said. Liz when the big roads like freeways are black you can travel, when the big roads are white you have to stay home." "What about the little roads?" she asked "Oi vey!"

To determine if a behavior is inappropriate ask yourself, "What is the child trying to communicate?"

We use a distraction strategies. Out of the blue we pose a question, "I wonder what --- is doing?" or "What are your plans for ---- Friday night?" Keeping a normal or softer voice at a slower (but not overt) pace provides Liz time to settle and think.

Liz often misinterprets firmness as yelling. If I remain calm and keep my own sirens silent we make progress. I am human. I fail. When I fail, Liz does too and the sirens with red lights become part of our life.

FINDING THE PIECES
AMONG THE CHAOS

Skill potential depends on three issues:

1. Extent of damage to the brain.

2. General health of the brain.

3. Potential of the brain to form new neural pathways.

Contrary to the myths, many children with FASD are high functioning by IQ measurement and do not qualify for services. This measurement is deceptive in that socially, behaviorally and academically they continually fail. Without intensive, extensive, comprehensive and continuing supports Liz appeared uncaring and lackadaisical to others. We appeared to be parents with poor skills. The reality lay rooted in hidden cellular damage. My heart went out to the children with brain differences, their parents, families and educators who work with them.

Liz attended private small schools for preschool through first grade. These loving and talented school systems lacked the resources or staff to continue to help Liz. She did not qualify for special education and she watched as the other students zoomed past her in reading, writing and arithmetic. Our local public school provided quality services and teachers trained in special education. For three years they worked with us to help Liz. Liz became despondent in school and aggressive at home. In fourth grade, fourth quarter we began homeschooling. Liz came home. I had spent eighteen months

Liz avoided reading because it was mentally painful, taking an inordinant amount of effort. Each word was laborous. While other students advanced Liz remained mired in Stage 1.

researching teaching methods while Liz spent the last year trying to read.

- How many other children sat in school daily like Liz had – sullen, sad, unfocused and withdrawn?
- How many other children fell on the floor enraged and exhausted when they entered the security of their homes?

Extraordi-NAIR-y
READING MEASURES.

How could Liz be so fluent in language and fall apart in reading? Weren't the two systems intricately linked?

Before I began homeschooling Liz, I attended the *Reading Works* and *Grammar Works* training program for teachers. This week-long program, presented by Jay Patterson, utilized his reading remediation work along with the pioneering work of Dr. Samuel Orton, neurologist (1879-1948), Romalda and Walter Spalding, Oma Riggs and Jeanne Chall. With Jay's teaching, practical experience and spirit I went home armed with new ideas to help teach Liz to build letters without reversal (**manuscript writing**) and attach the letter to its sound (**phonological awareness**).

Liz's spelling and reading skills grew. She understood the 44 sounds of the English language and connected those sounds to symbols – the 70 basic sound pictures (**phonograms**). We progressed with *Reading Works* by Jay Patterson, *Spelling & Reading with Riggs* by Myrna McCullock and *Writing Road to Reading* by Romalda Spalding. Liz's neurodevelopment program increased her working memory and vision therapy allowed Liz smoother reading without stopping. She now saw a page of letters and isolated words and sentences. Regardless of all the advances, we hit another roadblock. Liz would struggle in adult life with the reading skills she had. I needed to understand reading from a brain perspective.

Initial English (Phonograms) Sound Pictures

Single Phonograms

a	/ a, <u>a</u>, ah /
e	/ e, <u>e</u> /
i	/ i, <u>i</u> /
o	/ ah, <u>o</u>, oo /
u	/ uh, <u>u</u>, ah /
y	/ y, i, <u>i</u> /
b	/ b / (not bah!)
c	/ c, s /
d	/ d / (not dah!)
f	/ f /
g	/ g, j /
h	/ h /
j	/ j /
k	/ k /
l	/ l /
m	/ m /
n	/ n /
p	/ p / (not pah!)
qu	/ kw /
r	/ r / (kiss your goldfish with your lips)
s	/ s, z /
t	/ t /
v	/ v /
w	/ w / (with a feather)
x	/ ks /
z	/ z /

Double and Multi Phonograms

sh 'sh' two letter 'sh'
th / th, th ^{2}/
eigh /<u>a</u>/ four letter <u>a</u>

By providing explicit sounds with rules and letter construction (manuscript writing) Liz finally connected sounds to letters and could write.

Professor Jeanne Chall, retired from Harvard University as an expert on reading. She suggests there are five stages of reading development after the discovery of the world of print, when a child begins to see symbols on road signs, billboards and food packaging as having meaning. A child moves from learning to read to reading to learn.

Five Stages of Reading by Jeanne Chall

Learning to Read

Stage 0:   **Prereading** – Child pretends to read a story that was previously read aloud or retells a story while looking at the pages of a book previously read.

Stage 1:   **Initial Reading and Decoding** – Child learns the relationship between printed and spoken words and gains understanding of basic spelling rules. The child can read about 600 words and can understand more than 6,000.

Stage 2:   **Confirmation and Fluency** – Child is reading simple, familiar stories and selections with increasing fluency. Advanced decoding skills are delivered through continued direct instruction. The child can read about 3,000 words and can understand about 9,000+ words.

Reading to Learn

Stage 3:   **Reading to Learn** – Reading is used to learn new ideas and gain new knowledge through comprehension. By the end of Stage 3 reading and listening vocabularies have both increased and are even with each other 10,000 - 25,000+ words.

Stage 4:   **Multiple Viewpoints** – Student is reading a broad range of complex materials with a variety of view points. For good readers, the reading comprehension surpasses the listening comprehension for complex material.

Stage 5:   **Construction and Reconstruction** – Read and comprehend even more difficult materials, write well thought out papers, essays and other forms that call for integration of varied knowledge and points of view. The person can integrate his or her knowledge with that of others, synthesize and create new knowledge.

Evolutionarily speaking, reading is new. The written word was invented in early history to take inventory of property and record local and family history. Silent reading is first documented in the 4th century AD by St. Augustine as a curiosity. I needed to know more. Since it was an invented system, how does the brain learn to see print and read it? I wanted to know how to allow each child to be a separate entity and still teach in such a way to help a group of children grow. It would be unreasonable to think that all children learn the same way or at the same rate; after all I seemed to have a child who learned everything differently, needing explicit structure and instruction.

Stage 0

As a young child, Liz was immersed in reading. Karl and I both love to read and we read to her for hours. She preferred books over television, and her love for books and reading evaporated in first grade when she discovered her inability to learn like other students. She was devastated. Teachers encouraged us saying, "some students take longer, don't worry." By second grade Liz was still not reading or writing. We were not yet far enough behind to qualify for remediation, Liz however, was far enough behind to qualify for a broken heart and spirit. Her desire to read like mommy and daddy was squashed. Books became enemies.

A year ago Liz didn't understand how words rhymed, now she was flowing in freestyle rap and enjoying it. At the US post office Liz loudly rhymed "I wanna get paid. I think I'll get laid." A grey-haired grandmother dropped her jaw and looked aghast. Liz noticed her reaction "Mom, didn't she like my rhyme? I made the words work together. That was cool huh?" I looked at my painted eyebrowed young lady with a skimpy dress. We had a long way left to go. This would have been much easier if we were still interested in Cat in the Hat.

Stage 1

Speech has no symbols and formal instruction for speaking is typically not necessary. Written language, however, is not an innate skill that develops spontaneously. A precise neurological record of each letter and it's sound are necessary prerequisites to comprehension for reading.[43] Explicit rules for reading and writing needed to be learned to get on to Stage 1 – **phonemes** (sounds), **graphemes** (letters), **spatial concepts** (letter structure and placement), **phonograms** (sound pictures) and beginning root words and spelling rules.

Reading Works and *Writing Road to Reading* parallels Chall's work. It builds the necessary structures and attentional capacities for early readers utilizing metalinguistics. It breaks writing, reading and spelling of the English language into its most simple forms. Nothing in Stage 1 is left to chance.

speak

see

hear

motor & skin

Spalding teaches:

- Acute Auditory and Visual Discrimination
- Precise Speech and Articulation
- Logical Thinking
- Comparative analysis
- Correct Pronunciation
- Syllabication
- Neat and Legible Handwriting

It works through the four doors to the brain – visual, auditory, kinesthetic and vocal. It was the kickstart we needed to help Liz, but it wasn't the whole answer.

There are specific centers in the left side of the brain responsible for the two basic coding language processes – by sound (**phonetic word analysis**) and whole word by sight (**eidetic analysis**). Both areas are important. *Writing Road to Reading* advanced Liz from very poor 'sight only reading' and 'license plate printing' (I cn nt rd vre wll translated to I can not read very well) to beautiful controlled handwriting and mastery of the phonetic sounds of the English language.

Liz's handwriting in fourth grade (April 1998) before we began Spalding. Her very best effort.

43. Patterson, Jay. *Reading Works.* The Grammar Works People, RR 2 Box 318, Henning, Minnesota 56551

This method provided Liz a visual road map to create her phonograms with explicit page and letter structure. Each letterform has the same series of logical repeatable steps. All round letterforms are based on the face of a clock and are connected at the two on the clock, the four on the clock, the eight on the clock and the ten on the clock. By beginning a letter like an 'o' on the two on the clock point, it took very little time for her to achieve a nicely rounded letter. We worked on the dynamics of writing 'l, i, and o.' Soon she was writing all the phonograms – her name 'Elizabeth' the most beautiful of all. Beautiful handwriting proved essential for Liz to believe she was capable of academic learning and growth.

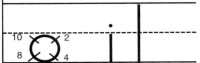

"Mom, how come if a pen stays the same when you turn it, does a p, b, d, q change into something else. Too many letters do that Mom . . . 3, m, w and 7, L, r and 2, 5, S . . . Mom it makes me crazy."

Liz (age 8)

Good spelling is critical for recognizing words. *The Writing Road to Reading* program builds a person's understanding of the English language sound by sound, along with explicit spelling rules. Letter sounds and spelling rules are important to understand exactly what you are reading. For example, the phonogram 'e' has two sounds /e/ē/ and so its name becomes its sound – short sound first, because that is the sound used most often in the English language, and long sound next. The phonogram 'i' follows the same process. This simple strategy eliminated the 'e' and 'i' sound confusion encountered in reading simple text.

Another example is the double phonogram sounds 'au' and 'aw.' Both letter combinations sound the same, however 'aw' is always used at

1,262,000

is raise proceed
now request practical
little truly preliminary
did cities receipt
hat sail possess
not whose restaurant
was attempt parallel
ran search physician
told consider kerosene
sold complete pneumonia
hope piece
Room system
light national
stamp refer
push absence
third majority
few unfortunate
wire session
fox discussion
there experience

Liz's handwriting and spelling January 2000. Though she was capable of spelling these words correctly she was unable to read what she had spelled or write them in a sentence.

the end of English words because English words do not end in 'u' or 'i.' This is the same way 'oi' and 'oy' and 'ai' and 'ay' also work. English words do not end in 'i' or 'u.'

We utilized Drs. John Griffin and Howard Walton's[44] work to strengthen Liz's reading, writing and thinking abilities to send data back and forth between the main brain areas used for language skills - speaking, reading and writing.

We worked with Liz's toolbox – her mouth, eyes, ears, skin and motor skills.

We focused on building capacity in her

(1) **motor cortex** - storage of motor programming to allow for duplication of symbols for writing and controlling speaking

(2) **auditory area** - increasing her processing and listening capacity

(3) **visual area** - training her to process what she was seeing and utilize her eyes. Then we began integrating the areas utilized for reading in her brain.

(4) **Broca's area** - production of words, speech formation and articulation;

(5) **Wernicke's area -** auditory-visual integration area for language with a focus on sound (phonetic word processing - word attack). This is where words are associated with their meaning;

(6) **Angular gyrus**- visual-auditory integration area for language with a focus on sight. (sight-sound word processing). This is where the letter shape, word recognition, sound and meaning synthesize.

The work of Griffin and Walton is helpful in the remediation of Dyslexia. Could my understanding of it also be helpful in teaching Liz?

Regardless if a person is right or left handed, about 97% process language in their left hemisphere of the brain.

www.brainconnection.com

Language Processing Areas of Brain

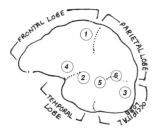

Though specific areas may be necessary for language they are not sufficient. Language is probably located throughout the brain with extensive crosstalk between areas.

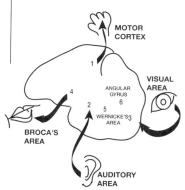

---

44. Drs. Griffin, John R, and Walton, Howard N. (1987) Dyslexia Determination Test (DDT) Examiners Instruction Manual. IMED.

I learned in training that when handwriting, the child will need to access motor memory for symbols to be used in the copy work. It is common for children to reverse letters in the early stages of their academic training. In writing the alphabet A-Z in capital letters, then in lower case letters and finishing with the numbers 1-10 children . . .

- *First grade may get up to five reversals,*
- *Second grade three reversals,*
- *Third grade one reversal and*
- *Fourth grade letters and numbers in correct orientation.*

Following is a simplified explanation of their work for further review and research for yourself.

LISTENING TO WRITING OR SPEAKING:

Being able to write a word in response to a spoken word or verbally spell back a spoken word.

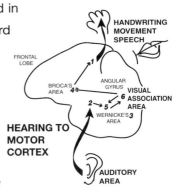

An audio frequency is received by the ears. It becomes a neural impulse traveling from the **(2) Auditory Area (temporal lobe)** which is on either side of the brain behind the ears to **(5) Wernicke's Area** where an interchange takes place with **(6) Angular Gyrus (left brain)** is determining a sound-sight match or a "word attack" with each syllable reprocessed with phonetic sounds, blends and structural analysis. Once the sound has been processed in the visual association area, the impulses travel on to **(4) Broca's area** of speech formation and then onto the **(1) Motor Cortex** to either the specialized area for **writing** (spelling words) or **speaking** (spelling words).

ORAL READING and COPY WORK:

A visual configuration of letters is seen by the eyes. It becomes an electrical signal and travels along the optic nerve to the **(3) Visual Area (occipital lobe)** which is in the back of the brain. It is then transferred to the **(6) Angular Gyrus (left brain)** where a sight-sound match is made if the word is known. If a match is made it is processed as a whole word or sight words **(eidetically - encoding)** usually within two seconds. If the word is not familiar then more extensive analysis of the word must be performed. This 'word attack' **(decod-**

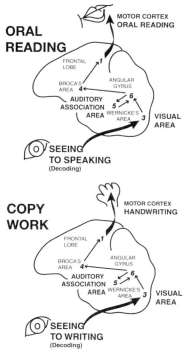

ORAL READING

SEEING TO SPEAKING (Decoding)

COPY WORK

SEEING TO WRITING (Decoding)

ing) is the function of the **(5) Wernicke's Area.** This takes a bit longer time, as each syllable is sounded out, phonetic sounds are blended together and/or structural analysis is performed. The impulses then travel on to **(4) Broca's area** of speech formation and then onto the **(1) Motor Cortex** to either the specialized area for **speaking (Oral Reading)** or **writing (Copy Work)**.

There is a difference between **imitating** or reproducing a form after watching someone else draw it and **copying** after being shown a completed design. Preprinting skills have a developmental pattern beginning with the **ability to sit upwrite in a chair** with enough balance to focus on writing instead of worrying about falling over. The child's **shoulder girdle development** must be strong enough to allow arm movement and control with additional **ability to move the arm** with precision and to vary the strength of the movement. Once the child has this ability an **efficient pencil grasp** becomes possible, though many children continue to use an energy expending power grasp which limits precision. **Bilateral hand skills** provide the child the opportunity to use both hands at once – writing and holding the paper still, or cutting while holding the paper. The final step is combining their eyes, arms and hands in **visual motor coordination** allowing the child to begin to learn to write shapes and lines.

When all these skills are complete, the child is ready to develop their pre-printing skills beginning with **random scribbling**. This random scribble evolves into a **directional scribble** that can be horizontal, diagonal or vertical. The child may imitate a parent or other child with this directional scribble.

Griffin and Walton believe encoding and decoding are interdependent and both are needed in reading. Liz needed sight-words (whole word) memorization/ visualization and phonetic/ memorization explicit teaching (Spalding-Orton; Writing Road to Reading). I introduced and reinforced these two to three grades levels lower than her current reading level, working with multi-sensory phonetic teaching for retention.

The transition from directional scribble and imitation to **copying vertical and horizontal lines** in a big developmental step, followed in order by first imitating and then copying circles, making a cross or plus sign, diagonal lines, a square, a triangle and finally a diamond. Until this foundation is laid it is too much to ask of a child to begin printing letters and numbers.

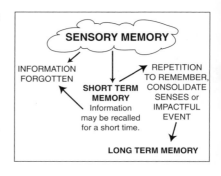

Most children learn to print in kindergarten and develop these pre-printing skills by about six-years-old.

At thirteen, Liz wrote each phonogram with precision. She knew the sound each made and began blending sounds together. The ability to sequence words into a sentence, to sequence a sentence into a paragraph, to sequence ideas explained into a tight essay all involve sequencing verbal information. Liz tried to grasp all the intricate pieces of knowledge needed to master Stage 1 reading. We worked on building her reading skills for seven years. Some days it felt like I was pushing a rope.

- Why did she spell well if we 'only' worked on spelling?
- Why could she read words as long as they were not in sentences?
- Why could she not understand rhyme or hear the differences in word endings?

It was a puzzle and we found five pieces.

1. Working Memory
2. Sensory Integration
3. Midline Crossing
4. Visual Processing
5. Auditory Processing

1. The first piece of the puzzle was working memory. Most children begin school able to hold five to seven pieces of information in their minds. Other children begin school unable to repeat back multi-syllabic words in the correct sound order. At age thirteen, Liz's working (short term) memory was three pieces

When a reader reads silently, there is electric activity in the larynx muscles. The implications of this odd fact is that Broca's area is producing word sounds in order to keep them in working memory, and that these word sounds are closely linked to speech. But because the reader is reading silently, the motor cortex does not signal the mouth, lips, tongue and lungs to carry through with speech.

www.brainconnection.com

of information or equivalent to a three-year-old, so to succeed in reading we had to build short term memory.

Short term memory is important for holding any concept in the brain long enough to do something about it — 3 seconds to 24 hours. Short term memory will stay based on the length of time it is needed. When it is no longer needed, it is gone. For some of us who lose keys, eyeglasses and transpose phone numbers we know intimately how short it can be.

Children with auditory processing difficulties have a particularly hard time processing sounds and their blends.

A longer working memory decreases levels of impulsivity, frustration and emotionality. Limited capacity short term memory simultaneously stores and manipulates information to accomplish a task. Knowledge of the world, vocabulary, sentence construction (**syntax**) and the ability to comprehend the written (and spoken) word are all linked to working memory capacity. Liz needed a working memory to understand spoken language, comprehend what is read, do problem-solving tasks, write words, sentences and paragraphs and perform math operations. Longer working memory provides sustained attention and memory long enough to hear the endings of words. As her memory increased Liz heard how words rhymed and began writing poetry. She held onto word definitions, associations, syntax and inferences (her own ideas) in her mind while she read a sentence. She comprehended what she was reading and recalled information (**comprehension**). Eventually she recalled the proper order (**sequencing**) of what she read, could think about it and integrate her own ideas.

2. The second puzzle piece was sensory integration. Her brain didn't know exactly where her hands were and what they were capable of doing. Different types of paper hurt her skin — paperback books, telephone directories, newsprint, coloring and puzzle books were rough to her touch. Though I didn't hear a sound, she

Liz's Daily Reading Program

- Biography of historical or scientific person read to Liz by Mom.
- Liz reading silently 2 levels below ability to strengthen skills.
- Reading aloud at new reading skill level.
- Spelling in various games and activities.
- Grammar and rules of language.
- Vocabulary within daily living and reading materials.
- A journal for her own private thoughts.
- A communication notebook between Liz and mom.

THE HANDLE™ INSTITUTE

DIFFERENTIATION

Differentiation of response is the inhibition of reflex and more. It is the ability to direct one part of the body to move according to plan while all other parts remain still. It is the precursor to the development of lateralization and helps the brain to establish specialized centers.

Individuals with immature differentiation may demonstrate an apparent weakness in kinesthetic memory, since the overflow movement defocuses the brain's processing of the intended movement.

Individuals with immature differentiation of response and irregular tactile perception may not realize that they are kicking, knocking over, or in other ways disturbing people and objects in their environment. They disclaim responsibility for these actions and may be viewed as liars. It is usually evident that there was no malice in their actions. However, after prolonged periods of receiving blame and punishment for these problems, an individual may begin to exhibit the behaviors his/her peers seem to expect.

It becomes easier to see how irregularities in differentiation can cause poor academic learning and also serious social problems.

The following are issues that may occur in a person experiencing difficulties with differentiation:

- Overflow movement to the head or jaw when eyes are tracking
- Overflow movement to the opposite hand when one hand is engaged
- Overflow movement to the legs when one hand is engaged.
- Tics that involve more than just the eyes, including Tourette's Syndrome
- Inability to sort out each finger for fine-motor coordination
- Overflow movement of the tongue and/or mouth when concentrating
- Knocking things over at the table
- Startle reactions
- Difficulty "turning off" obsessive-compulsive thoughts and actions.

This information is provided by the HANDLE Institute, www.handle.org

did. Tactile sequences and deep pressure improved her writing ability. She fatigued less often. The holes from her pencil lead ceased in her paper. Her pencil grasp was lighter. For some FASD students they can begin keyboarding and succeed very early, we had tried keyboarding and the computer flicker assaulted her.

3. The third puzzle piece was midline crossing. Our exercises in **midline crossing, differentiation** (page 146), posture and breathing allowed for better writing form. She wrote from one side of the paper to the other and moved only her hand – not her shoulder and legs, the chair or paper – her body and the paper remained stationary. Her head still moved to follow a sentence. She did not **track** (separate her head and eye movement).

4. The fourth puzzle piece was visual processing. to develop Liz's ability to move her eyes smoothly across a line of text instead of turning her head to follow the word. She saw the foreground from the background. She saw individual words within sentences and did not need to stop at each word waiting to cross to the next word. Letters and words finally stood still on her paper. A page of writing appeared as it looks to most people. We soon noticed Liz reading silently her lips moving as she read the words. Then her lips were silent. Her body no longer rocked.

Reading requires we utilize all our decoding skills at once – phonological skills, spelling skills, vocabulary and morphological skills. Liz had no bridges between spelling, reading and writing to read **(decode)** smoothly.

Taking neurodevelopment information, Liz and I worked from her motor cortex to her language processing areas. We exercised her brain building neurons, myelin and connections. If I couldn't open the door one-way, she and I swung it the other.

The more I understood how her brain worked, the more opportunity I had to help Liz get from point A to point B, breaking each step into tiny baby steps. If making a tuna fish sandwich involved 15 steps then how many steps were involved in reading. I kept look-

Jay Patterson's Reading Works program combines the research and results of spelling and word lists developed during the last 100 years. His list add to the Extended Ayres and Dolch lists to provide a child with a functional vocabulary of over 3,000 words.

Liz learns with a balance of love, challenge, innovation and reward. There is no technology today that will replace human presence, touch, kindness and encouragement.

"Liz, Dad and I think you are ready to go back to school with other students."

"Mom, I can't! They will think I am stupid! They will think I am dumb! I hated it there! I hated it." Crocodile tears streamed down Liz's cheeks. Tears with emotion was a new developmental step.

ing for smaller pieces and different routes to enter data.

We searched for auditory processing piece five. My entrepreneurial spirit understood that many strategies could get the same job done. Some were more efficient than others. I believed in working with a diverse team to utilize and build upon a person's strengths and weaknesses for the success of the whole. I thought of Liz's brain in that same structure — unlimited possibilities for performance mixed with combinations for achievement. I was sure there were neurons waiting to do a new job function hiding in the nooks and crannies of her brain.

Stage 2

To read comfortably in Stage 2 knowledge of root words (**morphemes**) must become automatic, almost as though the words were pictures or objects. Rules for spelling, syntax (how words legally live together), capitalization and punctuation come together to make reading a more fluid experience. Individuals at this stage begin increasing their reading, writing and speaking vocabularies utilizing morphemes (the smallest units in language). Free morphemes – root words – can stand alone, but bound morphemes – **suffixes** (ment, less, ness, ly, ed, s, es, ies, 's, s') and **prefixes** (un, pro, pre, dis, in, ex) – cannot. As a child's reading and language develop derivational morphemes of prefixes and suffixes, that change the word's meaning are added. For example, 'ship' to 'shipment' turning the verb 'ship' into a noun. The vocabulary and reading leap forward with the ability to derive words. Silent reading and the beginning of creative and non-verbal writing begins at this time.

CREATIVE AND NON-VERBAL WRITING:

This is primarily a memory of movement function and occurs after earlier ability in reading and spelling has been developed.

Henry Kao, Ph.D. at the University of Hong Kong has done extensive studies on how the practice of calligraphy has been shown to be of significant

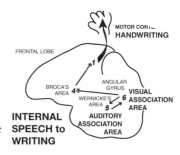

value to persons experiencing cognitive and behavioral problems. Liz and I discovered that learning to write beautifully was fun.

Callirobics (www.callirobics.com) was developed for the older learner wishing to have more mature handwriting. It comes in two level with music that is upbeat. I continued to study how the brain worked when dealing with basic academics: seeing to speaking, hearing to writing, seeing to writing, hearing to speaking and thinking to writing.

- What was the order of the brain's processing?
- Could we strengthen or access those areas?

Blom's Taxonomy (Appendix 6) offered clues in challenging Liz with the right developmental level of questions her brain processed without creating frustration. We encouraged higher levels of thinking by asking questions she could process. We added Greek and Latin roots, learning root words slowly. They surrounded us in daily life — tele (far) phon (sound) or tele (far) gram (write). I taught prefixes and suffixes and history of their meaning.

" Mom, my hair's falling out!" Liz shrieked. Not paying any attention I rambled "Maybe you need to wear it down more, and not pull it so tight in your hair dos. Did you pull it out in anger? Maybe you damaged the roots and they let go? Did you use a friends hair product? Maybe it wasn't good for your hair?" I asked. Liz answered. "Mom, I used some hair cream Kathleen had, that said 'NAIR' in big letters and 'hair' in little letters. I did not read the rest."

"Mom, I'm hearing things in my head. Voices Mom are talking to me," Liz worried. I probed deeper and discovered Liz had finally accessed her inner voice. The voices she was now hearing were her own thoughts. She no longer said everything she was thinking. An inner world was now hers.

I taught Liz with intensive, individualized, comprehensive and systematic strategies using incremental, multisensory metalinguistics. At the beginning of each quarter we tested Liz's knowledge of the Extended Ayres List. Mastery needed repetition. Each quarter Liz tested at a higher level, understanding more definitions, syllabication and reaching higher levels of analyzing a word with proper marking. We built a functional core vocabulary — one she could spoke, read and understood.

Every creative brain entry provided opportunity to find a neuron that was idling and waiting for a job to do. Novelty and variety kept Liz engaged.

Action Based Learnng

- I showed it, told it, whispered it or shouted it.
- We sang it, acted it, rapped it, wrote it and danced it.
- We could cut it out, glued it on, painted it or stuck it – flash cards with flash.
- We formed it in the air, drew it in the sand, and stretched it with our bodies.
- We twisted it with our tongues and molded it with our hands.
- We mixed it, baked it and ate it.
- We crushed it, stomped it and threw it.
- We jumped on it and teetered with it.

When Liz was young we practiced writing spelling words on her back. I reintroduced this and soon we were spelling words in written capital letters with a feather on her palms, soles, face, neck and eyelids. Toni taught us to verbally spell words to Liz — p - r - o- m- o - t - e . This encouraged Liz to remember the letters, put the letters in sequence order, and visualize the word. She said the word and spelled it back to us. We passed six hundred words in *The New Reading Teachers Book of Lists* printed by Prentice Hall.[45] We 'said the word' and 'wrote it on paper' or 'spelled it back'.

"I hate reading. Reading is stupid!" Liz yelled.

"Liz, I want you to keep your hair." I smiled, "No more NAIR hair remover for you."

We played games. I wrote the phonograms on a blank set of dice. Each day we shook the dice cup and said the phonograms rolled. We played *Elision* I stripped away parts of a word and challenged her to answer. What's basketball without the ball? What is frog without the 'r'? We played *Simon Says Opposite* if Simon said stand still Liz moved quickly. Each of these methods exercised a different area of her brain and made her think. We stretched Liz's reading level with *New Practice Readers* by Phoenix Learning Resources designed for older struggling readers.[46] My hope: connections and automaticity – wires fired get wired.

"Liz, until you can give me ten good reasons why you should not go to school in writing, I am not going to listen to you," Karl said.

Practice makes permanent. We needed practice to speed the process and myelinate the connections. I

45. Fray, Edward Bernard, PhD., Fountoukidis, Ed.D., Polk, Jacqueline Kress, M.A. (1985) Prentice Hall
46. New Practice Readers are a seven-book series intended to provide reading interest along with the development of comprehension skills for readers who need additional practice to achieve mastery.

People who become blind after having sight, activate these same areas of their brains while reading Braille.

www.brainconnection.com

wanted Liz to enjoy what she read and not struggle with processing the words. I wanted her to comprehend what she was reading. For her to do that she had to relax and enjoy the story. Academic Therapy Publications offered a wide range of high interest reading materials written for older readers needing remediation. I chose reading Levels 1 and 2. Within six weeks, Liz read *White Fang, Swiss Family Robinson, A Man Without a Country* and was working on *Hunchback of Notre Dame.* Proudly I overheard her tell her impressed high school friends what "she" was reading. The door to wanting to read cracked open.

The brain physically changes as it learns. Each change enables new learning and allows for more changes. Liz exercised specific regions of her brain in neurotherapy with biofeedback. Dr. Nash encouraged her, with kindness and humor, to regain her focus and attention without frustration or anxiety. With his help we began refining the foundations laid with neurodevelopment and vision therapy. We built new connections and exercised existing pathways so they could myelinate for faster data transmission.

Liz's ten reasons to return to school:

1. Meat new friends.
2. Luern new things.
3. Try new things.
4. Get you to grops of people.
5. Get a chance to go more places.
6. Do more acctivids.
7. Get be to recanized.
8. To give avice to others.
9. Maybe popular.
10. Get you to new teachers.

Liz could ace these words in a spelling test, but not when writing.

Liz faced a quadruple learning whammy.

"Mom, why can't I listen and take notes? How can I ever go to school, if I can't take notes?" Liz worried. It is still hard for her to think and write.

1. Limited working memory (three-year-age level)
2. Difficulty hearing and sounding out words
3. Inability to sequence what she heard
4. Plus, her words danced

Liz's eyes sparkled now wanting to write. Creativity emerged as Liz gained practice in reading things of interest to her. She gave friends gifts of personal rap lyrics. She made cards with poetry. She wrote her first creative story. She tried using the Internet to find information and asked if she could make her own web page.

Liz still struggled with reading. She worked at sounding out whole words. Previously a longer word starting with 'pre' could become anything from 'pre'his-toric to 'pre'vious based on whatever popped into her mind. Her reading vocabulary increased. She no longer lost her place on a page. She read without the guidance of her finger. Liz's large handwriting reduced in size and increased in readability. We began school days with a 'full' page of creative journal writing ending the page with a pencil that was unbroken. She had gained six years in reading comprehension in eighteen months. Understanding what she was reading was the first important step in beginning to build speed, structure and efficiency.

Little by little Liz began to believe in her capabilities. She past the basic state Reading Writing and Math tests without accommodation. The struggle was worth it. Liz may be six years of practice behind her peers, but life is more than childhood and I was still learning. She had years to catch up.

A person must have increasing levels of vocabulary both **syntactic** (how they are used - grammar) and **semantic** (meaning of word used) to gain higher levels of reading. Just as we had learned with all the other developmental work we were doing with Liz — the brain was happy to do what the brain was ready to do. It was our job to figure out how to get her brain ready to make the transition from learning to read to reading to learn — the gate to access advanced knowledge.

Karl and I noticed Liz's reading progress. She read the menu at restaurants and asked what things were instead of what it said. She looked up telephone numbers for ordering pizza, to see what movie was playing and to make a hair appointment. She read signs along the road as I drove. She wrote deeper and more meaningful song lyrics countering her friends with non-cuss lyrics because they were more difficult to write. She explained to them she 'preferred' to write more difficult pieces and cuss words were shallow. She read

"Liz, come to dinner!" I shouted.
"I can't Mom, I have to finish reading this chapter of this new book," Liz shouted.

storybooks to young children and enjoyed them herself. She had an internal voice. These were simple things — but in the bigger picture of life they were leaps. I upped academic required reading. She didn't notice. I bought magazines she was interested in and left them on her pillow. She read them instead of tearing out the photos and adding them to her wall. Her walls were organized and clean. So were her closet and drawers. Whose child was this? Was this the same child we had thought of institutionalizing?

Liz was unable to integrate vision, auditory and motor at the same time. Note taking was impossible. She copied data but did not know what she had written. She listened and if she tried to write notes lost the content of the lecture. Her reprotoire of skills had increased including integration of her eyes and ears. Someday we would integrate sensory motor. We kept plugging a little bit of reading into Liz's life — we needed a different hair-raising experience.

ENGINEERING A LEARNING ENVIRONMENT

Liz's Learning Strategy

- Globally introduce the topic on the first day.
- Gain emotional interest with activities, games, easy projects, humor, videos, music.
- Read a story of a person involved with the topic.
- Make comments through out the day when you make a connection to the topic.
- Organize the information and make a topic mind map.
- Do experiments, field trip, make a model.
- Reinforce the topic.
- Discover patterns and connections you already know.

It was time to change our homeschool environment. Street noise, delivery persons, the phone and the door all contributed to sudden auditory disruption and spontaneous combustion from Liz. The neighborhood sidewalk, squirrels and birds provided visual distractions. Urban neighbor children begged to be tutored; yet when I attempted to help, Liz's retention rate dropped to half. I moved our school to a small corner upstairs away from the household traffic patterns. I divided this room with bookcases: one side for academics, the other side for activity, movement, therapy, floor time and casual study.

In the tiny academic area Liz had a comfortable chair with armrests providing her stability and physical boundaries. Once in the chair it was difficult for her to get up. My chair sat alongside. All of our current learning materials were within easy reach. Everything else was on shelves or in cupboards. There were no windows. There was nothing for distraction. An incandescent lamp varied our lighting.

On the other side of the bookcases, I added a gray piece of carpet and beanbag chair. At the

Physical reminders help children know where they need to be:

- Footprints on the floor to line up at the doorway.
- Handshaped stickers on desks to know where hands should be.
- Hula hoops, cardboard boxes or rug squares for circle time.
- Pictures of what is inside a drawer or cupboard.
- Photo stickers of the child on things that belong to them.
- Post-its with pictures for reminders with what to do and how to do it.

computer was a balance ball to sit on. Two windows provided natural lighting and we replaced the fluorescent lights with full spectrum bulbs.[47] Her harp stood in the corner. A white board covered the books on the bookcase (we had learned long ago chalk was not tactile friendly). The room was bare and available for whatever we needed moment by moment. Our new space was small, simple, safe, flexible, organized, consistent, predictable and comfortable.

The change provided structure for separate academics, therapy and life skills. We balanced active and quiet time, free and structured learning, and large and small motor skills. Liz's ability to focus and learn grew without distractions. We created a sheltered learning world.

We taught Liz pattern recognition with two to three pieces of data. The ability to make sense out of randomly appearing data is critical to understanding and motivation. Each pattern can be added to a learner's 'perceptual maps' and the brain can leave that state of confusion, anxiety or stress. Liz progressed slowly at first. We worked with simple shapes, then we moved on to tiny 3"x4" puzzles. Four months later Liz worked 150 to 500

piece puzzles. Liz was finding peace among the chaos and enjoying it.

We role played social situations. I told and showed Liz what to do. She practiced. Without focused training she would not 'get it.' We created an educational fantasy world that existed in very few places - a secure, quiet learning environment with a one-to-one teacher ratio, a combination fiscally impossible to in duplicate public schools.

A child with brain damage may master a task many times and lose it many times before it is permanent. You will need to teach it repeatedly and in many different ways.

Support successes.

47. Full Spectrum Bulbs produce glare-free light – reduce eye strain, greater visual acuity, less fatigue. Also help with Seasonal Affective Disorder (SAD). www.fullspectrumsolutions.com

We continued asking questions:

- How can what we learned be converted to teach groups of children like Liz?
  - Could IEP's (Individualized Education Plans) be executed in ways that would encourage growth in children with FASD?
  - Could professionals and parents form collaborative partnerships to provide ongoing support and respect for both the family unit and the professional community?
  - Did parents know they had 50% of the power in IEP meetings – that only one more vote was needed in their favor to make the differences they were requesting for their child?
  - At what point should we reintroduce Liz into group learning.
- How do we empower individuals with FASD to live safely and independently as a part of society?
  - Could we help to change the 10% success rate for individuals with FASD?
  - Could we contribute to slowing the number of suicides, child abuse cases and homeless people?
- Could we keep them out of holding tanks – confined to hospitals, mental health wards, prisons or other institutional gulags?
- Could we develop safe and creative respite programs?
- Do parents of children with FASD ever retire?
- Can we have group homes for married couples?

  - ***Is not the child's future also the parents' future?***

I tried to tackle a spelling test in a fetal alcohol brain simulation exercise. Fluorescent lights and audio noise flickered. A shower cap and twine necklace irritated my neck. A winter mitten on my non-dominant hand numbed my coordination. I proudly wrote the word I heard — penis. What a disappointment when the only word I figured out was wrong. The workshop leader said HAPpiness and I missed the HAP. Oh well, off to the principal for Jodee.

EVERYDAY THINGS THAT TEACH

Develop skills without the child even knowing it! Keep it simple. When playing games we begin with only one rule. Add one more rule as a child learns the game. Keep it fun! Keep the time short and play often. Practice makes permanent!

BASICS

Blocks, beads, lacing cards
GeoBoard, Pattern blocks
Lego & construction sets
tangrams, pentaminos
puzzle books, puzzles
puppets, sandbox, Tinker
Toys, Kinnex

STREET GAMES

Jacks, jump rope
hopscotch, Four Square
pick up sticks

YARD GAMES

Bocce, badmitton
croquet, tetherball

CARD GAMES

War, Speed, Uno®
Solitaire, Go Fish
Concentration,
Shapiro's EQ Games

IN THE CAR

Collect each state license
I'm thinking of something
I'm going to grandmas, in my
suitcase I will bring.

BOARD GAMES

Checkers & Chinese
Checkers, Sequence
Boggle®, Yahtzee®,
Dominoes, Ungame®
Mindtrap®, Blurt®, Gestures®,
Jenga®, Pictionary®, Twister®
Barrel of Monkeys®
Magnetic Darts®

FUN STUFF

Whistles, koosh balls
bubble blow, bean bags
Krazy straws, water noodles

GROSS MOTOR

Pedal-Go, Teeterboard
Disk Dizzy Junior
Rollerblades/Skates
Bikes/Trikes
Balance board and beam
Hula Hoop,
Balls of all sizes
Trampolines

AROUND & ABOUT

Hammock & swing
water play area, tent
garden paths, tire swing
trees to climb, play house
climbing play structures
obstacle course, sensory
trail, chalk for sidewalk
games, basketball hoop
slide, climbing bars
hammers, screwdrivers
saws, nuts, bolts, locks
keys, tweezers, tongs
blankets, pillows and boxes
turning pages, picking up
coins, beans

CRAFTS

Clay, Crafts, BloPens®
Paints, Colored pencils
Drawing and Writing paper
Paper punches, Yarn, Beads
Decorator scissors
Rubber stamps, Stencils
and Templates, Controlled
tearing, folding, wrapping
and unwrapping.

AROUND THE HOUSE

Cooking, Groceries, Cleaning
Laundry, Sewing, Gardening
Shopping, Yard, Building &
Maintenance

MAKE BELIEVE

Store, Kitchen, Dress-up,
Restaurant, Hospital, Dentist
Party, Circus, Zoo
Traffic Officer, Airport,
Carpentry, Camping, Farm
Service Station, Car Wash
Stand up and balance toys
(people, soldiers, animals)

PROGRAMS

Community Services
Youth Groups, Chior, Church
Groups, Scouts, YMCA,
Campfire. Sport Programs
Boys Club, Girls Club
BrainGym®
    www.braingym.com
Suzuki Music

*Visit www.betterendings.org
for fun ideas and information.*

GROSS MOTOR SKILLS

Side Walk Games and Walks in the Rain.

Catching and Tossing:

Bean bags are easier to toss and catch for a beginner.

1. Toss up, catch.
2. Toss higher, catch.
3. Toss, clap, catch.
4. Toss, clap twice, catch.
5. Toss one hand, catch with other hand.
6. Toss, touch knee, catch.
7. Toss, touch shoulder, catch.
8. Toss, touch ground, catch.
9. Throw and catch with partner.
10. Balance bean bag on parts of your body.

Spring arrived. It had been a long winter. Liz and I grabbed rakes to clean the yard. The sun beat on our faces as we laughed and worked outdoors. I glanced at Liz who was raking like she had done it her whole life. Seven months earlier she could not cross her midline. This made raking, shoveling and sweeping very difficult. She was smiling.

What I do you cannot do; but what you do, I cannot do. The needs are great, and none of us, including me, ever do great things. But we can all do small things, with great love, and together we can do something wonderful.

—Mother Teresa

Patterned repetitive activity results in patterned neural activity that changes the brain. Enjoyment and engagement in activities or play helps speed the learning process. Play is how children integrate their senses to move on to higher developmental levels. We completed nine months of clinical and visual therapy and her eye-to-hand coordination, which began at four years in one eye and zero in the other, was now at a seven- to eight-year-old level. Liz had completed 18 months of neu-

rodevelopment. She skillfully performed basic 'even' locomotor skills of hopping and jumping and the 'uneven' skill of skipping. We worked on walking, running and leaping (even), learning how to slide and gallop.

Balance is the integration of the inner ear (vestibular) system. The inner ear functions as a motion detector and visual stabilizer during head and eye

Balance Beam:

The child must be able to perform on solid ground, then on a line of tape, next on an 8 ft 4x4 on the floor and finally an 8 ft. 2 x 4 – 4" off the ground. With each stage the same spotting (holding, touching, surrounding and finally letting go) is mandatory.

1. Balance on both feet.
2. Balance on 1 foot.
3. Balance on 1 foot, hands at side.
4. Balance on1 foot, hands like airplane.
5. Balance on one foot, eyes closed.
6. Walk the beam heel to toe.
7. Walk the beam not looking at feet.
8. Walk sideways.
9. Walk backwards.
10. Walk on tip toes.
11. Step over a stick while walking.
12. Try to skip.
13. Pick something up.
14. Walk and toss bean bag.
15. Carry a book.

movements. Vision provides the reference for the surrounding environment and motor control provides postural stability and coordination. These balance components all work together and are integrated in the brain.

At 15, Liz joined in instead of standing on the sidelines trying to process what was going on, being laughed at or being disappointed with her attempts. Her memory, sequencing and balance system was developed so she was able to play games and learn basic sport skills. It was time to build visual/ motor skills and coordination. We enlisted teen friends as team members. Together we prepared our summer school program. We focused on play – art (drawing and crafts), phy ed (skills, games, fitness) and auditory (experiences in listening).

A child who cannot stay on the sidewalk, but climbs the walls, walks on the curb, then the gutter is still teaching herself muscle control, depth perception and visual integration skills. The child instinctively knows that her balance needs more practice. To be still is impossible.

We initiated things Liz struggled with:

- **play opportunities** — laughing, rolling, skipping, hopping, jumping, leaping, running
- **sidewalk play** — jump rope, hula hoop, hopscotch, jacks and four square
- **yard play** — bocce ball, dice throw, croquet and catch
- **park play** — crawling, climbing, hanging, spinning and sliding
- **street games** — hoops, balls and rackets

REFLEXES - OFF WITH THE OLD ON WITH THE NEW
We designed activities to enhance skills and normalize reflexes.

Head Raising
Prone (lying face down)
Supine (lying face up)

Lying on Your Side
Turning
Supine - sidelying (from back to side)
Supine - prone (from back to tummy)
Prone - supine (rolling over)

Crawling
Puppy dog
Static - make amphibian movements no
    forward motion of body
Belly Crawl - make amphibian
    movements moves body forward
Bunny Hop - assumes 3 point crawling
    using complete rotation
Creeping - assumes 4 point crawling
    using complete rotation
Creeping - uses partial rotation up to
    sitting then assumes 4 point
    crawling using complete rotation

Sitting
Maintains
Assumes using complete rotation
Assumes using partial rotation
Assumes using symmetry

Standing
Kneel stands
Kneel walks
Pulls up to standing
Stands unassisted
Walks hands in air
Walks hands down
Walks cross pattern
Hop with both feet

Advanced Mobility
Run hands up
Run hands down
Run cross pattern
Hop one foot
Gallop
Skip
Jumping Jacks
Tricycle
Strapped foot pedals
Can pedal
Bicycle with training wheels
Bicycle

Arm Hand Control
Reflexive grasp -
    no eye-hand coordination (0-4 mos)
Conscious grasp - pronation (4-8 mos)
Crude
Between palmer and finger ulnar
Corralling reach
Arms use asymmetrically control
    from shoulder and shoulder griddle
Radial palmer grasp (7 mos)
Scissor grasp (8 mos)
Thumb envelopes objects (8 mos)
Elbow flexible (8 mos)
Crude pinch-pincer grasp (9 mos)
Advertent release of grasp (9 mos)
Wrist flexibility (9 mos)
Use of forearm between mid-position
    and pronation (9 mos)
Pincer release
Supination more frequently (11 mos)
Opposition (12 mos)
Supination-cortically controlled (12 mos)

Cross Crawl Alternatives: Step Aerobics, Swimming, Mountain Climbing, Stair Stepping

Eye-Hand

Coordination Games

- Air Hockey
- Badminton / Tennis
- Jacks, Tiddly Winks
- Hot Potato
- Horse Shoes / Bocce
- Kaleidoscopes
- Basketball
- Puzzles

Toy Store Games

- Operation®
- Jenga®
- Don't Spill the Beans®
- Kerplunk®
- Twister®

I interviewed personal trainers and visited health clubs. The lights, noise and busyness of the clubs assaulted Liz's senses. Liz's nutritionist is also a chiropractor who works with sports injuries and rehabilitation. He introduced us to the *Body by Design*® program and provided us with a repertoire of exercises for aerobics and weight training to help Liz's posture, walk and reflexes. We integrated his program into our daily regime and adapted it to our yard and neighborhood.

We learned different ways to move our body. In stretching we paid attention to our breathing – inhaling as we stretched and exhaling as we released the stretch, loosening our muscles and other tissues, paying attention to any sensation at all, including heat, color, emotion, irritation, memory, your body parts, feeling the movements and our body's reactions.

Liz learned to do exercises to normalize her early reflexes. When she was able to smoothly execute the movements she added one pound weights. Her goal for leaner thighs and a flatter tummy proved incentive for development of better muscle tone and posture. She complemented her weight training with *The Listening Program*®, her auditory neurodevelopment therapy wearing her power headset.

We walked. Walking is vital for our bodies. In addition to exercising our hearts, it helps relax us, energizes us and reduces the stress in our lives. Liz learned to let her arms swing back and forth in opposition with her feet. We played with our feet as we walked trying to discover a gentle heel to toe rolling motion. We quieted ourselves trying to walk and belly breathe – imagining

Hula Hoop Fun:

Hula hoops come in a number of sizes. Those filled with water are the easiest to use.

1. Jump in and out of the hoop.
2. Jump backwards out of the hoop.
3. Jumping Jack in the air and jump in hoop.
4. Roll hoop to friend.
5. Friend rolls hoop and you throw ball through rolling hoop (try different types of balls).
6. Friend rolls hoop, you jump through.
7. Friend rolls hoop, you run around it as it is rolling.
8. Hula hoop 20 seconds.

our breath going all the way down to our heels and walking it out. We tried to notice small things — a rabbit in a garden, a crack in the street. Walking provided talking time. We begin learning to run by power walking. Liz power cross walked faster than our dog. We added short sprints to our walk, building stamina and challenging Liz to cross-pattern run, she was now able place her arms to swing in opposing direction from her legs. We added distance keeping our focus on being together.

Liz began walking and doing acivities with friends, well chosen friends provided an external brain, ill-chosen friends sent us into disaster. On the surface, we never knew whether the relationship with another would be positive or negative. It was so easy for Liz to overreact, get out of control or impulsively do something that caused pain, suffering or trouble.

Karl designed and built a teeter board with six different fulcrum inlays. We changed the supporting beams on the bottom of the board to change the levels of difficulty and balance. We played catch, counted backwards, recited rap lyrics, spelling and cross-tapped. Like Sea World with Shamu we develop activities for visual motor

Log Rolls

- Place hands above head, eyes closed and roll on mat.
- Try eyes open.

Forward Rolls

- Begin with one roll, have child stand and look at feet, squat down in front, place hands in front, head and chest down. Push with legs and roll.
- Roll. Stop. Roll.
- Work to continuous forward rolls.
- Work to continuous forward rolls with eyes closed.

where Liz succeeded and enjoyed — then we raised the bar. We learned skills standing on firm ground. Then we moved to the teeter board. She stood like a flamingo and danced on her board, our girl had talent!

Our challenge was to increase Liz's balance and integrate visual motor skills. Liz sat on the balance ball for posture while she practiced typing, listened to stories or worked Brain Builder®. We added variations to sit-ups and back bends by doing them on the ball. We did helicopter spins. As her balance increased I added front and back rolls, leaps and challenged

TEETER BOARD PIECES

3" 2" 1"

BALL

ROCKER

TEETER BOARD
With 3" Fulcrum

Teeter Board pattern is available for download at www.betterendings.org

her to cartwheels.

On aerobic days Liz's chose a workout tape from our small, but diverse video library. We purchased fun fitness videos. We learned Jazz and Hip Hop Dances to current hits, the ChaCha, Salsa and Macarena to Latin Music, and a step workout with a beat. We stretched with beginner yoga tape and Pilates. We punched the air with TaeBo. Liz's friends joined us. They taught Liz segments to help her enjoy the activities, instead of feeling frustrated as she was bombarded by new information.

Brain imaging research has shown that musicians have a bigger corpus callosum, connecting the two sides of the brain, in addition to the primary cortex and cerebellum which are involved in the movement and coordination of playing an instrument. Perhaps what began as Liz's desire to play a beautiful instrument and my desire to help her learn to hear better was actually building a better brain.

"Toni, Liz wants ankles. You helped her get arches on her feet. Now she wants ankles like the other girls," I requested.

"Who do you think I am Ankles-R-Us? Sure I can give you exercises so Liz can get her ankles. Got any more requests?" Toni laughed.

Liz took Suzuki harp lessons for eight years working on Book One. Prior to our brain training camp Liz learned only one to two new notes a week. Learning a new song took months and sometimes years.

Liz now learned complete measures in more than one song each week as her working memory increased. She began to read music and to develop rhythm. She transferred notes from the harp to the piano. She wrote lyrics and thought of the melodies to go with them.

We utilized the calligraphy and the brain work of Henry Kao, Ph.D. I wondered if calligraphy didn't work similarly to music, in that you utilized the preciseness of line with the flow of beauty — the mixture of creative with technical application. What other mediums could I use to adapt that concept?

We played with calligraphy pens and wrote beautiful letters. We worked with painting and colors and learned

"If Liz likes it, other kids will," Toni stated. "I've learned from Liz, if it is not fun, don't bother introducing it into her program. It won't get done or the battle to accomplish it will take all the joy out of doing the neuro work. Liz challenges me to come up with ideas to help her grow without knowing she is doing a specific exercise program."

to stay within the lines. We mastered the task of working with a paintbrush.

Liz's drawing and craft skills were finally at the level of a seven-year-old. This was an open door to begin teaching her to create and draw. I had used the work of Mona Brooks *Drawing With Children* and *Drawing for Older Children and Teens* when developing my *Art for the Master Program* for K-4th graders. My students loved learning and even the kindergartners created delightful works of art. Liz was 12-years-old when I taught that class. I had used her skill level to build my program and much of it was far above her capabilities. I reintroduced the program to her. Liz processed what she saw and coordinated fine motor skills with it. Art was no longer so stressful.

We created art projects. I kept everything simple and fun. Liz made snuggly blankets and scarves for gifts. We worked with fine line black markers and water color pencils. We learned to draw hatch lines and stipple. We worked with color theory by using only red, yellow, blue, white and black media. We

Playing an instrument with both hands is a complicated developmental task, especially when each hand may be playing a different note at a different time. "Liz would you like to learn the right hand of a new song, the left hand of one you already know or put another song together with both hands?" Liz's harp teacher asked. "I guess the left hand, I don't like both hands together," Liz replied.

worked with brushes and Blo-Pens®. Liz created the rainbow of colors she would use each day from black, white, yellow, red and blue. I provided an art environment where Liz could create and explore without fear. She had an adversion to chalks, charcoal and pastels, but clay and cookie dough were enjoyable sensory experiences. The kitchen provided a wealth of opportunity to stretch Liz's skills in art and science. Decorating cookies provided opportunity to mix colors, develop shapes and blue tongues.

Antonia Rathbun, M.A., A.T.R is an art therapist in Vancouver, Washington who works with persons with prenatal exposure. She believes using art to show others what it's like may be easier than finding words to tell them. Art materials are consistent. Each material has different properties the child can count on. She recommends teachers focus on the process of materials, instead of the product being made. Liz was often disappointed with her finished product, together we found something good about each piece of her

Rathbun provides these tips for failure proof art:[48]

- **Preparation:** Keep the physical environment simple and safe. Don't be afraid of a mess. Keep a choice of simple media.
- **Invitation:** Follow the person's instinct about what will work best that day. Soft music, nature objects, photographs can spark sensory exploration.
- **Encounter:** To observe is to participate.
- **Acceptance:** Suspend judgment.
- **Ownership:** Responsible in clean up, materials care, take project home

creative work — even if it was only an opportunity for her take time to be quiet and remain calm while she created it.

Scientists are discovering that physical activity alone is enough to trigger a boost in brain cell proliferation and that specialized exercise programs may help repair damaged or aged brains.[49] For twelve years in Denmark an experimental School in the Forest for kindergartners proved an innovative and effective way for children to develop school readiness skills. The children climbed trees, ran, played games, developed their imaginations, explored and learned about their surrounding world with their teacher. The results were first graders ready to learn.

Getting your arms and legs moving and the heart beating faster increases the blood flow to the brain. This blood keeps our brains healthy by feeding our neurons with oxygen and nutrients.

Our yard became a playground with balance structures, hammcks, tire and porch swings, hula hoops, bubble blowing sticks, chalk and jump ropes as neighborhood teens joined in the fun to help Liz. We all had a reason to go back to child's play and have fun doing it. Who said any of us should outgrow childhood?

The sun smiled on us as we climbed new mountains and planted gardens. Fourteen years after Liz joined our home, she finally rolled down hills and played sidewalk games. Liz smiled at the snowflakes as they fluttered down on a cold night. She stuck out her tongue in a rain shower and caught raindrops on her face. The time arrived to make snow angels and take walks in the rain.

---

48. Antonia Rathburn is a Registered Art Therapist and Certified Mental Health Counselor. She works in adoption support and has a keen understanding of working with children with FASD.
49. Society for Neuroscience (www.sfn.org)

TO SEE OR NOT TO SEE.
WHAT WAS THE QUESTION?

Neurodevelopment therapy continued to help Liz; she was happier and more secure with who she was. She controlled some of her emotions and she was no longer attacked by her senses. There were still missing pieces. We continued to plod along in reading. She was now skilled at decoding words but tired quickly and was easily frustrated. She had mastered English spelling rules and phonograms but could not put the pieces together. She skipped words and whole lines, getting lost in the unmanageable sea of moving letters on a page. She had trouble copying information from one place to another. Her comprehension was exceptional when I read and fell apart when she read aloud. On the visual acuity test, she read the 20 foot line beyond 20 feet, she had to back up 10 feet in order to get the letters to stand still – the test chart was located under a fluorescent light, the sound vibrations and blue color causing all letters to jiggle. No one checked how her eyes actually worked. She did not need prescription glasses.

We took our little eagle for another vision test. Three trained professional optometrists spent two hours testing and examining. Their findings – Visual-Perceptual-Motor Disorder. Their conclusion – they could remediate.

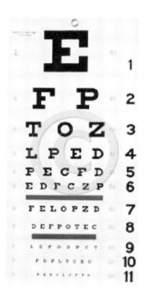

Two thirds of all the information we receive is visual.

Visual acuity is the ability to 'see clearly' whereas vision is the ability to interpret, identify and process what is seen by the eye

Your eyes are an extension of your brain. The optic nerve and retina grow out of the brain before birth, rather than forming separately and connecting to it during embryonic development.

Vision therapy is an organized therapeutic regimen utilized to treat a number of neuromuscular, neurophysiological, and neurosensory conditions that interfere with visual function. Vision therapy encompasses a wide variety of procedures to improve a diagnosed nueromuscular, or neurophysiological visual dysfunction. The ability to learn in school, achieve on the job, and enjoy sports and recreation depends on efficient vision. Optimetric vision therapy assists individuals in developing visual abilities and efficiency most suited to their needs. It enables those individuals to achieve maximal levels of visual performance. Optimetric vision therapy can help individuals achieve and maintain good vision for life. [50]

The exam concluded what Toni had discovered; Liz suppressed the function of one of her eyes and moved her head instead of her eyes while reading. She had poor depth perception and difficulty perceiving relationships between herself and another object. She was unaware of right and left and did not understand directional concepts such as up, down, above or behind. Her fine motor/hand to eye coordination was underdeveloped. She could not separate the foreground from the background, was unable to focus on selected information and ignore what was irrelevant. She could not visually recreate an event or object in

Early experiences can have a dramatic effect on the brain's wiring process, causing the final number of synapses in the brain to increase or decrease by as much as 25%. Wiring for vision takes place in the brain the first few months after birth. [51]

her mind's eye. Of no surprise to us, they discovered a short attention span, distractibility and perseveration. Visual therapy was recommended to break down faulty methods of using her eyes and replace them with functionality.

Dr. Don Sealock, O.D., F.A.A.O. explained to Karl and me that the eyes are connected to everything we do: thinking, feeling, moving, planning and emotions. The eye examination must be more than determining if a child can see the wall. The child must be able to get the whole picture, sequence the picture, and then develop timing and rhythm.

50. Four Season Eye Care, Plymouth, Minnesota, (763) 559-7358
51. Starting Smart: *How Early Experiences Affect Brain Development: An Ounce of Prevention Fund* (1996) www.smartstart-nc/org/news/newsletter/braindevelopment p3

The ability to visualize, and to hold a picture in her brain, empowered Liz to make better choices in dress. Black was no longer her favorite color, like the survivors of the Kobe earthquake in Japan she regained her color sense as she gained visual skills. Abundant jewelry and sparkles became fascinating as she tried various looks and enjoyed seeing things differently. Bangles and bobbles and fancy hair were a new hobby.

Four essential perceptual processes frequently impaired in underachieving children:

1. Capacity to receive stimuli
2. Capacity to hold stimuli
3. Capacity to scan stimuli
4. Capacity to respond to stimuli in a meaningful way

The eyes, *which are actual extensions of the brain,* are more intricate and complex than any humanly conceived system to date. To illustrate this point the space shuttle Columbia, with its 5.2 million parts, could be compared to a single eye, containing 137 million photoreceptors and more than *1 billion total parts.*[52]

The way visual information travels from our eyes to our brains is different from the way sensory and motor information travels to the brain. Unlike the body, where the nerves on the left side are con-

Visual Readiness Steps

(Dr. Lyelle Palmer, Winona State University, Minnesota)

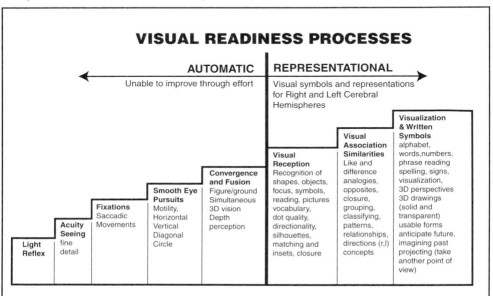

52. Liberman, Jacob, OD, PhD,, *Light: Medicine of the Future.*

nected to the right hemisphere of the brain and the right side are connected to the left side of the brain, our eyes are wired so that the left visual field of our total vision (both eyes) goes to the right side of the brain and visa versa.[53]

Growth of visual synapses appears to slow down by age five. By that time it is thought that the basic brain wiring is established. If this were true, could we "turn on" an eye that Liz had suppressed long ago? Could she develop binocular vision? Could she learn to see in 3D?

The eyes and brain represent only 2% of our total body weight, yet they require 25% of all our nutritional intake. The eyes alone use one third as much oxygen as the heart, need ten to twenty times as much vitamin C as the joint capsules involved in the movement of extremities, and require more zinc (our intelligence chemical) than any other organ system in the body. Housing 70% of the body's sense receptors, the eyes are the entry point for approximately 90% of all the information we learn in a lifetime (with the exception of blind people, who receive much of their knowledge from their other senses).[54]

Nearly all humans are born with the potential for good eyesight, but vision – the ability to identify, interpret and understand what is seen – is learned and developed, starting at birth. In learning to walk – developing gross to fine motor control – a child begins by crawling, creeping, standing, walking with assistance, walking unaided, hopping, skipping and finally developing the ability to sit still. A similar process takes place in the development of vision; one visual skill builds on another as we grow. Many people miss a step or don't complete a step. Children may begin to perform academics or other visually demanding tasks before an acceptable foundation of basic visual skills is in place. Because Liz was able to see well, everyone had overlooked vision, yet Liz was having difficulty in every visual capacity. Everything a normal child learns automatically Liz had to be taught or retaught to change from her unique adaptations. Her coping methods restrained her.

The critical flicker frequency (CFF) is the highest frequency, in cycles per ssecond (cps), when a flickering light source can be detected. At frequencies above the CFF, the light source appears to be continuous even though it is actually flickering.

53. Siever, Dave CET, *The Rediscovery of Audio-Visual Entrainment Technology.* (2000)
54. Liberman, Jacob, OD, PhD,, *Light: Medicine of the Future.*

Liz adapted for fourteen years with limited, spastic and chaotic wiring. Now those wires were being untangled and connected. We retaught her the most basic skills including vision. We jumped in, up to our eyeballs, in a daily vision-training program. We worked with puzzles, mazes and hidden pictures at home while the professionals worked with lenses, prisms and computer programs at the office.

Children move from simple wooden puzzles to cardboard puzzles and then to printed-paper puzzles. "Mom, I can't do a puzzle on that paper. It hurts me!" Liz looked fearful. I discovered Liz's tactile defense issues had prevented her from touching anything printed on cheap paper — paperbacks, newsprint and phonebooks. She told me color crayon paper hurt her skin and the sound of a class of children coloring made her head crazy. She avoided cheap paper just as she avoided the computer because of flicker. I introduced 2 for $1.00 5"x7" Playmore® puzzle books[55] two pages a day until she tolerated the paper's texture.

> "Our daughter had trouble with eye contact. After an eye examination by a trained eye doctor, we discovered our daughter had double vision within about 30" of her face. If people got within that distance, they developed four eyes and two overlapping noses. Vision exercises and glasses helped. I still get a chuckle from memories of all the professionals who wanted to plant a psychological meaning to her refusal to make eye contact.
>
> Delinda (FASD mom)

A short duration of practice — one to five minutes — made bigger gains for Liz than overtaxing her. We played games, did puzzles and gave directions patching one eye for one task and switching eyes for the next task. We practiced right and left until they became automatic. Liz got frustrated. She yelled. She stomped. Papers were torn and crumpled. She succeeded.

> "I quit. I hate this. This ****. I can't do this." "Liz, you know what Dr. Sealock would say? Can't doesn't live in this room." In time, with practice and sometimes with developing smaller incremental learning steps . . . Liz could.

Within a short time Liz flew through puzzle pages and looked forward to the exercises. She no longer feared the telephone book and she could handle the TV schedule. She separated the foreground from background. She saw the bigger picture instead of being

55. Playmore Puzzle® Books can be purchased at most dollar stores.

Things families can do for fun to improve a child's vision:

- **Dot-to-dot:** Muscle control, eye-hand coordination, creating and completion of task.

- **Mazes:** Perceptual path work, eye-hand control, planning, sequencing, pencil control, visualizing a path, solving an unknown, completion of task.

- **Hidden pictures:** Seeing a form within a form – perceptual training.

- **Word search puzzles:** Organization, ocular skills, visual discrimination, letter recognition, spelling and vocabulary.

- **Pattern blocks:** Spatial reasoning, visualization, develops problem solving.

- **GeoBoards:** Visualization, hand skills, bilateral control, perceptual skills, memory.

- **Wicki sticks:** Add flexibility and creativity for dot to dots and mazes.

- **Other Toys:** String games, pick up sticks, slinky, etch-a- sketch, making balloon animals: ambidextrous (two-hand) play.

---

attacked by a million details. For the first time in her life, at fourteen we played checkers. Liz was winning as each individual square became a piece of the game board. We introduced the game Sequence®.

Visual therapy turned on Liz's suppressed eye. She saw with binocular vision – both eyes working as a team learning to process smoothly, accurately, equally and simultaneously. This allowed her to utilize both eyes to view two sep-

Liz's colorful vocabulary subsided as she became less and less frustrated with her surrounding world. She was beginning to think before she overreacted – at least once in a while.

arate images and combine them into one three-dimensional image in her brain. She saw stereo! (Stereoscopic vision is a by-product of good binocular vision.)

Life was simpler while we had kept vision, sound and movement separate. It was time to begin mixing modalities and integrating them. We pursued what she considered an attack on her senses. Each system worked fine in isolation and rebelled when forced to work tandem. We introduced jacks and added jump rope drills to workouts. We caught

*In our journey through vision we realized how hidden most of Liz's disabilities were. I wondered how many other children faced the same issues in learning. They **could** see well, but **could not** process what they were seeing. It was useless to have Liz try harder.*

bubbles. We dusted off jump rope rhymes and elementary hand-clapping games. We watched short seqments of dance videos and tested sequences.

We found super visual motor ideas in the book *Classroom Visual Activities: A Manual to Enhance the Development of Visual Skills*[56] by Regina G. Richards, MA. Regina Richards manual is filled with ideas we could do at home to enhance the visual therapy being done in a clinical setting, where she was seen three times a week over a nine month period. Her homemade materials were easy to create and fun even for a teen. Karl's built a teeterboard (pg 161).

As Liz's vision skills increased we incorporated Ms. Richards ideas into our daily lives. We reintroduced physical education skills in a developmental sequence. We gradually added Concentration and Listening CD's developed by Advanced Brain Technologies[57] into our silent school environment.

Our classroom, like the world was no longer silent and serene. We talked during therapy. We mixed senses together. At 14.5, the computer was reintroduced into our schedule, along with auditory and timing, the screen no longer assaulted her vision and made her dizzy if she used it only in short duration. We found a $30.00 musical keyboard on a clearance table. She was able to watch a full television movies and sit in a movie theater. The rhythmic stimulation of flickering lights, computer screens and light flickers still gave her headaches. The spinning board

The ability to see objects move through space is a key aspect of vision. We encouraged development with toy car play and rolling a hula hoop and throwing bean bags through without knocking it over.

I met with Bob DeBoer at A Chance to Grow - New Visions School. His educational model followed the same path we had followed with Liz. Nutrition, academics, nuerotherapy, vision, OT, PT, auditory training, parent support groups. He had realized and executed my dream — a public charter school which provided these special children a real chance to grow without stripping the parents' pocketbooks.

Liz is a super star. She has come a long way. She is where most of my patients initially start out after four months of vision therapy.

Dr. Don Sealock

56. Published by Academic Therapy Publications, 20 Commercial Blvd., Novata, CA 94949-6191 (www.academictherapy.com)
57. Advanced Brain Technologies (www.advancedbrain.com)

Peripheral vision decreases as a child fatiques or when the child is stressed. That is one reason a child may move more or appear to fidgit later in the day, they are trying to see.

made her dizzy and nauseated. The metronome sound turned a pencil into a projectile missile. I listened to expletives.

I added chapter book reading. Liz learned to order her own pizza using the telephone book. She used a dictionary to find a word. Words on a page no longer assaulted her. She read menus at the restaurant. She made her own change. She began reading music and understood how notes fit with the strings on her harp. I caught her fingering the piano keys with her harp songs. We simplified her room and added a wall of five inexpensive door mirrors to watch herself dance, exercise and do aerobics. This encouraged smoothness in body action.

Seeing the world with both eyes while trying to listen at the same time, Liz shouted, "Will you shut up, so I can see?" her purple hair flying. I introduced another period of silence without chaos for her to regain her emotional and academic footing. Then I began mixing motor, eyes and ears again — bit by tiny bit. Payback time had come; it was my turn to introduce the chaos into her life!

Soon it would be time for group learning. Someday she may even take the city bus and reach independence!

Our eyeballs are only the beginning of vision.

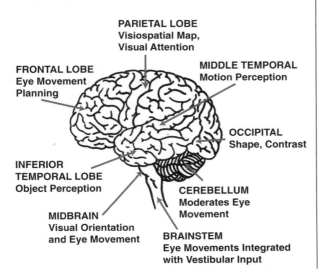

PARIETAL LOBE
Visiospatial Map,
Visual Attention

FRONTAL LOBE
Eye Movement
Planning

MIDDLE TEMPORAL
Motion Perception

OCCIPITAL
Shape, Contrast

INFERIOR
TEMPORAL LOBE
Object Perception

CEREBELLUM
Moderates Eye
Movement

MIDBRAIN
Visual Orientation
and Eye Movement

BRAINSTEM
Eye Movements Integrated
with Vestibular Input

Vision development

first six months of life:

1. Acuity

2. Accommodation

3. Peripheral Vision

4. Binocular Vision

5. Depth Perception

Liz was 14 when we begin developing some of these skills. At 15 years of age, it was time to move on.

ALL ON BORED!

We discovered Dr. John Nash - as we had all our other health professionals – while we weren't looking. Dr. Nash is a biologist, biochemist, neurotherapist and psychologist. In addition he is the examiner for Neurofeedback Providers and advanced instructor for Lexicor Medical Technology. He has been a consultant to NASA. We didn't know we needed him, but we are grateful he joined us on our journey. His practice, Behavioral Medicine Associates, Inc. *(www.qEEG.com)* provides

We don't know yet the extent that neurofeedback can help people with FASD improve their lives . . .We know what we are seeing in terms of behavior . . . continued improvement in functioning.

Ken Dunning, M.S., C.M.H.C.
Northwest Neurofeedback
Associates

Currently there is no research that shows brainwave feedback is effective treatment for FASD. However there are studies that show FAS and FAE individuals have different brain patterns compared to individuals without FASD.

Steven Rothman, Ph.D.

Quantitative EEG (3 dimensional) recording. In contrast to MRI or CT scanning of the brain (which reveal structural abnormalities), qEEG reveals brain wave performance characteristics reflecting actual functional or cognitive abnormalities. He uses state of the art cognitive behavior therapy coupled with advanced neurofeedback, neurodiagnosis and neurotherapy. He works with tough teens. His eyes sparkled meeting Liz. It was obvious he enjoyed adolescents.

EEG technology is not new. The first paper published on electrical activity of the brain was in 1929 by Hans Berger. Three-quarters of what we now know about EEG was already known by 1934.[58] More than half a century passed and only a few wrinkles

58. Hughes, John R., M.D., Ph.D. and John, E. Roy PhD. *Conventional and Quantitatitive Electroencephalography in Psychiatry.* The Journal of Neuropsychiatry and Clinical Neuroscience. May 1999

were added. Then the rapid advance of computer technology surged into the EEG and biofeedback research making it relatively inexpensive and accessible. Unregulated by a professional community, this freedom of accessibility and lack of methodical standards gave an undeserved bad reputation to EEG and Quantitative EEG methods of brain mapping. Over the last 20 years however, vast databases of information have been accumulated. Powerful statistical comparisons are now available between normal operating brains and persons having different diagnoses. These databases accurately address neurological issues – thus helping to make a difference in lives.

We honor the men and women who are researching the brain and advancing neuro technology.

Liz enjoys learning how her brain works and what areas she has trouble with.

Quantitative EEG is a non-invasive measurement, using digital technology, of electrical patterns at the surface of the scalp. QEEG brain mapping can contribute in the distinction of separating social and motivational issues from organic issues by revealing marked abnormalities as the brain is in its constant state of flux. It can aid in assessing cognitive, attentional and developmental disorders.

When millions of neurons discharge in unison to a stimulation they produce sweeping electrical charges called brainwaves. These rhythmic electri-

Brain Wave Frequencies and Reported Experiences

Name	Cycles Per Second		Person's Experiences
Delta	1-4	**SLEEP**	sleep, disassociation, (disconnection from body-very slow waves)
Theta	4-8	**DREAM**	diffuse focus (fuzzy, foggy), creativity, strong sense of being alive
Mu	7-9		Thalpha, insightful, personally transforming (can be harmful if stuck)
Alpha	8-12	**RELAX**	peaceful, calm, relaxed, under activated, slushy
SMR	12-14		narrow focus (mild) Sensory Motor Rhythm (SMR)
Beta 1	14-16	**ALERT**	narrow focus (moderate)
Beta 2	16-20		narrow focus (intense)
Beta 3	20-24		hypervigilant, extreme anxiety, panic
Beta 4	24-28		robotic, compulsive, little or no sense of self or others
EMG	28-32		often used with muscle control, no reported feelings with this

cal impulses from the brain are broken down into frequencies and measured in cycles per second called Hertz. When we are engaging in a mental task, the normal brain responds with quicker **Beta** waves (14 H_z or higher). **Alpha** represents a sort of daydreaming state and typically disappears when we get busy (8-12 H_z). **Theta** waves typically predominate as sleep begins (4-8 H_z) and gradually give way to slower **Delta** waves (0-4 H_z).

Neurofeedback (neurotherapy) is not experimental. It was first introduced in 1957. Neurotherapy is a method of exercising the brain's ability to modify its own brainwaves. The basic premise is to strengthen weak brainwaves and relax too tense brainwaves. The goal of neurotherapy is to bring order to a disordered brain's physiology through operant conditioning. Simple computerized games are played using the person's own ability to modify brain wave production.

A stretchable elastic electrode cap was placed on Liz's clean hair and the recording electrodes were filled with a water soluble gel. A computer cable popped out the top and transmitted the electricity from her brain to the computer. No electricity from outside touched her. The procedure was non-invasive. Liz tolerated the application of the gels and the cap. A year earlier her tactile defensiveness and other sensory integration issues would have prevented even a few minutes of access by the technician. Her impulsivity and frustration would have appeared as noncooperative.

Liz and I watched her brain waves change as she stuck out her tongue, blinked her eyes or lifted an eyebrow. When Liz was comfortable with the cap and how it worked we proceeded to record eyes open, eyes closed, math, reading, listening, and drawing. Dr. Nash's technician also had Liz do a Continuous Performance Test and another test for additional comparisons. Two hours and fifteen minutes into the assessment Liz hit meltdown. I was proud of her — our previous time barrier had been less than an hour. The data would be sent into a national database that would compare Liz's brain information to that of other teens her age with brains considered normal. The deviations would be diagrammed onto mappings.

Presently there is more to the brain that scientists don't know than what they do know. Measuring and manipulating brain waves is only one piece of the brain research. It was important for me to see how Liz's brain worked, not what it looked like.

Her brain wave reports were compared with a computer library of medical, neurological and psychologically evaluated normal subjects.

By now, we had discovered that specialized health practitioners had experience, tools, and discernment that could make a difference for Liz. None held a complete answer, but each added another element that helped us put the pieces together.

Data reports showed:

- What is her ability to respond and pay attention to what she saw and heard in her environment?
- How quickly she decided what to do?
- If she could repeat tasks. Did her mind wander?
- Was her performance erratic?
- If she processed better with seeing or hearing?
- If she could maintain interest in a subject if she fatigues?
- Did her brain go on standby and wait for incoming information?

Ten days later, Karl and I met with Dr. Nash to review a half inch thick report containing her brain mappings. It was fascinating to see her brainwave patterns and brain functionality. What was most interesting to me was the areas she was having the most difficulty in — frontal left lobe, right and left hemisphere connections and slow response times — the exact things I had pinpointed as her parent and teacher. These disordered areas were two to four levels below the norm. On the other hand, she excelled in areas above her normal peers. Armed with printed information we could now target her weak areas. We were no longer isolated on a FASD island. We were ready to "beam Liz up to Dr. Nash" and take off.

Toni arrived for her one year evaluation of Liz and met with Dr. Nash to discuss Liz's brain mapping results and collaborate in the development of her next quarter's neuro program. It was going to be hard work; the goal would be to increase her ability to focus and concentrate.

We could see that Liz's brain was on and off task multiple times within one minute from the reports. Instead of engaging and becoming active Beta waves during a task, Liz's brainwaves intermittently slowed daydreaming Alpha waves or foggy Theta waves. As her teacher, I had watched her tune out and tried to reach her. Sometimes I made contact, other times my call "earth to Liz" reached out into a chasm in her

Why? You should never ask why. It sends the person into a room of mirrors with no answers.

Dr. John Nash
Behavioral Medicine Associates
www.qeeg.com

unchartered universe. Nash's program would help Liz learn to keep from getting herself lost in the space within her head.

We needed an initial 20 sessions of her full cooperation to establish whether this would help Liz. Karl and I developed an incentive program. When the full 20 sessions were completed Liz and a friend could enjoy a weekend of relaxing by a pool in a warm climate. This provided incentive for Liz to cooperate, it also created a cheerleader peer to encourage and check up on the progress after each session.

Dr. Nash gave me a fossil when I shut down in therapy. You should have seen the difference when my attention turned on. I can see what happens to me now, but I still don't understand it.

Liz adapted to the neuro-feedback and soon ordered her flying super girl around the computer screen. Super girl soon flew through her Theta waves and beat her initial scores. Her Alpha's were becoming the desired Betas.

Dr. Daniel G. Amen, founder of the Amen Clinics, is a clinical neuroscientist, a psychiatrist, and the medical director of The Amen Clinics. He is a nationally recognized expert in the fields of the brain, behavior and attention deficit disorders. Dr. Amen has pioneered the use of Brain SPECT Imaging (Single Photon Emission Computed Tomography) in clinical psychiatric practice. His clinics have the world's largest database of functional brain scans for neuropsychiatry. www.amenclinic.com

Each therapy we had introduced took some adjusting in our parenting and Liz's lifestyle. Neurofeedback was not without adaptations. Liz's emotionality increased during the initial sessions, but she soon regained her composure. This appeared, however, to be a new level of emotionality. Suddenly she wanted names for her feelings so she could identify them. She wanted to know 'why' she was feeling them. Twenty sessions allowed enough access to believe in further research in this therapy for children with FASD. Liz, however, quit cooperating.

"This is boring!" Liz drooped, her super girl powered down to slower Alpha waves and crashed.

"Great!" Dr. Nash exclaimed, "That's the whole purpose, to help you stay on board when you are bored. We don't want to lose you. Your job is to beat down boredom and learn to concentrate and focus."

12. AUDITORY

DO YOU HEAR
WHAT I HEAR?

I guess when you make noise you don't have to listen. Liz delighted in making noise, loud noise. Yet if the blender or vacuum cleaner ran she left the room. The sound of a group of children coloring hurt her ears with the paper scratching.

Liz grew up amid diverse sounds, but the seconds that David relished and understood Liz avoided. We thought it was a gender issue — boys being attracted to motors, engines and horns, mimicking the changing noises they make. The noises David squealed at with baby glee, Liz blocked out by covering her ears. On the other hand, Liz loved music. She loved singing and laid on the couch — as she explained to us — 'eating classical music' with her ears.

At four-years-old, Vivaldi was her favorite composer — not for her music, but because of her hair.

Auditory Readiness Steps
(Dr. Lyelle Palmer, Winona State University, Minnesota)

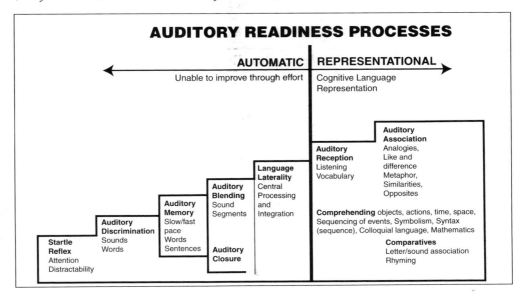

AUDITORY READINESS PROCESSES

AUTOMATIC | **REPRESENTATIONAL**

Unable to improve through effort | Cognitive Language Representation

Auditory Association
Analogies, Like and difference Metaphor, Similarities, Opposites

Auditory Reception
Listening Vocabulary

Language Laterality
Central Processing and Integration

Auditory Blending
Sound Segments

Auditory Memory
Slow/fast pace Words Sentences

Auditory Closure

Auditory Discrimination
Sounds Words

Startle Reflex
Attention Distractability

Comprehending objects, actions, time, space, Sequencing of events, Symbolism, Syntax (sequence), Colloquial language, Mathematics

Comparatives
Letter/sound association Rhyming

Liz danced, sang and talked her way through preschool. At age six, Liz, developmentally age three, sat mesmerized watching her cousin Piper's fingers deftly glide across harp strings making beautiful music. She wanted to play too. The Suzuki Music harp program at the MacPhail School of Arts accepted Liz as a student knowing her difficulties in learning. They assigned the Minnesota Orchestra's first chair harpist, Kathy Kienzle to us. In addition, they provided a special education consultant and Kathy offered lessons in her home to limit distractions. For Liz's first formalized listening program Suzuki was the right choice.

The Suzuki method teaches children as young as three to play instruments by listening to music. Teachers in Suzuki are trained to work with very young children with patience, love, commitment and tiny baby step by tiny baby step. Liz dreamed of being a famous harpist. Those dreams were shattered at eight-years-old when the new group of four-year-old students surpassed her.

INNER SPEECH

The development of inner speech is the process by which we hear ourselves think and can listen internally. We must be able to silently dialogue with ourselves to attain skills in reasoning and reflection. Inner speech becomes a tool for self-regulation of behavior, reasoning, reading skills and higher-level cognitive thought. Children with normal development must talk in order to think with words until about age seven. Liz was still talking to think at age twelve. Our little chatterbox was silent only – when she was in deep sleep. The work of Chris Brewer and Don G. Campbell, *Rhythms of Learning, Creative Tools for Developing Lifelong Skills,* provided a sequential program to encourage listening, not just hearing for Liz.

What was the key to Helen Keller's breakthrough from wild child to wonderful woman? *A mentor. Annie Sullivan was someone who was insightful, dedicated, committed and consistent. She had reasonable expectations for Helen to reach her potential and release her spirit inside. Our children have whole spirits needing to be nurtured and nudged, with patience and perseverance. Just as Annie worked with Helen incessantly until she got the concept of language, we must work with our children and also the world, to "get it" when it comes to FASD. And just as Annie worked intensely and closely with Helen, each child with FASD needs a mentor to achieve success in reaching higher potential.*

Teresa Kellerman, *FASD Mom*

Listening requires the ability to focus on sounds. It isn't always desire that allow a person to hear. A person may look without seeing or hear without listening. Background noise may be too distracting: fans, venting, outside noise, telephone, animals, other people, chairs rubbing across a floor. For some children separating foreground from background noise is impossible. Poor ability to listen equals poor learning. High reverberation makes it difficult for a student to comprehend what is spoken. Chance to Grow School in Minneapolis emphasizes curtailing noise distraction for its students. They put tennis balls on the bottom of chair legs and cover most areas with hypo-allergenic carpet, curtains, bulletin boards and other materials designed to absorb reverberation.

I can't lose Liz. I find her by listening for her voice. She has no volume control. How many times have I said, "Please, Liz, use your indoor voice."

The work of Brewer and Campbell provided insight into teaching Liz listening skills. We isolated ourselves from external noise. If she had trouble listening, I taught her listening tools. She cupped her hand and made a megaphone around her right ear to receive information. She tried listening with only one ear by covering one ear with her hand. She covered both ears with her hands to muffle noises assaulting her. These were only band aids to the underlying problem. Reading presented the most difficulty as it requires synchronizing the eyes and the ears. If we were to help Liz with organizing, processing and interpreting auditory information (**auditory fusion**) we needed more help than I could provide. We returned back to Liz's first concert hall — the womb.

Ear infections in young children can impair a child's ability to hear subtle differences between sounds.

According to Dr. Alfred Tomatis, a French physician, educator and psychologist, good hearing is necessary, but is not sufficient to produce good listening. The sounds we hear in the womb are very different from the sounds we hear after birth. The mother's voice sounds to the unborn child like a series of S's, Sh's and Zh's, similar to the high frequency chirp of a bird, rhythmically patterned. This is because the amniotic fluid absorbs (filters) the low pitch sounds. It is why the S, Sh and Zh sounds have a calming effect on an infant.

First I chose the words or words with sounds we were working on. If Liz misread a word, I whispered the correct word first in her right ear and then her left.

The initial phase of the Tomatis listening program reintroduces the sound the fetus hears in the womb. The program progresses with the sounds of a mothers voice with less filtration simulating the passage of sound from the liquid in the womb to sounds in the air (**audition**).

Infants who come into the world with the ability to hear have the potential to learn to listen. Separation from the mother, early infant or pregnancy trauma, major life disruption or prolonged emotional distress can cause the child or even an older person to close off from the world of listening. A child will lengthen the response circuit in order to withdraw and introduce distortions and fadings in sound to close off the ability to listen. As a result the child becomes a prisoner of these tricks initially instigated for protection.

We do not hear and listen through air conduction alone. The important, yet subtle, stimulation to the skin and through the bones greatly changes the manner how we receive information. Tomatis realized that vibratory stimulation in the womb beginning in the sixteenth to eighteenth week after conception, created important links for lifelong communication. The eighth cranial nerve pair, which carries auditory information from the ear to the brain, is the first sensory pair to develop. Although it takes another couple of months for the nerve to mature, the early charging of the brain with these high frequencies seems important in language development. Sound is a nutrient. We can either charge or discharge the nervous system by the sounds we take in through both bone and air conduction. Tomatis proved that the voice only represents what the ear can hear. This is known as the

Like musical instruments, all languages use the same basic tones. The base tones are generated by our vocal chords. These range from 125 to 250 Hz. The overtones, however, differ from language to language. That is why English, French and Spanish sound very different. And that is why if a Spaniard speaks English you hear the overtones.

The mouth cavity acts as a sounding board. Our tongue is divided into two parts providing two sounding boards. If you have ever tried to speak a foreign language you may have discovered you're literally tongue tied trying to enunciate sounds you are unfamiliar with.

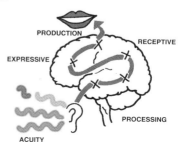

Tomatis Effect.

To illustrate this, spend a long period of time quietly bombarded with noise, typical of a modern office environment. Depart last so that you are responsible for turning off all the equipment. As each piece of equipment is turned off you will feel an 'ahhhh' of noise relief.

Liz begged me to take her to the fireworks. She wanted to sit in the front row and feel them. Previously we watched behind a window miles away.

In Toni's evaluation of Liz, she discovered Liz's dominant ear was her right ear. The dominant ear is the ear you use most often, it is the ear you turn toward the source of the sound to hear better. The right ear is the information ear and the left ear is the tonal or more effective ear. Sound that is captured by the right ear is directly transmitted to the language center in the left hemisphere of the brain. Sound captured in the left ear goes first to the right hemisphere, before it is transmitted to the language processing centers of the left hemisphere. Thankfully, right ear dominance put Liz at an advantage.

It finally made sense why adults naturally change the frequencies of their voices when speaking to an infant and young child.

Liz accepted information and processed better if she closed her eyes. When her eyes were open, information reception was discombobulated as it merged, crashed and criss-crossed in an information traffic jam.

We receive millions of sensory impressions each minute, but only a few reach the conscious attention in the cortex. We helped Liz manage her emotions **(limbic system)** and access her cognitive thinking functions **(cortex)** by separately teaching to each receptive sense. The limbic system functions as a kind of switchboard, reading sensations and sending them on to the neocortex for expansion. We organized the data in small segments before we bombarded Liz with new information. This provided a safe haven for her to learn without having her switchboard become a tornado and my teaching area a disaster zone.

Loud noise can affect our delicate hair bundles. After exposure to loud noise, the hair bundles (cilia) in the ears disappear, fuse together or fall over.

Liz struggled to 'tune out' extraneous sounds and focus on the task at hand — conversation, learning, or executing a task. Whereas high pitched sounds stimulate the

Advanced Brain Technologies has designed CD's for background music to enhance learning, concentration and productivity.

brain and the desire to communicate, base sounds excite the vestibular system and generate body movement, consume and exhaust the body. Liz preferred the low sounds. Toni taught me how to separate visual teaching from auditory teaching. I wrote reminder notes on a white board. I introduced new vocabulary first saying the words, then by silently writing the words I spoke and finally asking Liz to read what I had written. I showed and did not speak. I spoke and did not show. I introduced material we 'would learn' tomorrow. I told her she didn't have to pay attention to learn today — she listened attentively. We developed hand signals as cues to eliminate verbal interruptions. These methods helped curb frustration. As time went on, Liz and I discovered another avenue to input new information — tactile. I wrote on her skin (spelling and math) with a feather. She did not look. I did not speak, instead she visualized in her mind what I wrote, said it back to me or gave a math answer.

Toni prescribed therapeutic listening for Liz. We purchased *The Listening Program*® and executed the program in our home for thirty minutes each day under her supervision. This eliminated adding five more weekly therapy sessions with professionals to our already busy schedule. Liz, unable to sit still complemented auditory training with weight-training. Wearing the headset she exercised her auditory system while she normalized her reflexes and built her strength, balance and coordination.

Auditory training is based on the pioneering work of Alfred Tomatis, MD. The goal being to restore listening, making it possible to read, learn and communicate. Listening is a key to that success. In nature, there is no pure sound. Natural sounds are a mixture of high and low pitched frequencies. The ear must be able to distinguish between them.

I put on The Listening Program's® headset and

Education (educare in Latin) means to 'draw out.' Instruct (instrure in Latin) means to 'pile upon.' When we pile upon we do not honor the creative process, for we do not allow time and space for incubation, illumination, or the synthesis involved in creative intelligence. When we instruct, we merely provide facts and answers. Educating implies drawing out, an active participation in creating intelligence, and awakening of inner thought process.
Brewer, Campbell
Rhythms of Learning (1991)

picked up the manual knowing my hip-hop, ghetto rap teen was going to need some encouragement. Music filled my ears and brain as birds flew from one side of my head to the other, rain fell and classical music filled my head. Then as I was prepared to hear the next measure of a familiar classical piece I received an auditory surprise of a sanctuary of sounds, blessing the mind and ears of a very tired mother. I had to know more.

Just as seeing is related to vision, hearing is related to listening. Vision and listening are the brain processing pieces of sensory information through the eyes (seeing) and the ears (hearing). Listening and vision are active focusing processes.

There are a number of different programs currently being used based on the work of Tomatis. Among them are Samonas, Sound Therapy for the Walkman, Auditory Integration Training (AIT) and Auditory Enhancement Training (AET).

Sound is the basic sense we use to communicate just as sight is the basic interpretive sense we use to navigate within our world. Memorization of words and numbers have an abstract quality without the ability to integrate sight and sound. A Chance to Grow School in Minneapolis uses the auditory training work BDRL (Baltic Dyslexia Research Lab) of Kjeld V. Johansen (www.dyslexia-lab.dk) of Denmark effectively. Johanson's CDs are mastered from ROTNA Music individually for each child's specific auditory issues based on audiometric testing. The training is adapted as the child grows. Visiting a Chance to Grow School I had the opportunity to experience BDRL. Lying reclined – head slightly downward – wearing glasses and a headset, I closed my eyes and listened relaxing with the combination of sight/sound therapy.

The quality of a person's vision and listening ability will affect their creativity, alertness and focusing. Remediating Liz's listening and vision contributed to increasing her self-image, normalizing her emotions and enhancing her social development.

AUDITORY PROCESSING DISORDER

Auditory Processing Disorder (APD) is not a hearing problem. The American Speech-Language Hearing Association (ASHA) defines APD as "the inability or decreased ability to attend to, discriminate, recognize or understand auditory information." Most language is learned by listening. In neurotherapy we watched Liz's brain waves slow down as she tried to attend to listening. In order to learn, a person must be able to attend to, listen to, and separate important speech from all the other noises in the surrounding environment. When auditory skills are weak, a person may experience overload. This makes learning more challenging, frustrating and sometimes too difficult to continue, resulting in shut down or explosive behavior. Like all the other developmental models auditory processing also has a sequential hierarchy, even though many of the skills overlap and are essentially inseparable.

Very similar to the hierarchy of vision, the ear first must be able to perceive sound **(sensation)**, discriminate the differences in sounds **(discrimination)** and determine where the sound is coming from **(localization)**. To do this the brain must be able to keep its attention on the sound **(auditory attention)** and identify one sound from another **(auditory figure**

"Can we learn the states and capitals?" Liz's teen friends pleaded and I offered to teach them in 6 days. "No way, man. Our brains don't work that good," they chorused. "Sure they do. I'll prove it." In two lessons 13 states were memorized. These special ed kids began to believe in their own potential and the power they held between their ears.

Insight into the world of a child who has ADP (Auditory Processing Disorder)

- It takes increased effort to follow what is happening in a classroom, the child may 'switch off' or 'act out' when it becomes too difficult to concentrate.
- A printed homework /chore timetable, list of assignments and expectations for completion helps the child organize.
- Be specific in your vocabulary, 'clean up' is abstract; 'put the pencils in the holder' or 'put the books on this shelf' is specific.
- Speak clearly to ensure understanding. Ask child to explain back in his 'own words' not repeat back to you like a tape recorder.
- Group conversations and debates are difficult. When addressing first use the child's name, then make eye contact to let her know you are talking to her.
- Present instructions in small, easy steps. Let the child begin a process and require a 'one minute check in' to secure she is on task.
- Provide a quiet, non-distracting environment, especially for testing.
- Telephone conversations and computer audio may be confused because the sound quality is often degraded and no facial or body clues are available.
- Build coping routines, start small and praise repetition, encourage self-advocacy.

ground). A more advanced level of auditory discrimination allows a person to distinguish between words and sounds that are similar. Higher up the ladder is auditory closure which allows a person to understand a whole word or message when a part of it is missing. Beyond that, auditory synthesis provides the ability to blend individual letter sounds **(phonemes)** or units of sounds **(morphemes)** into words **(phonics)**. It is at this point vision begins to integrate with hearing and auditory analysis is used to identify these phonemes or morphemes within a word **(reading)** and finally attach a meaning to it **(auditory association)** with comprehension. The grand finale **(auditory memory)** is being able to recall the sound after it has been labeled and stored. This is not a simple process.

Stomping on bubble wrap can be a wonderful sensory precursor for children facing loud and noisy situations, but must be executed with caution to avoid hearing damage.

Auditory processing to vocalization occurs in many areas of the brain. Damage may have occurred in any one of millions of cells in prenatally exposed children. The focus of auditory training is to re-educate the ear and the auditory pathways. It is a combination of art, science and engineering that improves the ability to perceive the full range of auditory frequencies (20 Hz-20,000 Hz cycles per second) that results in active listening. Active listening improves auditory tonal processing, and this helps the ear and brain better support auditory sequential processing as well as language processing. The integration of auditory function in the ear with the brain achieves changes in listening, communicating and learning.

Chance to Grow utilizes Audio-Visual Entrainment (AVE) with excellent results to exercise the brain. AVE discovered that the electrical rhythms of the brain tended to assume the rhythm of a flashing light stimulus, a process called entrainment.

www.actg.org

In humans, hair cell bundles are arranged in four long, parallel columns on a gauzy strip of tissue called the basilar membrane. This membrane, just over one-inch long, coils within the **cochlea,** a bony, snail shaped structure about the size of a pea that is located deep inside the inner ear. Soundwaves generated by mechanical forces cause the eardrum, and in turn the three tiny bones of the middle ear, to vibrate. The last of these three bones **(stirrup)** jiggles a flexible layer of tissue at the base of the cochlea. The pressure sends waves rippling among the basilar membrane, stimulating some of its hair cells.[59]

These cells send out a rapid-fire code of electrical signals about the frequency, intensity and duration of a sound. The messages travel through auditory nerve fibers running from the base of the hair cells to the center of the cochlea and from there to the brain. After several relays within the brain, the message reaches the auditory areas of the cerebral cortex that processes and interprets the human voice, musical phrases, rain or any of the myriad sounds in the world around us.[60]

Compared with the 100 million photoreceptors in the retina of the eye, there are only 16,000 extremely vulnerable hair cells in the human cochlea. David Corey and James Hudspeth of Massachusetts General Hospital have videotaped the dance of this tiny patch of 16,000 hair bundles arranged in four long parallel columns. Looking like miniature antennae these cells quiver to high-pitched tones of violins, sway to rumbling kettle drums, and bow and recoil like tiny trees in a hurricane to blasts of rock and roll music. In our high-decibel society of traffic, loud music and man-made noise, life takes a toll on these tiny hair cells. People tend to lose 40% of their hair cells by age 65. Once destroyed we can not regenerate them.

I thought Liz was listening quietly to hip hop music I approved of. Little did I know until I listened she was bombarding her mind and heart with lyrics degrading to humanity. I cried. She liked the way this woman rhymed, the sound of her voice and the beat. "Ok I will listen then we will find a person with decent lyrics who compares."

"Crazy hair, clothes to wear!" two-year-old Liz sang repeatedly watching herself in the mirror. "Mark my words, just wait until she is 14," Karl winked. Crazy hair, clothes to wear Liz at 14 honored dad's prediction.

Liz's tolerance to sound improved. She remained frustrated and confused in group environments, but attended for short duration on given tasks, even if interrupted by noise. She was learning to work with groups of teens — participating and contributing instead of standing on the sidelines. Loud noises no longer startled to her. She made fruit smoothies in the blender and vacuumed her room. She laughed at the 4th of July fireworks show. Her musicality improved and her senses

59.-60. Seeing, Hearing and Smelling the World. www.hhmi.org

Points of reference measured in dB or decibels

0	Softest sound person with normal hearing can hear
10	Normal breathing
20	Whispering at five feet
30	Soft whisper
40	Quiet residential neighborhood, library
50	Normal conversation, refrigerator, dishwasher
60	Sewing machine
60-95	Power lawnmower, vacuum cleaner
70	Freeway traffic, TV audio
80	Ringing telephone, whistling kettle, machine tools
85	Heavy traffic, noisy restaurant
100	School dance, snowmobile, motorcycle
110	Shouting in ear, baby crying, busy video arcade, power saw, car horn, squeaky toy held close to ear
112	Personal cassette player on high
120	Thunder, chain saw, band concert, ambulance siren, jet plane
125	Auto stereo
130	Stock race cars, air raid, jackhammer
140	Airplane taking off
150	Jet taking off, firecracker, capgun, balloon pop
160-170	Rifle, handgun, shotgun

Decibels are measured on a logarithmic scale. Each increase of 10 on the scale represents a tenfold increase in loudness. 20dB is 10 times louder than 10 dB, 30 db is 100 times louder than 10 dB, etc.

---

began integrating with her motor skills. She learned a new harp song with both hands in five months, whereas previously we had worked two years on one song. She sang while she danced.

Rhythm and memory have effects on our ability to learn. Songs, raps, games and chants helped enhance developing rhythm. Liz held auditory rhythmic patterns in her head. She memorized lyrics and music. Dr. Seuss was no longer an auditory onslaught. She was free style rapping, writing lyrics and poetry. She found a producer and organized a hip-hop rap and dance group. She tried complicated dance steps and she almost was able to stay on beat.

Mixing listening and timing is a further step. The work of Jim Cassily and Interactive Metronome helps children gain control of their bodies and thought processes, thus improving the mind to music link. Like Brain Gym, Interactive Metronome has proven successful for many children once earlier developmental steps

"We will make the whole universe a noise. The melodies and silences of Heaven will be shouted down in the end."

C.S. Lewis
The Screwtape Letters

Noise is the leading cause of hearing loss in 28 million Americans, and it is happening at younger ages.

are achieved. The child must be able to clap hands together, pat knees with alternate hands, toe tape and then integrate these movements with timing.

For more information visit their website at www. interactivemetronome.com.

So many of Liz's systems were subtly compromised, I didn't want to risk hearing damage on top of processing damage. The CD personal stereo systems seems to be permanent headgear on teens. If Liz cannot hear us talking to her in a normal voice from three feet away, her headphones are too loud and may be damaging her ears. We check periodically if her ears ring or buzz – an early warning sign of hearing damage. Unfortunately US Government guidelines of 85 dBA to protect workers' hearing is not enforced to protect our children. If turned up all the way sounds can be produced as loud as 105 to 120 dBA. Noise levels above 85 dBA will harm hearing over time, noise levels over 140 dBA can cause damage in one exposure.

Liz may ask me to 'needle the thread' and hope I don't 'finger my prick.' It could lead to an emergency trip to the hos'tip'al. I wonder exactly what she hears. She bagan to catch her raucous blunders and laugh.

Someday perhaps Liz will hear what I hear, meanwhile her statements are often the very fodder cartoons are made of.

Liz could finally use the vacumn cleaner. Kirby had withstood the abuse of fourteen other children in our home. The first month of Liz's new skill development, he ended up in the shop. A month later he made a return visit.

In the barrage of today's noise can we tune into the song of the cardinal or the coo of the dove?
Can we hear the symphony of the mosquito or the concerts of crickets? The kingdom of noise shouts out chaos and rebellion.
Can we tune in to listen to the kingdom of quiet as it whispers to us of order and beauty?

"There are two ways of spreading light: to be a candle or the mirror that reflects it."

Edith Wharton

FRIENDS
OPENING DOORS FOR GROWTH

The medical diagnosis of FASD brain damage changed our lives. Knowing the truth provided opportunity for understanding. Life was not going to get easier from this point on. **Liz dreams of independence.** She is a hard worker. She has an affect on people. She is an overcomer. Her music lyrics are poignant, piercing minds and hearts. The diagnosis was a gracious gift opening up our present to realistically set a course for a future.

My daughter, my student – outgoing Liz does not comprehend 'stranger danger.' She passed out our phone number to anyone looking like a possible friend. Teens tell me she is a magnet of energy. Her sense of humor and friendliness quickly attract people. On the other hand she leaves people abandoned and shattered in her wake with impulsive, outrageous behaviors and random statements. It is important to train her to be the best she can be and not hide behind the excuse of brain injury. It is difficult and sometimes impossible to know the difference between 'rude' teen behavior and neuro 'gas passing.'

Liz is a real friend to me. When I am sad or angry she helps me calm down. She has really good ideas. I guess that is because she has to deal with hard things herself. I know I can call her and she will listen to me and help me. The hardest part is when she gets mad and can't understand something.

Leekplay - Liz's friend

Life is relationships. Each day we must dance our own dance as we interact with others. Our interpretation and expression of another's actions is vital in the maintenance of long-term and healthy relationships. When Liz's brain is working better her selection of friends improves. She is not vulnerably drawn to peers using her impulsivity and innocence to do their 'dirty' work. Their smooth talk no longer fools her. She discerns between friends who hold her emotions hostage and friends who encourage her to be her best. When her brain is not working well (stress, tired, nutrition, medication, chemical abuse, depression, etc.) her dangerous choices as an older teen can be deadly.

Liz is different. She stands out in a crowd and is singled out by more traditional peer groups. Her resiliency to public rejection from peers astounds me.

- Does her lower IQ protect her from this negativity?
- Does her inability to understand double meanings and puns isolate her heart from destruction?

I believe some of Liz's strength comes from knowing we won't reject her. We try to guide her versus use our natural tendency to criticize or condemn inappropriate friends. Like many other skills, friendship building takes practice. For some youth, sports, fine arts or church clubs, offer supervised and structured access to quality peers, and regularly scheduled respite for parents. As an early teen rollerblading provided Liz opportunity to blow off steam and have fun with others without the need for conversation or close relationship. As an older teen non-alcoholic, adult supervised teen dance clubs offered supervised recreation. Karl and I provided transportation keeping our ears open for problems. We try to make ourselves available, listen with interest and guide thinking without lecturing. We provide projects to earn money for movies, sleepover snacks, and film for the video camera for teens.

Friday night sleepovers in our home blend into Saturday mornings in front of the bathroom mirror over baskets of makeup and hair supplies. The girls trade clothes, posters and boy stories. They talk into wee morning hours. They sing and dance, laugh and yell, watch and make movies trying to discover who they are. We dine together, play pranks on each other and work to provide a safe, supervised space for them to grow. They see us at our best. They see us at our worst.

We do not hide the medical diagnosis of FASD from Liz's friends, their parents or the community. I explain behavior issues, provide a copy of Liz's book and give them ideas to enjoy Liz when she is with their

Liz and I are sisters for life. Our hearts are related. I can tell her anything. When I am with Liz I can 100% me. I don't act different. She loves me the way I am - my good self and my bad self.

Kathleen - Liz's friend

Being with Liz is fun. You never know what she is going to do next. Malica - Liz's friend

I like it at your house. I get attention and I don't get to do everything I want to.

Anna – Liz's friend

family. As families have gotten to know Liz, she has been invited to participate in their outings. Parents skilled in working with a special needs child pull it off well and everyone has a good time. Unbelieving parents of more normal children call us before the visit is up to fetch Liz.

My old friends 'wiley' (rile) me up Mom. My new friends calm me down and help keep me safe.

Liz

Friendship with a teen with FASD is tough. The subtle nuances of relationships are invisible to Liz. We use role-play to expose negative social behaviors and to reinforce and dramatically practice positive social behaviors. I focus on one aspect of friendship at a time. When I notice it happening in public, on television or at the movies I point it out. I try hard to frost it with humor.

Friends provide fun and excitement. Liz compounds the equation. When Liz has a FASattack Karl or I are accessible to provide friendship support ideas. We try to guide Liz's friends as they guide our daughter. We teach her friends sensory integration exercises and keep communication open to tough teen issues: depression, sex, gangs, violence and substance abuse. We offer rides if they are in trouble and ears when they need a shoulder to cry on.

By age fourteen, Liz progressed from emotional outbursts to emotional synergy. If a friend was angry, Liz was angry. If a friend cried, Liz cried. We celebrated that age two milestone, but Liz did not separate herself from another's emotions, she could not outreach to provide sympathic care, if someone was ill, hurt, or in need, she was overwhelmed and stagnated. She cared about 'only' herself, her universe of one. But her friend's who 'ate up' her concern, misread her responses as 'totally supportive' and loved it. She had not yet developed the skills of compassion and safe boundaries between people in relationships.

Real friends enrich your life and can provide lifelong satisfaction, standing by you during difficult times. Friendships don't just happen. They are nurtured — to have a friend you must be a friend. Friends provide an opportunity to learn to deal with conflicts and differences of opinions. Friends become allies in times of trouble, and stability in times of stress. They become the ears and hearts to talk to about problems. Liz can be all ears. She can also be all mouth. Being Liz's 'real' friend is not easy.

"Mom, all my friends are broken. I'm bored." I discovered in probing deeper all her teen buddies were grounded.

In our last year of homeschool, we discussed how to get friends, how friends influence our lives and life goals. We worked with Liz to understand that it was her friends who would get her into the most trouble, not her enemies. We talked about 'real' and 'not real' friends.

The word GOal begins with GO and ends with AL, Liz and I figured out how to get started wtih AL the tiny steps to achieve. Her choice of friends would influence her ability to achieve her dreams. Liz dreamed of being a famous rapper. I explained gently that she may do better in hairstyling and enjoy rapping as a hobby. Unstoppable Liz was shocked. I didn't believe in her and she grandiously found a music producer on her own. She told him she had a group and they were ready to perform. She was ready to "GO!" At that moment there was no group and their only performance was in the backseat of my car. They talked the talk. Could they walk the walk?

One spring day, I went to the garden shop to purchase $30.00 in plants. The total was $2.00 over, "Aren't these on sale?" I asked. "No," said the clerk. "I'll take them anyway," I answered.

Liz ran to our car sobbing, "You, you, you took those plants Mom. You took them. They weren't on sale!" Liz thought you could only buy things in stores if they were on sale and not everything in the store was.

SISTERS AND BROTHERS

The doors to a child's heart are precious. It is far better to open those doors than to close them.

Liz chose Nina as her new exchange sister from Czech Republic. We enjoy hosting independent thinkers and Nina was a star plus. Nina loved life and beauty. Her parents sent her to the USA to encourage positive change. Nina changed our family, she provided Liz a reverse role model, sneaking behind our backs with adverse teen behaviors. Two years younger, Liz counseled Nina in what she thought was safer behavior. Liz asked Karl and I for ideas to use with Nina. For once, Liz felt like a role model and vicariously thought about behavior, consequences and reactions without being the person falling apart. Nina was a challenge to keep safe and the two girls made quite a pair as Karl and I struggled to teach them to survive in a world with menacing potholes: Liz fell headfirst without knowing how she got there; Nina jumped in

It is the children who have broken my heart and shaken me to my very being, and who have given me wisdom.

because it looked fun. Despite the challenges, Nina was a sweet spirited teen who wore me down as I guarded her life. While I headed off the pass as the meanest mother in the world, my friend Liv adopted her as a God-daughter, spending time shopping, dining and talking. Both of our relationships were vital. Nina needed Liv's unconditional love. She needed parents standing firm.

Toni moved us to the next level with group interaction exercises. We added Anna as a summer daughter and Dave returned for summer vacation. Our home was filled with siblings, neighborhood teens and group dynamics. We learned building unity had nothing to do with race or religion, it had to do with human interaction. The girls practiced praise dancing and American sign. They were joined by a group of boys stirring my pot of house, phone and mother rules. Being a part-time sister or brother to Liz was a heavy load, lucky for Anna and Dave, they had other homes for respite.

FIST T'CUFFS . . . NIMBY

"I've gotta go to the bathroom!" Liz announced. No restrooms were in sight down the mile long white sand beach.

"See ya in the ocean!" called her best friend.

"Bitch!" Liz bellowed.

"What did you call me? I'm gonna kill you!" running from the waves.

"Try it!" Liz countered as her friend marched towards her and shoved. Ken and I hustled to intervene. POW! This was no longer a pushing match. Fists were flying and blood was flowing as beach boys gathered to cheer and watch the excitement. My leisurely day spontaneously combusted into chaos without warning. I was glad I was not alone to pry them apart. Two minutes earlier both girls were laughing together and taking pictures. I followed Liz as she stomped down the beach looking for tissue to clean off the blood.

What did you do to talk yourself into getting so mad?

Dr. Nash

Our family friend Ken harbored Liz's girlfriend trying to bring her back to her senses. "No one ever wins in a fight, no one!" he counseled. "No matter how badly

So many children fall through the cracks. Children are not disposable. Giving in and giving up is not an option. Supports must be in place to help families with complex children become the best they can be.

hurt the other guy is, no one ever wins. You both lose something. People will say and do things to you your whole life and you will get mad. Are you going to beat up everyone? An eye-for-an-eye makes the whole world go blind. Anger breeds more anger. Hatred fuels more hatred. Violence leads to more violence. It doesn't resolve anything. " Both girls had their own issues. I had three days left to go.

- Was I crazy? What on earth I was doing over a thousand miles from home alone with two special ed teens?
- How could we turn this into a learning experience?

Violence, the act of purposely hurting someone is a major issue facing today's young adults. In the hours after our school bells ring (3:00 - 6:00 pm), violent juvenile crime suddenly triples. All of our children are at risk of becoming victims. Statistics show that the incidence of violence caused by young people reached unprecedented proportions by the 1990's.

What causes someone to punch, kick, stab or fire a gun at someone? This is not a simple question. How could so much anger erupt in such a short time? How could they move from hugging each other and laughing to slugging and swearing within minutes? It was like their brains downshifted to a primitive functioning level.

An unbridled Liz threw a mean punch. It seemed like she combusted without any thought. My mind raced back to Liz's anxiety before flying to New York as an FASD expert for the Ricki Lake Show. Instead of hitting a friend she punched a stop sign. I grabbed her and she punched me. Huge bruises remained on my arm for three weeks.

Factors contributing to violent behavior include stress, peer pressure, need for respect or attention, feelings of low self worth, early childhood abuse or neglect, witnessing violence at home, in the community or the media and easy access to weapons. In living with Liz, I concluded she had constant triggers building one on another and firing when an unexpected seemingly insignificant trigger was pulled.

When Dave lived with us I gave him a 'fuss box'. It was simply an old cardboard box he could fuss in.

"Mom, sixty percent of the time it feels like my brain is fighting against me, like there are little men in my head switching switches. They turn things on I want off and they turn things off I want on. I hate Fetal Alcohol, Mom, I hate what it does to me!" Liz sobbed

It was important to know what was happening inside and outside of Liz to understand her violent reactions. Her constant daily triggers were the result of the primary damage she lived with because of prenatal alcohol exposure – slower abilities to process information, difficulty retaining information, inability to think ahead, sensory confusion and impulsive reactions. These constant and inescapable triggers isolated her and created a feeling of separateness from the rest of the world melting into the emotional triggers of being overwhelmed, humilated, embarrased, insecure, sad or scared. If her internal environment was compromised with hunger, anxiety, stress, sleep deprivation, abandonment, grief, sickness or pain the cockpin was engaged for rapid fire. A surprise event, change in plans, difficulty or misunderstanding from an external source (environment, person, job, machine) overloaded her capacity to maintain and she exploded.

When life changes Liz loses her frame of reference and does not have the ability to create a new beginning or an understanding that there can be another ending. She can't rationally understand that her anger often defeats her. Unexpected schedule changes disorientate Liz and create anxiety which foam into frustration and bubble into anger.

Some people use violence as a way to release feelings of anger or frustration, as Liz did on the stop sign or my arm - no thought just action. Other times, violence is used as a form of retaliation against someone who has hurt you, or against someone you love, as Liz's friend responded to the name-calling - drawing a line in the sand and making a decision for action. In other cases, violence is used as a method of manipula-

Warning signs that immediate violence is a possibility:

- loss of temper on a daily basis
- frequent physical fighting
- significant vandalism or property damage
- increase in use of drugs or alcohol
- increase in risk-taking behaviors
- detailed plans to commit acts of violence
- announcing threats or plans to hurt others.
- enjoy hurting animals
- carry a weapon

Except for the daily temper, Liz had none of these. **Why the interest in violence?**

Liz, what we are doing today may frustrate you. I need you to tell me when you begin to get frustrated so I can help you.   Dr. Nash

tion to get something a person wants - premediated violence.

Liz utilized violence to gain what she believed she needed. She struggled to manage her feelings when others hurt her. At times she believed that by having someone fear her, she protected herself and by acting tough she gained respect. In reality she lost respect and gained further isolation.

Liz, if you feel red hot, find a safe way to cool yourself off. Liz discovered sucking made an impact in self calming. Cold items like popsicles or ice worked best, but if they weren't handy her thumb would do. She never sucked her thumb as a baby.

Research shows that violence is often learned behavior. Where did the beach violence come from? Both girls had trouble controlling feelings of anger. Each girl had been a victim of bully threats, teasing and disrespect. Both felt rejected and struggled acadmically. Each girl had survived malicious rumors. Peers failed to acknowledge their feelings and often taunted with nasty words. As best friends, they promised explicit trust to support, watch out and stand up for each other. Were they so fragile that one wrong word broke that trust? Why did Liz use the b-word so spontaneously? How could one teach her to refrain from verbal abuse or violent action? Her future adult world would not put up with her rudeness.

Anger's most basic function is survival. It is necessary for hands-on fighting. It provides the incentive to struggle against the elements and accomplish what would be impossible without the additional strength that comes from anger. Adrenaline, the chemical involved in anger arousal, produces a numbing effect on the body, which allows the person to continue to fight when hurt. The dampening of pain makes the person stronger. Without pain, the body comes close to reaching its absolute strength potential. It also creates tunnel vision and concentration is focused on the opposing force. Self doubt or fear of failure do not impinge on a combatant's struggle. The individual does not experience pain until the adrenaline levels drop.[61]

Liz, successful people have problems. I guess you can be successful.

61. Bilodeau, Lorraine. 1992. *The Anger Book.* CompCare

For anger to be useful, people must do more than merely experience the feeling of anger and act upon the immediate feeling. Those whom anger motivates productively undergo a four-step process.[62]

Four Steps to Make Anger Useful

1. They feel the anger.
2. They recognize the situation that provoked it.
3. They identify a healthy, productive goal that would alleviate the situation.
4. They maintain the anger until they can take the first steps toward the goal.[63]

As a leader (teacher, mentor, coach, parent) you are influential. Your words, expressions and actions become magnified. Your criticism becomes devastating. Your approval motivating.

Liz was just beginning to learn about negative feelings and how to handle them. She asked me what she was feeling and what to do about it. Neurotherapy made a difference in strengthening her tolerance. The catfight on the beach proved we still had a long way to go.

Some people lash out at themselves. instead of others - suicide is the most devastating expression of violence against self.

It's normal to feel frustrated and angry when you've been let down, hurt, disappointed and betrayed. Anger is a strong emotion. It can be very difficult to keep in tow. As the parent of a child with FASD I do not always keep my own anger and frustration in check. Good judgment comes from experience, and experience, sadly enough often comes primarily from bad judgment. Day-to-day living can be overwhelming, but I try.

- Could she learn to understand what sets her off and I prepare for action instead of reaction?

Check myself:
- Was I calm?
- Was I working toward training the emotions of my child?
- Was she being stretched enough to grow but not torn apart?

HYJACKING THE AMYGDALA

According to EQ Today (www.eqtoday.com) there is a three to six second flood of electro-chemicals (peptides and hormones) which creates emotion and action. Dan Goldman labels this **"The Hyjacking of the Amygdala"** since it temporarily removes you from your thinking state. Luckily these chemicals do not persist.

62.-63. Bilodeau, Lorraine. 1992. *The Anger Book*. CompCare

They dissipate in three to six seconds. To remove the fuel you must use the analytical part of your brain for six seconds. Some examples include: recite multiplication tables, visualize six details of a beautiful place, think of six foreign or state capitals, feel six breaths of air filling your lungs and imagine what it looks like, count to six in a foreign language you are learning, remember six birthdates of friends or family, name six emotions you are feeling, find six beautiful qualities in the person you are fighting with or any other type of hard thinking.

Liz needed to learn to solve problems for herself. How?

I wondered if a child with slower processing and less access to analytical thinking could be trained to use this approach. Was six seconds in her brain the same or how was it different? Were Dr. Nash's words "What are you saying to yourself to get yourself so mad" reachable? Dr. Nash worked with Liz to help her understand anger and control the rush of adrenaline causing her heart to beat faster, her voice to sound louder and her fists to clench.

Three to six seconds of silence to refocus is not a huge investment to **STOP** a reaction that could cause major life changes. Liz's first step to calm herself down was to **STOP** (**S**top, **T**hink before you Act, **O**xygen, **P**roceed Safely). She needed to access her higher-level brain functioning in order to focus and overpower her lower-level fighting instincts.

Breathing is crucial in regaining composure. Deep belly breathing can flip the switch in your brain from flight or fight to relax. Six deep belly breaths with a long exhale on each breath can help build the bridge for thought versus action. Liz took a few slow, deep breaths through her nose and refocused – breathing in "I can think" – breathing out "while I feel." Liz transported herself into a more peaceful place. She coud seek a safe adult or friend to help her and she could pray for guidance.

I helped Liz by talking her through these statements. Later I helped her understand her reaction and worked through alternatives while the situation was still fresh in her mind.

Liz's expressions tend to be more external than internal. Usually we know what she is thinking.

- What could have happened if you argued/fought/swore?
- What are the consequences for those actions?
- What was the other person thinking or feeling?

- What reasons did the person have for saying/doing that? (Try to find neutral or positive reasons for a person's provocation.)

Instead of talking herself into higher levels of anger she needed skills in positive self-talk

"This is the 911 dispatcher, is this --our address---?"
"Yes."
"Is there a problem? Is everyone alright?"
"As far as I know. Let me run and check with the teens (who assured me no one had called and there was no problem).

- Liz, you can calm down.
- It's OK to be sad, hurt or mad.
- You can think and feel at the same time.
- Liz, you don't need to prove yourself.
- Liz, you don't have to let ---- get the best of you.
- Liz, you are stronger and more powerful if you don't fight.
- Don't argue. Think first. No one will win.
- Stay cool and think.
- Only you have the power to control your anger.
- Don't let your anger control you.
- I can defeat the problem not the person.
- I can be strong. I can be safe. I can be cool.

Liz's angry verbal reactions tagged right into fist fighting. I wondered how many violent dramas would play out in her life; initiated by her outbursts, name calling or flapping her lips before thinking. She was so vulnerable. She didn't know when to call for help, when to fight and when to walk away.

Liz needed to set boundaries of behaviors. We needed to get past Stanley Greenspan's two-way communication and move up the ladder to emotional thinking for Liz's safety and the safety of others. On her 15th birthday she received money. Her 'friend' stole it. We had practiced not hitting or fighting with people so instead of hitting the boy who held her wallet refusing to return it, she punched her fist through the window. "Mom, you told me not to hit him," blood poured from ugly gashes. "I didn't know glass would hurt me." An emergency trip to the hospital, stitches and her money gone Liz was the victim, the thief denied taking it.

It dawned on me, Liz had started taking her stitches out, and asked me to finish the last four from her window pane accident. Scared I would hurt her she screamed loudly before I touched her. "Don't murder me! Don't abuse me!" A summer breeze blew through the open window — a neighbor must have been concerned.

Independent living meant loving caregivers would not be there to supply encouragement, praise and attention when things were going wrong. It was vital to establish a group of quality friendships available for support, without enabling her behaviors.

"NIMBY!" my friend said.

"What?" I asked.

"Not In My Back Yard," he answered.

I guess it was good we lived on the other side of the earth. Liz had so many jumbled pieces. We were still organizing her emotionality. She needed stretching to help her think before she reacted. She needed to 'function.' I didn't want her little fists in police handcuffs.

DOORS TO HEARTS AND DREAMS FOR FUTURES

TRIBUTE TO NINA - MARCH 22, 1984 - JULY 7, 2001

"Mom, can I enter this contest? I can win $10,000 and go with you to Australia to teach about FASD?" I smiled taking The "Start Something" Target Tiger Woods Scholarship brochure. Perhaps we could do a homeschool study. Liz needed to learn about influencing others in a positive way, working with a group and making a difference. "Sure Liz, let's try it. You can fill out the form."

Liz was on a mission to challenge the world and stop FASD. She liked selling her books, getting attention for her cause and making money. She joined me speaking at workshops. She convened a group of friends to sing and dance at community events.

She provided real insight to help me understand living with FASD. "Mom, you can have everyone put tin foil on their heads like a hat and make it

Anger Management that WRRCCs:

• **Work:** knead bread, pull weeds, pick up sticks, stack wood, shovel snow, rake leaves, pound nails, throw laundry into the washer or dryer.

• **Recycle:** crumple newspapers for a future fire, stomp on aluminum cans, rip up some old sheets for the rag bag.

• **Relax:** take a hot or cold shower, breathing exercises, foot, hand, temple and face massage, read, lie down and listen to soothing music.

• **Communicate:** write angry words on paper or with chalk, write a furious letter, journal, talk into a tape recorder or video tape.

• **Create:** paint, sport, dance, sing, draw, clay.

cover their ears." We played with noises. "Yeah Mom, that was how it was. Like when the cell phone is going through a tunnel. Sometimes things were louder or softer or just not there." We tested a variety of CDs to find just the right mix of obnoxious. "Now turn off and on the lights. Mom do we have a strobe light. Everything was moving. I saw everything all at once. I heard everything all at once. It was all mixed together." She helped me understand what it felt like to live in her brain and together we developed a method for simulating the experience for others using tin foil hats and a raucous tape **(auditory)**, flickering fluorescent lights **(visual)**, bailing twine necklaces **(tactile)**, plastic bags on non-dominant hands **(fine motor)** to fill out a FASD word find maze **(kinesthetic)** while listening to an obnoxious trainer **(me)** who spoke to the ceiling, the wall, the floor, changed my tone and speed of voice to confuse and confound. Liz loved to join in these simulations, but before the exercise was over, she curled up on the floor. Overstimulated, she removed herself by shutting down. I usually finished the presentations alone.

That spring Liz completed all five levels of the Tiger Woods contest. She sealed the envelope and dropped it into the mailbox like a small child sending away for a secret prize. She was functioning at the highest level we have seen her attain.

It was a sunny July Sunday morning. Nina had returned to Czech Republic two weeks earlier. Liz and her friends were preparing their first performance of praise dancing at church. The phone rang. "Nina is dead. She was hit by a train yesterday at 5:00 am. The car stalled on the tracks. Nina and the two boys are dead. Her girlfriend is in a coma." In the blink of an eye Nina was gone. My morning changed as did my perception on the fragility of life and the incredible gift each child is to our home. I saw Liz and her friends with different eyes.

Statements to help an angry person:

• It's OK for you to be angry. I won't let you hurt yourself or others.

• You can be powerful and still ask for help.

• I will help you get control of your life and the feelings you have.

• You can think for yourself. I can think for myself. It is OK for us to think differently.

• You can think and feel at the same time.

• Your angry feelings are important to me.

• I will help you learn to ask for help.

• It's OK to cry.

• Let's find a safe place to talk.

Karl wrapped Liz in his powerful arms and gave her a bear hug. With his deep male voice he comforted her as he held her and helped her regain composure.

The summer progressed with another loss, Karl needed a triple bypass. Liz hid among her friendships, rehearsals and performances, while David joined me at the hospital to perk up Dad, attend rehabilitation classes and do Liz's tactile sequences on him.

Liz's hip-hop group performed at National Night Out Against Violence. It was their second perform- ance and the realization of a dream for Liz. They were fresh, sparkling and vibrant. The crowd loved them. I completed filming their set, congratulated the group and admonished my urban boys to not cause trouble when I left. I headed to the hospital to kiss my husband goodnight. I was gone less than an hour and all hell broke loose. Our main male rapper was escorted home by police. The other group mothers rounded up the young ladies and headed to my house. I rushed home to find Liz hysterical. "This was her group. This was her dream. It was ruined." She exploded into a limbic rage, it was time her 'friends' discovered why I pro- tected my daughter. They needed to understand what fetal alcohol exposure and brain damage do to a person. Liz was screaming and growling while pacing and pulling her hair and biting her arm. Another special needs group member joined in and then another. It was a huge emotional expres- sion. The tough young man who started the orignal fight wanted to help. "Your fighting caused it, you figure out how to stop it." He looked panicked.

Neighbors left their houses to watch the National Night Out Against Violence show in my yard. My parents peeked out the window questioning why they volunteered to help me while Karl was hospitalized. Did Liz react like this often? Why on earth did we live in such a neighbor- hood? The panicked young man returned "Miss Jodee, what can I do? I'm scared."

"Q, You had peace during your performance. What did you do to get that peace? Who brings destruction and chaos?" I asked.

His eyes lit up, "Satan, Miss Jodee. This is his doing. That moth** fu**er. We gots ta pray." He rounded up the

People who pass through my doors and live in my home are the sea- soning in my life. We add different spices with each new face. Because we are willing to open our hearts, we are able to enter the doors of other's hearts. We change with each person we choose to love.

fifteen teens exploding in my yard and they joined hands around a big white poplar. Their prayer was not for the little white church on the hill. It was more in the style I would have imagined from Peter when Jesus pulled him fresh off the boat. Except for the expletives it was rock solid. "Amen." A knife cut the darkness. The energy in the group changed to love. Fifteen urban teens entered my backdoor, putting out their hand to my seventy-seven-year-old, white haired, blue-eyed rural father and apolo-

"Mom, wake up! The cat stole my make up and I threw her into the trash and shut the lid!" That was to be the beginning of my morning.

gized. My father took each hand saying "I am glad to meet you, too." The night concluded peacefully watching the video of their performance. Thirty minutes later my house was quiet, everyone calmly returned to their homes. A fitting ending to the National Night Out Against Violence.

- What did Q's prayer do to cause such a change? What made the difference?
- How could these 'six second kids' survive in a 'one second world'?
- Could they step back from a problem, relax and discover safe solutions?

Tolerance and flexibilty are needed to manage in the adult world. This would take advanced thinking skills Liz and many of her friends lacked. Hopefully their decisions and experiences learned from bad judgment would build skills towards success.

Liz avoided change by hiding in her room . . . The dream of the Tiger Woods Scholarship had vaporized. Mom was leaving for Australia without her. Dad was recovering . . . then Dad was to shoot photos in Alaska. . . she would have a couple days with Nancy, her old nanny before Mom returned.

"911... two airplanes ...NYC...two more airplanes... PA... Washington, DC... terrorists...American...United . . ." the radio continued. Liz spiraled into the secondary disabilities of FASD ...alone ... her caregivers didn't care or they would call . . . Mom didn't care or she would be home . . . Dad was in the air . . . would he crash too? . . . Her respite provider had no clue what to do as Liz had her own emotional bypass surgery. Liz crashed.

It was two days before I accessed an Australian phone line to contact Liz. It was eight additional days to access a flight home. Liz gave up. Dad was lost in Alaska. Mom was lost in Australia. Nina was dead. Like the towers her world collapsed, Liz catapulted into high risk teen behaviors for comfort. She would learn to control herself. What if Mom never came back? She switched to processed and junk food. She quit taking her supplements. What if Dad never came back? She drank, smoked and spent private time with young men. She would learn to survive on her own.

My heart broke as I reached for my daughter amid the chaos and disaster in my own home. We would rebuild. It was no use to rant and rave. Liz needed compassion to return to a place of sanity and peace. Was this the beginning of the dreaded secondary disabilities listed on unlucky page 13?

Liz ripped out her alcohol stained carpet. Buckets of hot soapy lemon scented water scrubbed down walls. We added new paint and streamlined her room to look like a studio for group rehearsal providing a fresh start. We cleaned up the mess of eight days. The phone rang, "May I speak to Liz Kulp?"

"Mom, I won! I won the Tiger Woods Scholarship! I can pay for my books at the printer! What do I do with the rest of the money? You're already back from Australia," Liz hesitated.

"What is your dream Liz? That's what you do," I said.

"I want to make a CD and let people know about FASD! I want to write songs and music," her voice rang clear. "I think I can make a difference Mom. I think I can change the future."

Together with three other young ladies we became the Mo'Angels. The next two summers I ferried teens between practices and performances. I joined Liz in her dream.

The Mo'Angels recorded eleven songs regarding prejudice, fetal alcohol, early sexual relations, foster and adoptive care – and – of course, boys. They sang on television, at community events and at the state capitol.

Liz was right she could "Start Something" and "Make a Difference." What she couldn't do was reverse her brain injury and remain off the secondary disability path. It was time to move away from homeschool and let Liz experience the 'real world'. I went searching for the 'right' school.

John came home crying the teacher wanted 'all' his tickets. He wanted to save them to prove he is good sometimes. The tickets were like little pieces of self- esteem.

Annie

MOM I'M AN ALCOHOLIC

I was lulled into thinking we transversed the dangerous secondary disabilties in teen years. I didn't realize something far more insidious lay deep within Liz's very being. "Mom, I need to talk to you. It's important. Pinky promise me you won't get mad?" Liz pleaded. Years earlier Liz and I developed this signal promising whatever behavior or problem she had I would offer help not anger. I braced myself.

"Ok, I promise. What's up, Liz?" I asked.

"Mom, I'm an alcoholic. I know it. When I get sad or mad I think about alcohol. It is inside my head. It controls me." Liz continued, "I drink whiskey like milk. I like the taste straight. I like how it feels when it goes down. It is like something I already know about. I crave it."

I listened, trying to look supportive. "I can't stop. I have a problem. I drank last night again. Help me stop. Pray with me. I don't want to drink."

My mind raced back to the previous night. The smell of nail polish remover was a coverup for the reality. I thought she was wound up and overly tired. The idea of her drinking alcohol again after her experience after Sept 11, 2001 didn't register. Before I left for Australia she stood firm against smoking, alcohol, sex and drugs.

Liz's confession opened a closed door in my own life. My parents struggled with alcohol while I was a teen. Was I now destined to struggle with alcohol with a teen? I felt engulfed in a never-ending circle. Liz understood alcohol's ability to destroy. She watched our neighbor's beauty vanish as she died from alcoholism. She visited her uncle in jail, witnessed his struggle and celebrated his victories of sobriety. A local teen was killed by a drunk driver. Her sister Nina died from unsafe choices while using chemicals. Liz was her own testimony to the devastation of alcohol. Her daily

"I only had one drink Mom. That's all," Liz showed me the 16 oz. glass from which she drank straight Brandy. We headed to the hospital.

struggle was a constant reminder of alcohol damage. We added an AA modeled teen discovery program to our homeschool. I introduced Liz to the serenity prayer.

God, grant me the serenity to accept the things I cannot change, the courage to change the things I can and the wisdom to know the difference. Living one day at a time, enjoying one moment at a time, accepting hardships as pathways to peace, taking as Jesus did this sinful world as it is, not as I would have it, trusting you will make all things right if I surrender to your will; so I may be reasonably happy in this life and supremely happy with you in the next
                     – attributed to Reinhold Niebuhr

Mom, I died. I drank three quarters of a fifth of brandy. I saw a white flash Mom. My life passed before me — all the details. I don't get another chance Mom. Next time I don't get to come back.

We celebrated my parents' 50th wedding anniversary — 25 of those years sober. We embraced my brother's new family — a beautiful little girl born without FASD. They chose sobriety during pregnancy. I knew free will and self-control were possible. I also knew Liz was one of the most determined people I had ever met, once her mind was made up, it was casting in concrete.

To understand addiction we return to the **midbrain**. The midbrain is the seat of five basic drives: hunger, thirst, flight or fight response, sex and pain regulation. In the addict, it is believed that a sixth function – addiction – occurs. This sixth activity is a primitive push for the addictive substance or behavior that feels to the individual like a basic drive. But there are two fundamental differences between this sixth function and the basic drives. The sixth (addictive) function eventually grows so powerful that it eclipses all the drives. And whereas the basic drives push the individual toward self-preservation, the sixth "drive," the pressure to get drunk, high or engage in inappropriate behavior, leads ultimately to self-annihilation.[65]

Fetal alcohol exposure is a risk factor for adolescent alcohol involvement and alcohol-related problems otherwise attributed to family history of alcoholism.[64]

64. *Prenatal Alcohol Exposure and Family History of Alcoholism in the Etiology of Adolescent Alcohol Problems*, Baer, John S. PhD, Barr, Helen M, MA, MS, Bookstein, Fred L. PhD,, Sampson, Paul D. PhD, Streissguth, Ann P. PhD. Department of Psychology, University of Washington School of Arts and Sciences and Veterans Affairs Puget Sound Health Care System, Seattle Washington. Fourteen year data collection by Heather Carmichael Olson, PhD. For more information contact: Ann P. Streissguth, PhD, Fetal Alcohol and Drug Unit, 180 Nickerson St., Suite 309, Seattle, WA 98109.
65. Paul H. Early.. MD and Michael L. Fishman, MD. Ridgeview Institute, *Insight Magazine,* 3995 South Cobb Drive, Smyrna, Georgia 30080. (770) 434-4567 (800) 329-9775.

Alcohol is far and away the drug of abuse by american teens, children under the age of 21 drink 25% of the alcohol consumed in the US. More than five million high school students (31.5%) admit to binge drinking more than once a month . . . and the age of children drinking is dropping.

Joseph A. Califano, Jr, president of the National Center on Addiction and Substance Abuse at Columbia University (2002)

Why the cravings? One viewpoint is that the **midbrain** transmits pressure for alcohol or other addictive substances or activities to the cortex through the **motor cortex,** which controls movement. In a person with a normal functioning cortex, the interpretive area of the brain kicks in to analyze the action "You deserve a drink." The interpreter tries, in retrospect, to make sense of the action triggered by the midbrain and carried out by the motor cortex. The alcoholic (or addict) searches for alcohol (substance) and begins abusing its use. The discrepancy between the raw drive for a drink/drug/behavior and the individual's rational functioning are doomed to fail as errors in interpretation multiply, entrenching the person in denial, habit and ritual. These misconceptions and rationalizations are the hallmark of addictive thinking.

Liz's interpreter appeared to be on vacation. When the cravings hit, they took over and Liz's one-track mind focused on getting alcohol and drinking with gusto. AA meetings made her think of drinking and tortured her. The sponsor she was provided was ill equipped to handle a teen with addiction and a brain injury. I discoverd the SMART program in combination with the AA model to be an effective tool to help Liz manage her life in a way to remain sober.

- Could prenatally alcohol exposed teens with biological vulnerability for drinking overcome the addiction process?

Liz needed a strong NO to drinking. She needed to care for her body. Liz freely made choices to control her diet. By choice she did not eat wheat without enzymes and she carefully avoided corn syrup. The same tenacity was needed for alcohol. We kept a drug test on the counter.

- Was the door opening to other secondary disabilities - marijuana, unsafe sexuality, eating disorders, smoking or other at risk teen behaviors in the future?

Success for our children does not come without strategic planning of our own lives to make the child's life a safe one. It takes commitment, dedication and continuous vigilance.

Teresa, FASD Mom

The answer was yes.

OPEN UP . . . PEASE

It was time to move beyond homeschooling. The public high school with thousands of students was overwhelming. Liz would flounder. The private schools were cost prohibitive. I searched public charter and alternative learning centers. I discovered a treasure. PEASE (Peers Experiencing a Sober Education) Academy is a public alternative learning center for teens in grades nine through twelve struggling with sobriety or wishing to remain chemical free. It is based on the AA model and was worth a try. Each student signed a contact of sobriety to attend. A relapse was cause for expulsion.

Liz dreamed of catching up to her natural grade level. I made no promises as I handed in our homeschool transcripts. Homeschool without breaks had paid off, Liz's qualified for grade ten.

Eight qualified faculty members shared knowledge and compassion for 58 independent and expressive students. Behaviors intolerable in a larger setting, were handled with care. I watched a frustrated teen overreact. They were obviously used to handling teens with challenging issues. The staff was interested in learning about FASD and helping prenatally exposed teens. They felt Liz was not the only student who faced these challenges. She was the only one diagnosed. The eyes of the students were clear under the red, green and blue hair, multiple earrings, and creative attire. Would my sparkly teen fit with this crowd?

Group learning complicated Liz's ability to learn. She hyperfocused to get good grades. I tutored in the evening and drove to and from school. Liz struggled to learn, but eventually adapted and gained new abilities. Liz's social tolerance needed strengthening. She had to learn to deal with her own impulsivity and frustration in diverse group environments. The school learned quickly about the world according to Liz. And Liz needed to learn the world did not revolve about her. She was just one of many others. PEASE was very small and personal. Except for minor eruptions Liz behaved well.

Math story problems combine two distinct brain functions – reading and arithmetic. "Liz, maybe you should go out in the hall and take a break?" her teacher offered. A frustrated Liz, loudly pushed the chair yelling, "I'm a bad kid. I'm going to the principal." Her old elementary school tapes replayed as she escalated the situation. In elementary school Liz believed she was 'bad.' She was the only girl to get her name on the board or get yelled at. She was trying her best to behave. She was also the only one yelling.

Note taking combines visual, auditory, fine and gross motor skills. It was more than Liz could handle. "F***Y*** this is a F**** class" she wrote across her assignment notes. She did not care if the teacher saw.

Liz slammed the chair on the floor and stomped out of the room. "People can't act like that. People can't treat others like that. This school has some funny thinking females. I quit!" When things got rough, Liz ran and jumped off the end of the pier.

"Mom I have to talk to the school, this is wrong. I work harder than anyone else in that class and I got an NC (no credit). I need that grade." Liz called an IEP meeting. She addressed the teacher and explained her viewpoint. "The final test's first question asked me to 'imagine I am not human and explain phenology.' I can imagine. I can explain, but I cannot explain and imagine at the same time, my brain won't work like that." Liz was beginning to understand her brain and how it functioned. Her own self-advocacy skills were emerging. The school offered adaptations to assure she understood the questions. After the test was graded a qualified teacher read the questions she missed to make sure she understood what was being asked.

In order to graduate Liz needed to pass the Minnesota Basic Standards in math, reading and writing. Liz took the tests and failed. She studied and retook them that summer. She failed again. She took them a third time in the fall. She failed. Liz obsessed on her school and homework and her report card showed A's and B's. The IEP staff offered accommodations to help her pass and not lower the value of the testing as modifcations do.

Liz paused and looked at the six adults in the room **"You know it's hard not to take something free. But I am doing these tests for me."**

In the winter of her junior year Liz passed all three state exams. A month later a heart broken Liz relapsed, breaking one year and ten days of sobriety and her contract with the school. It was time to try to stretch into public school as a High School Senior. First we would regroup with a semester of homeschool working on understanding addictions, sexuality and other issues I preferred to teach her at home.

Though Liz's chemical use cost her the school, she gained the opportunity to participate in a real world high school and won.

ABCs and IEPs

The IEP meeting is a time of negotiation and collaboration to work together for the benefit of the child with special needs. Liz qualifies as Other Health Impaired Disability, Developmental Disability and has an Individualized Education Plan (IEP). This IEP is crucial in helping teachers, parents and support staff navigate the maze of the public education system and to help Liz transition into adulthood. Liz is the most important member on the team.

The IEP spells out the following

- **Current Performance** - How the child currently is doing in school.
- **Annual Goals** - What are the goals the child can reasonably accomplish in an academic year?
- **Special Education and Related Services** - What changes to the current school program or special services are to be provided to help the child achieve these goals.
- **Participation with Non-Disabled Students** - To what extent will the child participate in regular classes and in other school activities?
- **Participation in State and District Wide Testing** - Are current tests appropriate and/or are modifications needed? (i.e. separate room, read test to child)
- **Dates and Places** - When will services begin? How long will they last? Where will they be provided and how often?
- What **Transition Services are needed**?
  - At 14, what courses does the child need to reach post-school goals?
  - At 16, what transition services are needed to prepare to leave school?
- **Measure of Progress** - How will progress be measured? How will parents be informed?

We, as her parents are key members of the IEP team and it is our responsibility to supply information concerning our child's special interests, skills, strengths and dreams. In addition, it is important that we voice concerns, problems, previous successes and failures. We also check on the progress of the IEP, stay in contact with the teaching staff and work together for the benefit of our student. Liz attends meetings, as an older student's input is expected in the development of an IEP. It is an action in beginning self-advocacy and as the parent you become the supporting cast. It is important to prepare your child for the IEP to build self-determination and advocacy skills. The worksheet below offers questions.

The best IEP teams avoid adversarial relationships and remain focused on the needs of the child. The team members remain in communication

---

Student IEP Preparation Worksheet

What do I do best? ——————————————————————

I like to . . . ——————————————————————————

I need most help with my. ——————————————————

My favorite classes are . . . ————————————————

This schoolwork is easy for me . . . ————————————

I study best when I. . . ——————————————————

I get along best with my friends when I . . . ——————

I have trouble with other students when they . . . ————

Person who helped me the most . . .How?———————

Support services I need help with are . . . ——————

Worries I have are . . . —————————————————

Ideas to help work with me are . . . ————————————

Things I want to learn are . . . ——————————————

When I am done with school I want to be a . . . ————

Problems with my current program are . . . ——————

Things that drive me crazy in school are. . . ——————

"Liz had an outburst today and was banging her head on the wall, I put my arms around her and held her, I guess you can sue me if you want to for touching her?" said her teacher. "Ha," I laughed, "I'd call that complete wrap around support, thank you."

through telephone calls, parent-teacher conferences and e-mail. On any given day I may receive between one and three messages letting me know Liz's status. If she has had a difficult weekend I provide a short e-mail for the educational staff. If she has had a bad day at school they return the courtesy.

The IEP team supplies me with information concerning Liz, and we reinforce their efforts, using the same vocabulary at home. If Karl and I are working on something at home, we send an e-mail asking for similar support. Her mainstream teacher posts homework assignments just a click away for parents on the internet. There is no excuse for forgotten homework. Each Monday night I translate her week's schoolwork in language she understands, dramatize it and provide examples she is familiar with. We introduce vocabulary she will need for the week and Karl and I carry on conversations using new words.

Liz is required to complete schoolwork before outside friendships so she hyperfocuses on her academics. This positive hyperfocusing has helped her achieve a final grade of B+ in mainstream Economics and an A in Political Science. She completes all her homework and turns in extra credit. She tests poorly and her IEP allows for a second testing on each test making sure she understands the questions she missed. She maintains a GPA of 3.42 with a 70 IQ. She is determined to graduate, except of course on the days she impulsively decides to quit.

Liz is testing the waters of independence and looking forward to her own apartment in the near future. She is a determined young woman who will need a community support team to integrate into the adult community. As her parents, we struggle with conservatorship, semi-conservatorship, guardianship or independence. We look at trusts and services to help her navigate adult waters safely. We will not always be here. She will always need some support. She will always desire independence and self-determination.

When a new person joins our support team, we provide all the information we can about prenatal exposure. Liz's book bridges the knowledge gap. Still, the first face-to-face experience with a FASattack is a surprise.

LETTING GO FOR GROWTH

It is natural for teens to begin separating from parents on their path to independence and adulthood. Normal teens grow increasingly angry with parents who limit friends, time alone, unsupervised activities and driver's permits. There was no day care for a 17 year old and 24-7-365 supervision would handicap her adulthood. We did not have a personal care attendant or a mentor and Mom wasn't cool unless she needed a ride.

Liz needed life experience to be safe. She needed to 'tandem fly'[66] with an army of co-pilots to keep her from crashing. We had to risk letting go and challenge the big bad world. Our love and commitment would stifle her future. We would walk alongside her, scoop her up when she made a mistake, challenge her to make better choices and use her poor choices as real life experiences and opportunities to grow.

Liz functions well when things remain the same, yet everything in life changes. Life is noncooperative. It is not fair or gentle. A teacher may get sick. The road may be filled with traffic. An expected check may not come. The dinner may burn. You may wake up with a cold. The dog may eat your sandwich.

Young adults with FASD go through a stage that I can only call denial when they don't want to deal with FASD issues or acknowledge that it's a problem. The sad reality is that FASD does control the lives of these individuals, and our lives too for that matter. Perhaps the challenge is to not let FASD ruin our lives. One of the most frustrating aspects of FASD is its unpredictability and inconsistency. One moment they seem normal. Turn around and they are overly immature and inappropriate. Hopefully, we can laugh more times than we cry.

Teresa (FASD mom)

---

66. Teresa Kellerman beautifully illustrates the term "Tandem Flight" in her web article *"Broken Beaks and Wobbly Wings"* that can be found on www.come-over.to and www.betterendings.org.

Liz mastered ordering pizza, checking on movie times, coordinating bus schedules and shopping with a friend using bus transportation. A driver's license would be an unwise choice for her and the safety of the general public. We arranged supports from health care professionals along the busline.

Liz's level A friends were used as co-supporters to help her grow and keep her safe.

Learning to use mass transit came with surprises. She was vulnerable even when traveling with a friend. She collected thirty pages with phone numbers of new 'friends.' Some were appropriate, others were dangerous, she did not have the discernment to know the difference. Liz invited her new found 'friends' home - friendly thugs and drug dealers. One offered to help her be a movie star as long as she removed all her clothes. She could be a famous rapper and rich. Another 'friend' was featured in the paper accused of murder, rape and slicing a young women. It was his picture in the paper along with the young woman he killed that helped Liz face the reality of her poor choices.

Karl sat down with Liz and instigated a safety program using her thirty page phone book, he challenged Liz to categorize her friends.

People Liz knew fit into four categories:

A. People to help her achieve her life goals and dreams

B. People who neither helped or hurt her

C. People who hurt her or kept her from achieving her life goals

D. Dangerous people

Karl then had Liz keyboard a list of all her 'A' friends with their phone numbers, she had permission to be with her 'A' friends as often as she chose, we neither encouraged or discouraged those on her 'B' list. People from her 'C' category we required her to avoid and 'D' category people she was banned from with the threat of punishment or being glued to mom and dad.

Next Karl had Liz write down what her life would be like at forty, when she was 'really' old. At forty, she wanted to be married, have a car, live in a house, be a famous rapper and make at least $19,000 a year. Then she wrote what her life would be like at 30, 20 and in 6 months at 18. Together they worked on reality, breaking her life into tiny attainable pieces all the way the present. A surprised Liz realized she needed $20.00 an hour to have the lifestyle she wanted - food, makeup, CD's, movies, travel.

Karl worked with Liz on making a list of all her behaviors, he included simple things like brushing her teeth to having sex with a young man. Then he had her use her 'A-D' categories to determine if the behaviors were helpful or hurtful and add safe friends to participate. Growing into adulthood was going to be step-by-step with potholes deep enough to drown.

I settled down for the rare treat of reading the newspaper. "Mom! Help! The stove is on fire. The stove is on fire!"

"Turn it off!" I shouted.

"No, Mom! Help! It's on fire by itself! I can't turn it off!" I hurried into the kitchen to see the center of my stove glowing red hot. The burner was on under the cover. The ivory porcelain bubbled, turning black.

How do we keep young adults safe, allowing them the opportunity to learn without tragedy?

"Liz all you have to do is turn off the burner," I demonstrated.

"Mom, I can't turn if off. I didn't turn it on! How can you turn it off if you don't turn it on?" Liz, was frustrated. She would explode along with my stove if I probed deeper at that moment. I would wait to help her process what had just happened, I already knew.

She had been talking with a boyfriend on the phone and danced into the stove. Her posterior had wiggled with just the right press and turn movement and lighted the center burner of my gas stove. She couldn't turn it off, if in her mind, she had not turned it on. Even with all the therapy and one-to-one teaching we continued FAScinating daily experiences.

• Could Liz survive independently without burning down her own home?

Liz wakes at 5:04 am to prepare for school at 7:00 am. For two hours she fixated on minute details of hair and make-up. Prior to bed she bathes, brushes her teeth and spends another hour getting ready. Three hours of teen girl prep for school was excessive, but it did provide respite for Mom and Dad and I figured we had a cleanly, even if obsessive, daughter. I was wrong, in asking Liz to show me how long her natural hair had grown, she unwound her ponytail and it fell in a matted mess, she had not combed it for two weeks nor washed it. It took two hours of tender loving detangling and conditioning to return to beautiful tresses. She said it hurt to comb, getting it wet felt strange. Early **sensory integration** issues resurfaced.

• Could Liz care properly for her hygiene, health and safety? Her plan was to move out in less than six months!

SECONDARY DISABILITIES
THE UNWINDING

"I want to kill myself. Everything is going wrong. I hate the skating rink. It broke my glasses and my hairclips." Liz screamed wielding our kitchen knife. I could escalate the behavior with the wrong intervention. I knew from experience to stand back and distract. The time for discussion was when her brain was working better.

Liz has cautiously given love to her family and fell head over heels in a first love experience, eventually ending in betrayal. Grieving is abstract and difficult for everyone. Liz's concrete thinking struggled for nine months to make sense of it. I n her grief she took herself and our family on a harrowing ride of self-destruction - chemical use, poor relationship choices and eating disorders, before we came up for air. Our family unit was almost destroyed. We hope she was strengthened by her experiences.

Liz proved to herself she was not able to drink alcohol, it took a number of additional encounters of the third kind and she again had seven months of sobriety. Any addiction discovery (**SMART; www.smartrecovery.com**) or recovery (**AA; www.aa.org**) program requires patience, practice and persistance. Liz made a commitment to not drink alcohol and she was working her program. A month after she quit drinking a high school 'friend' introduced her to marijuana. She liked how it made her feel, her body no longer ached. It had ached all her life and smoking made the pain go away. She never knew she hurt, she always had felt that way. It was a pleasant thing to do with her friend, it took only a few minutes and helped her sleep. If she smoked a cigar or cigarette just before she came home it was hard for Mom and dad to smell the weed. Colored contact lenses disguised her eyes. It took Karl and I two months to catch her, force a drug test and enforce 'time-in' with Mom and dad if her tests were not clean on random future testing. Liz gave up the

Big Tobacco has long understood the commercial consequences of this reality: Its incredible profits depend on access to children and the addictive nature of its products. More than 90 percent of smokers are hooked before they reach 21, and less than 1.5 percent of teen smokers quit while they are teens.

Joseph A. Califano, Jr, president of the National Center on Addiction and Substance Abuse at Columbia University

marijuana, but she refused to give up cigarettes.

Cigarettes relaxed her, all the high school seniors smoked, she looked cool and it helped her think. Liz was self-medicating. She was also controlling her weight by throwing up, drinking diet sodas and chewing a pack of gum a day. Anything Liz did she did with gusto.

She was having a love affair and it was with chemicals. She couldn't control her life, but she could control what she put into or kept in her body. The years of investment in therapies and nutrition were being drunk, smoked or puked down the toilet. Her short-term memory was abbreviated sending us back into toddler emotions.

Role play smoking. Sit back, relax, put the imaginary cigarette up to your lips and deeply inhale, hold it and exhale. Do you feel more relaxed? Try it oxygen is the real thing.

Independence loomed on the horizon. Could we make the connections Liz needed to remain safe and healthy? Liz learns by experience. Perhaps experiencing these secondary disabilities while living in our home will help her avoid them when out on her own. Liz is a strong person and she is aware of right and wrong, even though she doesn't always consider both options. Karl and I walk alongside Liz as she crosses each barrier hoping to teach her the difference between rational thought that will keep her alive and help her achieve her dreams and irrational thought leading to a path of defeat. We struggle with the insanity of repeating and reteaching without solid learning. Sometimes we hug each other wondering when our teaching will sink in, as we hand off our 'external brain' responsibilities for her to other adults, trying to keep her safe from being vulnerable.

Adults with FASD struggle as they swerve and turn to avoid the complexities and daily abstractions of life. It is easy to buy a new car. It is hard to make the monthly payments. Credit cards seem like unlimited money providing instant purchases until the limit is reached. Check blanks work as long as

The first goal of 24 hours (1 day) is a huge step in breaking an addiction, the next goal of 72 hours (3 days) allows the body time to adapt to the change.

checks are in the checkbook. The banks have plenty of money. Rent money may go for a new stereo, afterall it was a deal. You can have all the sex you want as long as you don't fall asleep. Sleeping with someone gets you pregnant. Expensive ice cream and a fancy dinner tastes great but is little substitute for toilet paper, diapers or baby food. The department store has so much stuff, they won't notice if you take something. It doesn't belong to anyone yet - no one has bought it. I had to go with him or her because he/she was my friend, I didn't do the crime.

Teens and young adults like Liz seek approval and acceptance from poorly selected peers. Their need for immediate gratification, desire to please, limited short-term memory and abnormal sensory issues become compounded in a society that bombards them with sensuality and violence. Just as they can do the wash, but not fix the washing machine they often do the crime but don't plan it. And because of their loud and bold actions, they are the ones caught and prosecuted. The real instigators are left free to victimize again.

- Could Liz fall victim like a friend's son with FASD participating in auto theft in return for friendship? (2 year jail term, he refuses to tell on 'his' friend)
- Could she lovingly follow a boyfriend unknowingly to a murder? (accomplice to murder — 50 years imprisonment without parole).
- Would she willingly go to jail as long as her party friends joined her?
- Would she let anyone who needed a place to stay live with her, eat her food?
- Would she accept a ride from a known drug dealer instead of taking the bus?

Unprepared legal representation fails to see that behind the happy, normal looking presentation there is another problem. There is something wrong with the brain. They fail to check who or what has recently influenced the person or who he has been talking to last. They fail to check if their verbal goals and ideals are backed with idle chatter or with depth of thoughts. They fail to check if there is escalation in criminal behavior or if the offenses are moment-by-moment, regardless how bizarre. Parents who themselves have FASD need access to support services to keep their children safe and family healthy. Jails, mental health institutions, under a bridge, in a car, box or homeless shelters are not affordable housing solutions, though these solutions are creative, we can do better.

While, Liz soared in our restricted homeschool lifestyle — gaining academic and thinking skills as she participated in family life, church and scouts, that restricted lifestyle would handicap her in developing the skills to manage a life on her own and socially navigate the complexities of employment and extended relationships. She was already pushing Karl and I away, not wanting us to act as her external brain. Lovingly we had to let go of her in the care of others to allow the opportunity to learn to fly.

Transitioning to independence was going to involve many others. Liz would need a job coach to maintain employment. She would require a conservator to help manage her money.

SAFE HAVENS FOR GROWTH –
THINKING DIFFERENTLY NOT HARDER

Liz has the most stake in her transition planning and it is her input and participation that is vital for future success and commitment. It is 'her' life. She will need self-determination to make her needs known, but that very self-determination could become termination of her life. In order to succeed she needs to be realistic about the brain injury she lives with, knowing her strengths and limitations. She will need this information to develop adult coping skills to compensate and negotiate getting her needs met and protecting herself and her interests in home living, in employment and in the community.

Self-advocacy means taking charge of your life by making your own decisions and knowing where and how to get help. To be a self advocate Liz will need to understand her civil rights through legislation such as the Americans with Disabilities Act (ADA) and Section 504 of the Rehabilitation Act of 1973. People with disabilities have the same rights as any other person.

With support she will need to determine her current skills, decide on future goals and develop a plan to attain them. Participation does not come naturally, like everything else she has learned, she needs support and coaching. She has been given opportunities to make choices and experience the consequences of her choices. Like all of us, she does not always behave responsibly. Learning life skills comes with practice, support and mistakes. Liz's strongest learning come from her worst mistakes.

Liz loves routines and schedules. What could I implement in our family she would enjoy with me as an adult – I decided to join a health club and do once a month cooking.

• What type of independent housing can provide Liz the most adult freedom with the least amount of danger?
• What social skills are needed to navigate in society, avoiding temptations that kill or destroy?
• Are there semi-independent adult living opportunities available and how do you access them?
• What are the best supports to help community integration?
• How far should we as the parents step back?
• How much support should we arrange?

John McGee of Gentle Teaching, Holland (www.gentleteaching.nl) believes that the most challenging behaviors come out of fear or a broken heart, not a broken brain. Karl and I have also found that to be true. The Fairweather Model emphasizes a peer-supported model of interdependence and is used within the Task Unlimited Lodge system. We, as Liz's parents need to safely hand her off to others skilled in helping her be the 'best she can be' as a voting, productive citizen. As her family we wrap around her in love. As she grows out of our care others began to teach and lead her to independence. Her IEP team embraces and supports her as she gets ready to graduate. The Secondary Transition Team for 18-21 year olds stands waiting to take the baton and a school of business has accepted her application for a music business program if she so chooses to slowly attend. All are aware of FASD.

Liz and I have begun the journey to independence.
- *Her medical team is located along the busline, knows her and accepts medical assistance.*
- *Her hairdresser is also along the busline*
- *We are building an "It's My Life" Support Binder.*

A system of professional companionship/mentoring/coaching (external brain) for individuals with neurological dysorganization is one of the 'life skill training wheels' necessary to help persons like Liz grow and remain safe as they learn to navigate independently. The Psychology of Interdependence is more than being nice to someone. A professional companion is not domineering or punishing. The tools of companionship are a warm caring presence, a positive outlook and confident body language to help a person feel safe, engaged, loved and loving. Companionship expresses the feelings of belonging together while plaing value in the diversity of each individual.

We have come this far together. . . now is it her life.

McGee's eight basic human values are:

1. **Body integrity:** healthy, decently clothed, clean, nutrition
2. **Safe:** not being afraid of people, desire to be with others and relaxed,
3. **Self worth:** seeing yourself as a good person, expressing personal talents,
4. **Life structure:** sensing a life plan, having a daily routine,
5. **Belonging:** loving others and being loved, having friends,
6. **Social participation:** living among others, participating in the community,
7. **Meaningful daily activities:** enjoying your daily activities
8. **Inner contentment:** feeling inner harmony, free from traumatic experiences.

CLOSED CLOSETS - OPEN OPPORTUNITY

Two years ago I dreamed of Liz's complete independence and avoidance of all the secondary disabilities. I gave over my life and profession when Liz was an infant to help her grow and this became the work I needed to do during that time. On our journey together we discovered many opportunities to make a difference. The areas of development Liz mastered have remained strong and effective. Areas not as strongly developed atrophied. Today Liz can hug another human, she can take notes, she is able to work in groups and she will graduate from high school. She is becoming her own self-advocate and all of these are huge accomplishments. She is a better person and more able to navigate her adult life. That transition for her will be difficult, but it is possible.

As her caregivers, the greatest gift we can give Liz during this transition time is to guide her towards successful experiences, to build her confidence and skills rather than direct her to activities which will lead to disappointment and failure. The transition from supported home environment to small alternative school setting and finally high school was the beginning of this transition to adult independence. We expect new needs to arise as we enter the adult independence frontier. Time, life experiences and maturity may add additional knowledge and skills to Liz's life. They will not heal her fetal alcohol brain injury, Karl and I will continue to be her adult life consultants.

Toni Hager, NDS has opened a school, neurocounseling and therapy center in Spokane, WA. based on her work with Liz. Tom and Morgan have worked with Toni for four years in her clinic setting, they write:

"By the age of seventeen, I will have reached my Eagle Rank in Boy Scouts . . . I would not be the young man I am today without CAN LEARN. It has helped me develop skills I need to be a successful person. I have come a long way in my young life and I know that I will be an asset to society and will break the cycle of abuse and alcoholism."   **Tom, 2003**

"Today I am seventeen and have volunteered as a camp counselor all summer. I have been a leader for a new group of ten girls each of these eight weeks . . .My life will be filled with challenges, but I know I can accomplish my goals. I want to be a Marine Biologist. Thanks to CAN LEARN my dreams can be reached by hard work and dedication. Children with FAS do have promise. I am no longer that frightened little girl with thick glasses and no hope."   **Morgan, 2003**

Liz and I have spoken coast-to-coast and in her interviews she is forthright and honest. She boldly testifies in front of Senators and TV personalities. She is unafraid to perform in front of audiences or speak to groups of professionals about what it is like to live with FASD. She is not special, she is one of many american children – over 45,000 born each year struggling with the realities of prenatal exposure to alcohol. Many are less affected than Liz and some are more affected. Karl, Liz and I have navigated brain injury knowingly for five years, a medical diagnosis we recieved twelve years late.

I am saddened that some in the medical and educational commuity fail to believe this is a 'real' diagnosis. Some believe that the child will out grow it. That we, as a people, will not admit that FASD is devastating to society is as tragic as the infighting between researchers and professionals, the conflicts between teachers and parents, the sorrow between adoptive families and birth families, the misunderstandings between cultures and races. We judge each other, when judgment will not produce action. When I see competition for grants and financing tear apart opportunities for collaboration I am angry. While children and families suffer, we reinvent and restudy what we already know wasting precious resources and time.

There is hope for our children and families. Each family of a child with special needs will adapt with the skills they have and the opportunities set before them. **I believe** in early diagnosis and early support services. **I believe** in the whole child/whole family case-management model to help families understand and navigate the professional, academic and community at large to access effective support and services, and a single point of entry or one agency that stays connected with the family from the onset of diagnosis through death of the person. **I believe** in building public understanding and awareness. **I believe** in opening the closed FASD closet door, clearing the dust, throwing the junk out and organizing what left. I believe in truth!

There is hope on the horizon - the brain is the frontier of the 21st century and medical diagnosis of other brain differences will open doors for children and persons with FASD. The diagnosis enables treatment, which enables abilities, which optimizes outcomes – that saves lives, that changes poverty, that allows success, that saves taxpayers money. It will take a community willing to think differently and willing to see differently to begin to change the futures of persons with FASD. It will take a world-wide village.

Life is either a daarng adventure or nothing at all - Helen Keller

Today

by Liz Kulp - 9.15.2003

Today I'll be startin' ova

I'm gonna become sober

Not once, but for all time

I won't let my goal fall

Instead of giving in

I'm gonna over extend

My grounds where I stand neva' agin

Will I give myself to please a man

Girls think that they need love

So they go to thugs

Or start abusin' them drugs

No I said

'Don't let the devil over power you

You're just slippin' into hell

Like he wants you to do

Forget them boys

They don't do nothin' for you

They cheat. They creep.

They can't even support you.

They use you. Cause you pain.

Till you're emotionally insane

And you're locked up in jail.

Cause you can't maintain

That's such a shame

He's got yo' mind all twisted

You can't leave him

Cause you think you'll miss it

So you keep comin' back

Cause one day he'll change

And you'll get engaged

Just think

You'll be a nice beautiful wife

Then I realize

This is my life

And I don't know

If I want to live anymore

I don't even know what I'm here for

I feel like a dirty ass whore

That should be locked away

Till I can wake up to a new day

Wait for a new life

That I can be livin' in

Be a stronger woman

Where I don't need a man

Til I see the ring on my hand

But till then

I don't trust no one or myself

I just wish I could get some help.

Consider copying this sample card and adding a copy of your child's medical card to the frontside, then laminate together for your child to carry. FASD is not a moral or value judgment issue. It is a medical diag-nosed injury to the central nervous system. Prepare your child for the future.

APPENDIX

FETAL ALCOHOL
SPECTRUM DISORDER

FASD
RESOURCES FOR FAMILIES

Win-win solutions allow all parties to
feel good about the decision and
feel good about the action plan.

Win-win is based on the paradigm
that one person's success is not achieved
at the expense or exclusion of the success of others.

May this Appendix
enlarge the bounty of win-win solutions
for the person you love who
has been prenatally brain injured.

We pass a torch to light your life trail.

Appendix
Table of Contents

Disclaimer: This information should not be construed as medical opinion, consultation, or recommendations for course of treatment. The neurological problems of a child or adult with FASD are complex and require a complete psychiatric evaluation with a comprehensive face-to-face assessment by a trained specialist, such as a psychiatrist or a neurologist, even in the absence of a diagnosis of FASD. Families of persons who are already being followed by a specialist are encouraged to share this information with them. Families of persons who are only being followed by a primary care physician are encouraged to ask for a referral to a specialist, who can then formulate a treatment plan based on the individual assessment and on this information.

FASD RESOURCES FOR FAMILIES
ARTICLES, BOOKS & FILMS

ARTICLES
research you can trust

Connor, Paul D. and Streissguth, Ann P, PhD, *Effects of Prenatal Exposure to Alcohol Across the Life Span* (1996) Published in Alcohol Health and Research World, Vol. 20, No. 3.

Kaimal, Shanti B.D.S., M.D.S., et al, *Understanding and Managing Fetal Alcohol Syndrome* (Feb 2004) Northwest Dentistry, Journal of MN Dental Assn.

Streissguth, Ann P, PhD, Barr, Helen M, MA, Kogan, Julia EdM, Bookstein, Fred L, PhD. *Understanding the Occurrence of Secondary Disabilities in Clients with Fetal Alcohol Syndrome (FAS) and Fetal Alcohol Effects (FAE)* (1996) Published by University of Washington School of Medicine, Department of Psychiatry and Behavioral Sciences, Fetal Alcohol and Drug Unit, 180 Nickerson, Suite 309, Seattle, WA 98109. (206) 543-7155. www.depts.washington.edu/fadu

Streissguth, Ann P, PhD, Barr, John S, PhD, Barr, Sampson, Paul D, PhD, Bookstein, Fred L, PhD. *Prenatal Alcohol Exposure and Family History of Alcoholism in the Eriology of Adolescent Alcohol Problems* (1998) Published at the Center of Alcohol Studies, Rutgers University.

Siever, David C.E.T., *The Rediscovery of Audio-Visual Entrainment Technology.* Comptronic Devices Ltd, 9008 51st Ave., Edmonton, Alberta, Canada T6E 5X4.   www.comptronic.com

NEW! For Medical Professionals

Brick, John, Ph.D. *Handbook of the Medical Consequences of Alcohol and Drug Abuse* (2004) The Haworth Press

BOOKS
you can understand

ADOPTION/ATTACHMENT
get a better understanding

Keck, Gregory C. and Kupecky, Regina M, *Adopting the Hurt Child, Hope for Families with Special Needs Kids* (1998) Pinon Press.

Magid, Ken Dr. and McKelvey, Carole A. *High Risk, Children Without a Conscience.* (1998) Bantum, Doubleday Dell Pub.

Monahon, Cynthia. *Children and Trauma: A Guide for Parents and Professionals in Helping Children Heal,* (1997) Jossey-Bass.

ALLEGATIONS
prevention and survival

Kulp, Jodee, *Families at Risk, a Guide to Understanding and Protecting Children and Care Providers Involved in Out-of-Home or Adoptive Care,* (1994) Better Endings, New Beginnings, Minnesota.

ALLERGIES & NUTRITION
we are what we eat

Block, Mary Ann, Dr., No More ADHD, *10 Steps to Help Your Child's Attention and Behavior Without Drugs* (2001) Kennsington.

Larson, Joan Mathews, PhD., Seven Weeks to Sobriety, The Proven Program to Fight Alcoholism Through Nutrition (1997) Ballantine Wellspring

Lyon, Michael R. *Healing the Hyper Active Brain Through the New Science of Functional Medicine* (2000) Focused Publishing.

Rapp, Doris J. MD, FAAA, FAAP, Bamberg Dorothy, RN, EdD, *The Impossible Child In School At Home?* (1986) Life Sciences Press.

Schmidt, Michael A., *Smart Fats, How Dietary*

Fats and Oils Affect Mental, Physical and Emotional Intelligence (1997) North Atlantic Books.

BRAIN
books you can understand

Amen, Daniel G. M.D., *Change Your Brain, Change Your Life, The Breakthrough Program for Conquering Anxiety, Depression, Obsession, Anger and Impulsiveness.* (1998) Three Rivers Press, New York, NY

Diamond, Marian, PhD., *Magic Trees of the Mind: How to Nurture Your Child's Intelligence, Creativity and Health Emotions from Birth Through Adolescence* (1999) Plume

Doman, Glenn J., *What to Do About Your Brain Injured Child?,* (1994) Paragon Press, Honesdale, PA

Elliot, Lise, Ph.D., *What's Going On in There? How the Bran and Mind Develop in the First Five Years of Life.* (1991) Bantam

Goldberg, Stephen MD, *Clinical Neuroanatomy Made Ridiculously Simple,* (1997) MedMaster, Inc., PO Box 640028, Miami, FL 33164.

Lyon, Michael R. MD, *Healing the Hyperactive Brain Through the Science of New Functional Medicine* (2000) Focused Publishing

O'Brien, Dominic, *Learn to Remember, Transform Your Memory Skills* (2001) Six time World Memory Champion, Duncan Baird Publishers, London

Robbins, Jim: *A Symphony in the Brain, The Evolution of the New Brain Wave Biofeedback* (2000) Atlantic Monthly Press.

Scott, Susan: *The Brain: Fact, Function and Fantasy.* (1997) (Must be ordered from the author) Northwest Neurodevelop-ment Training Center, Inc., PO Box 406, 152 Arthur Street, Woodburn, Oregon, 97071. (503) 981-0635

Sacks, Oliver: *The man who mistook his wife for a hat and other clinical tales*, Summit Books, NY (1985) *An anthropologist on Mars; Seven paradoxical tales*; Alfred A. Knopf, NY (1995)

Stine, Jean Marie. *Double Your Brain Power.* (1997) Prentice Hall Press.

EDUCATION
ideas to help children learn

Blow, Susan E., Elliot, Henrietta R. *The Mottoes and Commentaries of Friedrich Froebel's Mother Play.* (1895) D. Appleton and Company. New York

Campbell, Don G. & Brewer, Chris. *Rhythms of Learning Creative Tools for Developing Lifelong Skills.* (1991). Zephyr Press

Greenspan, Stanley I M.D. & Wieder, Serena PhD: *The Child with Special Needs Encouraging Intellectual and Emotional Growth.* (1998) Perseus Books.

Greenspan, Stanley I M.D. with Breslau, Nancy Lewis: *Building Healthy Minds, The Six Experiences that Create Intelligence and Emotional Growth in Babies and Young Children* (1999) Perseus Books.

Kline, Peter. *The Everyday Genius, Restoring Children's Natural Joy of Learning – And Yours Too.* (1988) Great Ocean Publishers, 1823 North Lincoln Street, Arlington, VA 22207.

Pierangelo, Roger, PhD. 1996. *Parents' Complete Special Education Guide. Tips, Techniques and Materials for Helping Your Child Succeed in School and Life.* The Center for Applied Research in Education.
Tobias, Cynthia Ulrich. *Every Child Can Succeed.* (1996) *The Way They Learn* (1994) Focus on the Family Publishing
Shapiro, Lawrence E., PhD: *How to Raise a Child with High EQ, A Parents Guide to Emotional Intelligence.* (1998) Harper Perennial.

FASD knowledge is power

Burd, Larry, Ph.D. *Children with Fetal Alcohol Syndrome. A Handbook for Parents and Teachers.* (1999) (Must be ordered from the author) Larry Burd, PhD, 1300 S. Columbia Road, Grand Forks, ND 58202.

Buxton, Bonnie, *Damaged Angels: a Mother Discovers the Terrible Cost of Alcohol in Pregnancy* (2004) www.amazon.com

Davis, Diane: *Reaching Out to Children with Fas/Fae: A Handbook for Teachers, Counselors, and Parents Who Live and Works with Children Affected by Fetal Alcohol Syndrome.* (1994) Center for Applied Research.

Dorris, Michael: *Broken Cord: A Family's Ongoing Struggle with Fetal Alcohol Syndrome.* (1989) Harper & Row.

Federici, Ronald M.D., et al. *Help for the Hopeless Child: A Guide for Families.* (1998) Federici & Associates.

Kleinfield, Judith & Wescott, Siobhan: *Fantastic Antone Succeeds! Experiences in Educating Children with Fetal Alcohol Syndrome.* (1993) *Fantastic Antone Grows Up!* (2000) University of Alaska

Kulp, Liz, Kulp, Jodee, *The Best I Can Be, Living with Fetal Alcohol Syndrome or Effects.*(2000). Better Endings New Beginnings, 6289 Brunswick Avenue North, Brooklyn Park, MN 55429

Malbin, Diane: *Fetal Alcohol Syndrome.* (1993) Hazelden.

McCreight, Brenda: *Recognizing and Managing Children with Fetal Alcohol Syndrome/Fetal Alcohol Effects: A Guidebook.* (1998) Child Welfare League

MOFAS - Current Curriculums
a. Tools for Success: Program to support persons with FASD in juvenile justice
b. Project SOS: Seeds of Success Casemanagement tool for families.

Streissguth, Ann, et al., *The Challenge of Fetal Alcohol Syndrome: Overcoming Secondary Disabilities.* (1997) University of Washington Press.

Streissguth, Ann: *Fetal Alcohol Syndrome: A Guide for Families and Communities.* (1997) Paul H. Brookes Publishing Co.

FUN creative discipline ideas

Arp, Dave and Claudia, *60 One-Minute Memory Makers, Fun and Easy Ways to Create Family Memories that Last a Lifetime.* (1993) Thomas Nelson Publishing, Nashville, TN

Jasinek, Doris and Bell-Ryan, Pamela, *How To Build a House of Hearts, A Heart Level Home Makes Everyone Who Lives There Feel Good.* (1988) Comp Care, MN

Keating, Kathleen, *The Hug Therapy Book,* (1983) Comp Care, MN

Lansky, Vicki, *101 Ways to Tell Your Child "I Love You",* (1988) Contemporary Books, Chicago, IL

Simons, Laurie M.A. *Taking "No" for an Answer and Other Skills Children Need. Fifty Games to Teach Family Skills.* (2000) Parenting Press Inc., PO Box 75267, Seattle, WA 98125

St. Claire, Brita, *99 Ways to Drive Your Child Sane* (1999) Great ideas for dealing with RAD children. Order: Brita St. Claire, Families By Design, PO Box 2812, Glenwood Springs, CO 81602

ORGANIZATION
to make your life easier

Aslett, Don, (1984) *Clutter's Last Stand, It's Time to Dejunk Your Life!* Writers Digest Books, Cincinatti, OH

Barnes, Emilie, (1995) *Emilies Creative Home Organizer,* Harvest House, Eugene, OR

Campbell, Jeff, (1991) *Speed Cleaning Clean Your Home in Half the Time or Less!* Dell Books, New York, NY

SENSORY INTEGRATION
normalizing the senses

Ayres, A. Jean, *Sensory Integration and Your Child.* (1979) Western Psychological Services

Heller, Sharon, *Too Loud, Too Bright, Too Fast, Too Tight* (2003) Quill

Schneider, Catherin Chemin, *Sensory Secrets* (2001) Concerned Communications.

Kranowitz, Carol Stock, M.A., *The Out of Sync Child Recognizing and Coping with Sensory Integration Dysfunction.* (1998) Skylight Press *The Out of Sync Child Has Fun* (2003) Perigee

Quirk, Norma J. MS, OTR, and DiMatties, Marie E., MS, OTR (1990) *The Relationship of Learning Problems and Classroom Performance to Sensory Integration.* Order: Nancy Quirk, 131 Dumas Road, Cherry Hill, NJ 08003.

UNITED PARENTING
keeping it together

Coleman, Paul, Dr., *How to Say It to Your Kids: The Right Words to Solve Problems, Soothe Feelings and Teach Values.* (2000) Prentice Hall Press.

Eyre, Richard and Linda. *Teaching Your Children Values* (1993) Fireside. Richard and Linda Eyre have a series of Teaching Your Children and they are all wonderful.
Wyckoff, PhD & Unell, Barbara, *Discipline Without Shouting of Spaking, Practical Solutions to the Most Common Preschool Behavior Problems* (1984) Meadowbrook Press

Snow, Kathy, *Disability is Natural: Revolutionary Common Sense for Raising Successful Children with Disabilities*; Softcover, 640 pages, $26.95. Order: 1-866-948-2222

FILMS - FAMILY SAFE

FAS: Everybody's Baby Teresa Kellerman. Educational Video about FASD 34:46 min. FAS Star Enterprises, Fetal Alcohol Syndrome Community Resource Center www.fasstar.com

FAS/FAE: A Community Perspective,
FAS/FAE: Teaching Strategies for the Classroom
FAS/FAE: Coping with Challenging Behavior
Three videos exploring the challenges faced by families coping with FAS and find hope for the future. LCC Bookstore, Lethbridge Community College, 3000 College Drive South, Lethbridge, Alberta T1K 1L6 Canada

Journey Through the Healing Circle, Robin LaDue and Carolyn Hartness. Native American storytelling, a family resource.
1) *The Little Fox* (birth to 5 years)
2) *The Little Mask* (6-11)
3) *Sees No Danger* (12-17)
4) *Travels in Circles* (18-22)
Contact Washington State Foster Parent Training Institute 800-662-9111.

Family Viewing

Feature Films for Families offers positive alternatives in film viewing. Help instill values for our children. Feature Films for Families, PO Box 572410, Murray, UT 84157-2410 www.familytv.com 1-800-326-4598 for their catalog.

For older children consider watching:
Tim (1979) with Mel Gibson produced in Australia
Forest Gump (1996) with Tom Hanks

"The alcohol-affected child is like a garden. Some seeds need to be planted year after year, like the carrots and the radishes. The seeds the birds carry away have to be replaced almost immediately. But there are bulbs that grow in the garden and every year they come up almost without tending. It can be too easy to see what failed to come up this year and step on the crocuses close to the ground. The important thing is to be thankful that there is a garden. It is not a waste-land." **From: *Fantastic Antone Succeeds***

FASD RESOURCES FOR FAMILIES

INTERNET SUPPORT AND INFORMATION

NATIONAL FAS DIRECTORY – www.nofas.org

International Fetal Alcohol Awareness Day
"Ring Those Bells" September 9 @ 9:09 am - www.fasworld.com

ARC – FAS Resource and Materials Guide. http://thearc.org/faqs/fas.html and thearc.org/misc/faslist.html

Alaska Program on Fetal Alcohol Syndrome www.hss.state.ak.us/fas/

ARBI – Alcohol Related Brain Injury FAS/FAE Resource Site www.arbi.org

Better Endings New Beginning www.betterendings.org

CDC – National Center for Disease Control www.cdc.gov/ncbddd/fas/

FASALASKA www.fasalaska.com

Fetal Alcohol and Drug Unit - WA www.depts.washington.edu/fadu Fetal Alcohol Syndrome Diagnostic and Prevention Network - WA www.depts.washington.edu/fasdpn

Fetal Alcohol Syndrome Community Resource Center www.fasstar.com

FASCETS Fetal Alcohol Syndrome Consultation, Education and Training Services www.fascets.org

FASlink an internet list service to help families dealing with fetal alcohol. Filled with great downloads. www.acbr.com/fas/

FASFRI – Fetal Alcohol Syndrome Excellent information. Family Resource Institute, P.O. Box 2525, Lynnwood, WA 98036. (253) 531-2878 www.fetalalcoholsyndrome.org

FEN – Family Empowerment Network: Support for Families Affected by FAS/FAE (800) 462-5254, (608) 262-6590.

MOFAS – Minnesota Organization on Fetal Alcohol Syndrome, (612) 803-8746. www.mofas.org

NOFAS – National Organization on Fetal Alcohol Syndrome, (202) 785-4585, (800) 66-NOFAS. www.nofas.org

NIAAA – National Institute on Alcohol Abuse and Alcoholism www.niaaa.nih.gov

FASD ONLINE CLINIC www.online-clinic.com/Content/FAS/fetal_alcohol_syndrome.asp

SAMSHA – US Dept. Health and Human Services   fascenter.samhsa.gov/

This list is provided to give you a connection to links, support, education and information on fetal alcohol. It is by no means conclusive, nor does the author endorse everything these sites represent. Please see footnotes in manuscript for additional websites.

BRAIN

www.brainconnection.com
Simple to understand information about the brain. College credited online courses are also available

www.thebrainstore.com
Practical resources brain research.

MEDICAL

www.aap.org
American Academy of Pediatrics

www.megson.com
Dr. Mary Megson, MD, specializes in Autism working towards returning children to health.

NEURODEVELOPMENT

www.braingym.com
Paul Dennison, Ph.D. Targeted brain activities through movement.

www.handle.org
Judith Bluestone holistic approach to neurodevelopment. Therapy ideas.

www.iahp.org
Institutes for Achievement of Human Potential

www.inpp.org.uk/index.htm
The Institute for Neuro-Physiological Psychology. Peter Blythe and Sally Goddard Blythe.

www.kidscanlearn.net
Children's Academy for Neurodevelopment and Learning. Toni Hager, N.D.S.

www.llsys.com
Development of language software to help children with language issues.

www.movetolearn.com.au
Barbara Pheloung author of, *Help Your Class to Learn, Overcoming Learning Difficulties* and *Help Your Child to Learn.* Books may be ordered from author's site.

www.nacd.org
The National Academy of Child Development.

www.specialyoga.com
Sonia Sumer of yoga techniques to enhance the natural development of children with special needs.

www.stanleygreenspan.com
Development of emotional and social intelligence. Development of imagination, abstract and logic.

www.retrainthebrain.com
Using the hand to speak to the brain. Jeanette Farmer a handwriting remediation specialist.

www.zerotothree.org
Healthy development of babies and young children. Zero to Three, 734 15th St. #1000, Washington, DC, 20005. (202) 638-1144.

NEUROFEEDBACK

www.qeeg.com
Behavioral Medicine Associates, Dr. John Nash Website. Qualified links are available from this site.

www.eegspectrum.com
General site discussing neurofeedback

www.neurofeed.com
Neurofeedback system and information

www.crossroadsinstitute.org
Neurodevelopment center (AZ, TX, FL)

www.mindalive.ca
Brainwave Entrainment by David Siever

NUTRITION

www.americanheart.org
American Heart Association site is filled with heart and brain healthy ideas and recipes.

www.allergy.mcg.edu
American College of Allergy, Asthma and Immunology

www.autismndi.com
ANDI Autism Network for Dietary Intervention. Support for families on gluten free and casein free diets.

www.foodallergy.org
Food Allergy and Anaphylaxis Network offers a wealth of information.

www.foodnews.org
Environmental Working Group new on pesticide and toxic chemical load in daily food.

www.gfcfdiet.com
Gluten and casein-free diet information

www.nal.usda.gov/fnic/foodcomp
USDA Nutrient Data Laboratory - allows you to search vitamin and food source.

www.pureliving.com
Dr. Michael Lyon, a functional medicine physician and author of *Healing the Hyperactive Brain.*

ON-LINE FASD SUPPORT GROUPS

www.fasstar.com
Teresa Kellerman offers sound advice and support connections

www.fasflight.com
Run by Stephen Neafy an adult with FASD

PARENTING STRATEGIES

www.difficultchild.com
The Nurtured Heart Approach by Howard Glasser author of *Transforming the Difficult Child.* Recommended by Dr. Patch Adams.

www.disabilityisnatural.com
Kathie Snow provides professionals and parents with a wholistic and healthy viewpoint of raising a child with a disability.

www.parent-magic.com
1-2-3 Magic and other creative strategies to help you to love and work with your child.

www.nancythomasparenting.com
Familie by design parenting idea by Nancy Thomas

SCHOOLS

www.actg.org
A Chance To Grow – New Visions School

www.bced.gov.bc.ca/specialed/fas/
BC Canada, FASD Teacher Resource Guide

SENSES

www.hhmi.org/senses
Seeing, Hearing and Smelling the World. Howard Hughes Medical Institute.

www.tomatis.com
Ear training site with information to help you understand this pioneering approach.

www.mindalive.ca
Audio-visual entrainment program used successfully at A Chance to Grow New Visions School.

www.advancedbrain.com
Programs for building working memory, CD's, The Listening Program. Alex Doman

www.garylamb.com
Gary Lamb's 60 Beats Per Minute music.

www.new-vis.com
Marvelous Mouth Music allows a child to go back to prespeech with musical fun.

www.feldenkrais.com
The Feldenkrais Method teaches how we can improve our capabilities to function in daily life.

Other Therapies

* Hyberbaric Oxygen Therapy
* Breathwork
* Music Therapy
* Dance Therapy
* Light Therapy
* Art Therapy
* Hippotherapy (horses)
* Watertherapy

www.upledger.com
* Cranial Sacral Therapy

www.callirobics.com
* Handwriting support

FASD RESOURCES FOR FAMILIES
FAMILY TREASURE

As parents we pledge to:

- Strive to keep our young people safe.
- Focus on positives rather than negatives.
- Respect individuality in each person.
- Allow freedoms as responsibility, judgment, new skills and talents develop.
- Show we value each person's work and provide opportunity for learning.
- Not criticize or squelch a person's enthusiasm though we may need to redirect it.
- Help each other deal with failure and bounce back without being devastated.
- Talk about a person's strengths and figure out ways to maximize them.
- Provide support systems.
- Provide logical consequences.
- Keep ourselves healthy so we can be better parents.
- Accept FASD is going to change our life in ways we cannot control.

We make the commitment to each youth in our care that if they find themselves in trouble, they can call us and we will get them...no questions asked.
We discovered they are so glad to see us, we usually get details before we get home.

We determine family signals that keep everyone safe and respectful.
For some of our kids these have been very overt, and for others very subtle.

The table is safe for any discussion. If you bring an issue to the table before we catch you it will be discussed amicably.
This has always promoted honesty and openness in our family.

We strive to find the "right" balance of freedom and discipline for each family member.
Each child is on a different time line for being able to do things, and each child requires different discipline.

Tips:

- Discover your child's personality, learning and processing preferences.
- Don't discount the impossible. Children can surprise us. Things that irritate you now may lead to a future success for your child.
- Provide exposure and experiences. Coach and mentor them through life's challenges.
- Don't allow exposure and experiences to: alcohol, drugs, pornography, violence.
- Teach them slowly. Teach them patiently. Teach them again and again. Do not sacrifice the quality of your teaching to encourage quantity. (When teaching housekeeping skills consider teaching professional methods.)

TREASURE HUNTERS

My child hates herself, thinks she is stupid and ugly...what can I do?

My heart breaks for the self-esteem of these children. They try so hard to cloak themselves in a mask of normalcy and then dive into a social abyss with their dismal behaviors. They are misunderstood, misdiagnosed and struggle with normal daily life issues.

We went on a treasure hunt for both Liz and David. We wrote a proclamation and presented it to them with a medal. We posted our results on the refrigerator. We gave a copy to David's mom, to Liz's therapist and we told grandma and grandpa!

You won't regreat going on a treasure hunt for your child.

Common Good Qualities has been compiled from ARC Northland in Duluth. Their sources were from Clarren, Streissguth, Morse, Malbin, Rathburn, FAS Resource Coalition.

Common Good Qualities and Talents of Persons with FASE.

tactile and cuddly	friendly/happy
spontaneous	loyal
trusting and loving	gentle
affectionate	curious
persistent	willing
involved	loving of animals
enjoy gardening	enjoy constructing
kind and caring	helpful
concerned	sensitive
athletic	moral and fair
artistic	musical
highly verbal	rich fantasy life
hard workers	atypical strengths
nurturing	compassionate
sense of humor	committed
devoted as parents	determined
strong sense of self	creative
social	follows through

good with younger children
wonderful story tellers
good long term visual memory

Tips:

■ What turns your child on? What are the child's keen interests or talents?

■ Does your child know something no one else in the family does? Let the child teach others.

■ Does the irritating behavior demonstrate creative problem solving? Salesmanship? Leadership?

■ Try to provide ten positive comments to every negative comment you give your child.

■ If the child is having trouble learning or understanding something, take a deep silent breath, break it into smaller pieces and when they conquer the first piece rejoice and go on to the next.

■ Don't hinder the caterpillar from growing into a beautiful butterfly.

MN DHS Guidelines of Care

for Children with Special Health Care Needs: Fetal Alcohol Syndrome and Fetal Alcohol Effect recommends families stress the following:

1. **Structure** - Create a structured environment which includes limited choices. Have clear and set routines. Adjust the environment for slower development and understanding.
2. **Supervision** - Carefully supervise teens so they do not place themselves in dangerous situations.
3. **Simplicity** - State instructions briefly and clearly. Use simple directions and orders.
4. **Steps** - Break tasks down into small steps. Teach each step through repetition. Lists may be helpful. Use rewards as incentives.
5. **Setting** - Teach desired skills in the way in which they will be used. Teens with FASD may not have the ability to transfer skills from one setting to another.

Chores

1. Teach the child the best way you know how to do the chore. First learning is very important to children with FASD.
   - Use very small steps, voice process
   - Show the child exactly how you expect the chore to be done.
   - Make a checklist of steps.
2. Start on the last step or in the middle of the chore first to keep it informal and not so overwhelming. Build from that point backwards or forward.
3. Set up inspection checkpoints "Inspect what you expect."

Stranger Danger 7 Safety Rules

1. I check with my parents or person in charge before I go anywhere. I tell them where I am going. Who will be going with me. When I'll be back.
2. I check first with my parents before getting into a car or leaving with anyone, changing plans, accepting gifts or money or anything without my parents knowing.
3. I take a friend when I go someplace.
4. I say NO when someone tries to touch me in ways that make me feel scared, uncomfortable or confused. If someone touches me in a bad way I tell my parents immediately.
5. I know my home telephone number address and my parents work number. If there is an emergency I contact my parents as soon as possible.
6. I talk to my parents about problems that are too big for me to manage alone.
7. I have the right to be safe.

Music uses both sides of the brain for learning. One side for creating the music and one side for expressing it. Music at 60 bps (beats per minute) is near our heart rates and tends to relax a person. Music can change the atmosphere. Play with different kinds of music and notice its affect on you and your children.

Middle School is a hard time for teens with FASD. It can take 20-30 min. to assimilate change leaving very little time for class work. Your school may have a program available to eliminate the chaos and make transitions less frustrating. An in-school suspension room with natural lighting may be a blessing in disguise.

FASD RESOURCES FOR FAMILIES

TEACHING TIPS - GENERAL

1. Observe, refocus, reframe.

Misbehavior is often a neurological misfire. Take a deep breath, think about what might be going on. Is it the child can't or is it the child won't? Ask the child how you can help. You may be surprised at her answer.

2. Give your child only one direction at a time.

Multiple directions are confusing to a child with FASD. The student may forget what was said first, may not understand what was said or may be confused by a two or more part question.

   a. Give clear directions - say "put your coats on" instead of "get ready to go".

   b. Use fewer words - stop, walk, go.

   c. Child can repeat back what you say.

3. Model and mentor correct behavior.

Focus on behaviors you want the student to grow, not on behaviors you don't like.

4. Reteach, reteach, reteach . . .

Keep it simple....if they are not getting it break it down into even smaller pieces or teach something easier to build upon.

   a. Use repetition.

   b. Be consistent.

   c. Make smaller steps.

   d. Build on learning.

   e. Try backward chaining.

5. Teach replacement behavior.

   – Reframe

   – Thought-stopping, positive thinking

   – Deep breathing and relaxation

   – Fun, humor and laughter!

6. Use Motivators.

Encouragement, positive attention, rewards and incentives for appropriate behavior and meeting learning challenges. Set a goal to be accomplished. Some incentives work well small toys, money, time with friends, roller rink passes, special dinners, and movies.

7. Modify your environment for the child's success.

Discipline yourself to be sensitive to set up your child for success. This may mean changing plans if the child is too tired, irritable, or nervous. Never go out hungry or over stimulated. The environment is an absolute 'key' to the child's success. Prevent the meltdown from happening.

8. Keep yourself healthy.

Maintain the support of other teachers. Teaching children with FASD can be very frustrating.

9. Be a team player.

The parents of a child with FASD will have ideas of how to help you with their child. Listen carefully to what they have to say. Find a way to keep in touch with the family on a regular basis.

TEACHING TIPS – FASD BEHAVIORAL AND EMOTIONAL CONSEQUENCES

Adapted from the work of Robin LaDue and Ann Striessguth, Fetal Alcohol & Drug Unit – University of Washington School of Medicine, Jocie DeVries, Vicky McKinney and Ann Waller, FAS Family Resource Group

Brain Damage	Behavior	Consequences	Emotion
ATTENTION DEFICITS	Unfocused Distractable	Does not finish projects/goals	Disappointment Frustration

———————— What you can do to help ————————

Reduce distractions: Calm, quiet room. Remove excessive pictures and posters from walls, keep toys in containers, cupboards. Keep living or educational environment uncluttered. Make things visible but orderly, less is more. Sitting on a ball, using a weighted vest or chewing gum may help focus. **Provide Focus Pointers:** Color code notebooks to different subjects. Add concrete markers to hold space – footprints-lines, carpet squares-circle time, hand print-desk, pictures on cupboards to show contents, picture directions next to objects. Label everything – clothes, lunchboxes, school books so it can be returned if forgotten or lost. **Reward paying attention:** Notice when child is on task. Provide on-going encouragement because tasks may be very frustrating. Allow self-talk to encourage focus.

ARITHMETIC DISABILITY	Can't handle money	Bungles finances Assigned a payee	Resentful

———————— What you can do to help ————————

Develop fail safe systems: Provide coach to work with finances, autopay bills and autodeposit. **Encourage rigid adherence to rules:** Set standards and verify they are adhered to. Make bill paying chart to mark off when bills are paid. (We have let Liz handle her personal money since age five)

DIFFICULTY WITH SELF REFLECTION	Can't express needs	Does not get help Fails to have needs met	Feels like failure Feels dissatisfied

———————— What you can do to help ————————

Provide verbal feedback for expressed feelings: I can see you are frustrated, too many things are happening at one time. Let's take a break. I can see you are lonely, let's go for a walk and talk. I can see you are feeling happy, it is fun to be with you when you are happy. **Reward clear need expression:** Thank you for telling me you are unhappy. You told me you are frustrated. Can I help you make this easier? Provide a listening ear when they need to talk.

Brain Damage	Behavior	Consequences	Emotion
DIFFICULTY ABSTRACT	Does not accept consequences Does not generalize learning to new situations	Tries hard but fails	Disappointment Frustration

─────── What you can do to help ───────

Provide increased structure: Train people working with person with FASD about fetal alcohol brain damage, provide ideas to help person. Keep days and weeks predictable.
Modify goals: Break a task into smaller parts. Teach one part at a time. Encourage at each step. Set attainable standard then slowly raise the bar as the person can manage.
Provide alternative satisfaction: Provide supervised social activities person can succeed in. Persons with FASD like active fun! Provide boisterous fun opportunities without drugs or alcohol.

Brain Damage	Behavior	Consequences	Emotion
DISORIENTATION IN TIME AND SPACE	Misses appointments Difficulty with time Misperceives social cues	Disappoints people Lose employment Miss appointments Unpredictable	Feels unliked Frustration Feels like failure Lonely

─────── What you can do to help ───────

Develop coping strategies: Order telephone wake up call services, watch with alarm, pager. Daily schedule list with times, pictures or words. Provide digital watch. Roleplay facial/social cue understanding. Use personal daytimers, notebooks, wall calendars. Have professionals confirm appointment. Keep appointment times/days the same. **Have friends be part of the solution:** Have friend or mentor provide ride share or phone call. Set standards and verify they are adhered to. Keep daily schedules consistent. Make charts to mark off completed tasks. Plan morning routine night before – breakfast dishes on table, clothes ready.

Brain Damage	Behavior	Consequences	Emotion
IMPULSIVITY	Quick to anger	Gets punished	Feels picked on

─────── What you can do to help ───────

Teach to think before acting: Teach breathing techniques. Allow person a quiet place to go to regroup – quiet room with subtle lighting, pup tent, large box, bath tub.
Anger management strategies: Drink cold glass of water. Suck on ice. Sensory integration tactile. Stress ball. Breathe. Run. Shoot hoops. **Reward withholding response:** Provide incentives to child for not reacting. Encourage person to tell you when they have managed to hold back and stand on your head in excitement when this is accomplished. Help them want to do it again and again. **Prevent low blood sugar:** Provide high quality nutrition for person.

Brain Damage	Behavior	Consequences	Emotion
MEMORY PROBLEMS	Does not learn from experience	Makes same mistakes repeatedly	Confusion, Frustration

─────── What you can do to help ───────

Teach/Develop memory aids: Procedure cards, notebooks, crib notes, tape record classes, reteach in many situations – for example to cross a street teach at many, many street corners. **Develop rigid routines:** Break tasks into smaller pieces and teach from the bottom up, reinforce and encourage learned tasks. Use role play. Provide sequences for going to bed, going to school/work, Friday or Saturday night. Make checklist or picture sequence cards. This may seem to you like 'stuck in a rut' but will provide security and safety for the person with FASD. When teaching new behavior videotape and let the child watch it over and over. Reteach and practice. **Build working memory:** Play memory games such as concentration, I am going to Grandma's, repeat back numbers, letters, actions like Simon Says. Include person in strategizing 'show me how.'

PERSEVERATION	Does same thing over and over	Misses the rewards Rigid, resistive	Confusion, Frustration

─────── What you can do to help ───────

Find other behaviors to reward: Choose your battles wisely, person is not aware of behavior. **Provide opportunity to change:** DO NOT HUMILIATE! Video tape behavior so person can see. Interact with person when they are perseverating - Stanley Greenspan, *The Child with Special Needs Encouraging Intellectual and Emotional Growth*. (1998) has full chapters on ideas which really do work with our children – highly recommended reading. Praise when child manages not to perseverate.

POOR HABITUATION	Drown in stimulation Emotional overload Shuts down discriminations Behaved erratically	Disappoints people Embarrasses people Gets criticized	Defensive

─────── What you can do to help ───────

Decrease stimulation: Arrive late, leave early from gatherings. Provide comfort item child can focus on. Distract and redirect child to another area or activity. Remove from over stimulating environment. Provide transition cues - five minutes before dinner, one minute before dinner. **Teach ways to reduce stimulation:** Provide ideas to remove self from stimulating environment. Breathing techniques. Ways to self organize - paper and pencil (drawing or games), comfort item, bottle of water to sip on, playdough. **Neurodevelopment:** Normalize sensory system so child can handle and integrate stimulation. Have complete vision processing and auditory processing exam.

Brain Damage	Behavior	Consequences	Emotion
POOR JUDGMENT	Trusts anybody Behaves irrationally	Easily victimized Easily scape-goated	Confused, hurt Low self-esteem

What you can do to help

Develop coping strategies: Develop simple and specific cues between you and the child. Teach stranger danger. Get to know their friends, offer to take them to community events, encourage your role as supportive resource and confidant. Redirect child out of situation they are behaving irrationally in, provide counsel or role play and engage child in coming up with alternative behaviors that could be tried next time. Provide furniture that allows movement - beanbag or rocking chair. Encourage child you are there to help, but they are to learn to manage themselves. Notice behaviors they have changed. Howard Glasser's book *Transforming the Difficult Child,* provides a wealth of ideas. **Reduce expectations:** Lower your expectations to that of a younger child, but continue to encourage and set child up for growth steps. Create opportunities to succeed in making good judgment. Ask the child's opinion. Encourage interaction in developing choices. **Develop other sources of self esteem:** Provide opportunities for person to succeed by capitalizing on their strengths. Seek out peers (usually younger) who also have same interests.

POOR SELF REGULATION	Out of control behavior Act without thinking	Gets into trouble	Confused

What you can do to help

Teach techniques to stay in control: Practice **STOP** (**S**top, **T**hink before you act — *what's my problem?, what am I doing?, where am I?, who is affected?, how can I change?,* **O**xygen - increase the brain's processing ability by feeding it, **P**roceed safely. Consider a Big Brother or Big Sister program volunteer to mentor your child. Establish calming technique before bedtime. Avoid stimulating drinks or foods. Be aware of lights, sounds, smells, touches that overwhelm your child. Consider neurodevelopment to help your child develop abilities to manage better in the world when not in your care. Notice when your child is making an effort and compliment their attempts. **Reduce settings that induce out-of-control behavior:** When heading into a setting that could be overwhelming, make sure child is well fed, not stressed or tired. Encourage friends to come to your home and provide supervision, structure and control. Provide safety and supervision when playing on park equipment. Shop during less busy times of day, engage the child in the activity. Can they push the cart and remain under control, pick up the items from the list, bag the groceries or transfer groceries from cart to counter and carry bags or push cart to the car? Break events into manageable amounts. Visit a museum, craft fair or library for only 10-15 minutes, select a mission to accomplish and JUST do that! Monitor the child's response and talk with the child about how they felt when they were out with you. Carol Stock Kranowitz book *Out of Sync Child* provides great ideas.

Brain Damage	Behavior	Consequences	Emotion
SLOW CNS PROCESSING	Fails to grasp meaning Misses deadlines Forgets information short-term	Object of derision Lack of success Misses opportunities	Feels dumb Low self-esteem

―――――――― **What you can do to help** ――――――――

Give more time: Provide data in smaller pieces. Keep sentences short. Allow processing time by slowing your speech or pausing between sentences. Do not hurry person, stress will produce even more difficulty in processing. Consider reading test questions.

Reinforce learning: Teach in multiple modalities. Teach through each sense at one time without mixing senses. For example: Watch: show but do not speak. Listen: speak but do not show. **Provide one-on-one supports:** One-on-one tutoring allows the teacher the opportunity to know if the child is understanding and remembering what you have taught. Consider allowing calculators for testing. Consider allowing auditory books for reading and oral presentation of book with teacher and student alone for book report. Let child tell about book or teacher asks questions. **Reduce expectations:** Transferring data from blackboard to paper may be extremely difficult, from text book to paper or from test question to answer sheet. Workbooks or worksheets may be easier to handle than dealing with the data transfer. Taking notes requires integration of visual, auditory and fine motor system in addition to reprocessing the data, consider allowing a tape recorder for person to play back or allowing the sharing of notes from another student. Lower your expectations to that of a younger child. Break task into MUCH smaller segments and teach one tiny piece at a time. Reinforce learned material while learning new materials. Liz may take one year to learn to play one song on the harp. **Reward success:** Provide incentives to master new material.

Tips to help your adolescent cope:

1. Get to know your teen's friends, offer rides, offer counsel, offer activities - stay parent active.
2. Find teen or young adult group and individual activities your teen can participate in and be accepted: scouts, choir, church group, band, Big Brother or Big Sister / rollerblading, biking, skateboards, Special Olympics, walking, running, swimming.
3. Involve teen in care of animals.
4. Designate a mutually agreed upon friend or relative who will provide a safe house.
5. Designate a mutually agreed upon adult friend or relative who will be a mentor and provide an adult/teen activity once every six weeks or less.― hair appointment, concert, zoo, sporting event).
6. Delay the obtaining of a driver's license.
7. Find medical personnel who are willing to develop a relationship with you and your teen.

TEACHING TIPS
DO I HAVE AN FASD CHILD IN CLASS?

adapted from http://www.lcsc.edu/education/fas/signals

External signs

1. Daydreaming for more than 50% of the class time
2. Bitten finger, finger nails and lips
3. Silence
4. Forgetfulness on an hourly, daily basis
5. Anger (quiet until puberty)

Internal signs (what you may see)

1. **Confusion**
   a. What time is it?
   b. What class is this?
   c. What happened in this class the day, week, or mouth before?
   d. What is this?
   e. Where is my assignment? Is this finished?

2. **Emotional Breakdown**
   a. Tears, but no noise
   b. Retreat from everything, staring
   c. High anxiety, no verbalization*

3. **Sexual Activity**
   a. Marked increase as they become older
   b. Impulsive acts or inappropriate touching
   c. Will cause a sexual incident on a "dare"
   d. Consequences are not under stood, nor is a pregnant girl or girlfriend

Identified, Diagnosed FASD

1. All the above will be the same
2. These students should have a letter from a diagnostic clinic or a note to talk to someone who knows their history

Unidentified FASD Students

1. Seems lazy
2. Falls asleep in class on a daily basis
3. Continuously late for class
4. Poor eyesight
5. Small, skinny fingers, ears, or legs
6. Complains of pain in joints/headaches
7. Have history of normal physical problems in excess of usual occurrences (especially in head, kneecaps, fingers, ankles, and internal organs)

This changes as they become older, especially in boys. **Anxiety + Anger = Violence**, *sometimes to the point that it becomes a matter for school officials/administrators or the police.*

While this can be disruptive and sometimes frightening for everyone **AVOID PHYSICAL TOUCH AS THE FIRST WAY OF REACHING THIS YOUNG PERSON.** Talking quietly but in a steady tone of voice will be more effective.

TEACHING TIPS - COPING EXERCISES

INTRODUCE THE CHILL "DRILL" Here is a fail-safe anger control technique to help harness the power of your anger energy and channel it constructively.

CHILL: Calm your body's anger energy.
1. **Chill.** When you first become aware of your anger, tell yourself to chill.
2. **Blow!** Thinking "chill" is your cue to take strong, steady breaths as if blowing up a balloon.
3. **Relax Your Face.** Change the angry expression on your face. Smile.
4. **Get Some Space.** Take a step from the source of your anger. Take time to reflect.

CHOOSE: Focus your mind on positive action.
1. **Claim Your Anger:** Take responsibility. It is your anger.
2. **Name The Hurt:** Identify your hurt feelings under your anger.
3. **Name Your Anger:** Think about what else you can do to take the edge off your anger.
4. **Make a Plan.** Focus on solutions; take positive actions.

"The Chill Drill" was developed by James Sipe, PhD, a family psychologist for use by children and adults. © 1994 Project Family

ADULT FIVE MINUTE VACATION Be good to yourself, take three to five mini-breaks each day.
1. Become aware of your thoughts.
2. Switch thoughts to your breathing.
3. Take two deep nasal, belly breaths, exhale longer than inhale and imagine your stress being purged out of your body on your exhales.
4. Scan your body for tenseness. Start at your toes and fingers and work up to your central axis. If you feel a tight area, shake or wiggle to loosen it.
5. Gently rotate your head in a circle and roll your shoulders forward. Switch your head rotation.
6. Imagine a pleasant thought — experience, place, a good friend.
7. Smile — as you think about this. Smiling helps release tension.
8. Take a few deep breaths through your nose and return to your activity.

CREATE A TIME BOUNDARY VACATION Twice a day give yourself a time boundary vacation. Sometimes it is five minutes and other days you may get fifteen minutes. Allow no meetings, phone calls, child interruptions or worries. Pay attention to yourself. I have a list of 50 nice things I can do for "just me" hidden in my undies drawer. Some days are hectic with many FASattacks it is hard to remember how to be nice to myself. My list includes: take a hot shower, drink a rootbeer float or hide in the sauna with a good book. Challenge yourself to find 50 simple ways to be nice to you!

SMILING AND HAPPINESS Take a deep belly breath and play with your face. Feel the difference in your countenance as you smile and breathe, frown and breathe. Our facial muscles contain direct linkages into our emotions. Play with your body language and face as you practice the universal six basic emotions: happiness, sadness, anger, fear, surprise and disgust. Go back to smiling. Parents of brain injured children need to smile a lot. Not only is it good for our children and their growth, it is good for our own health. As I tell Liz, when I am old, my wrinkles will tell people I lived a happy life. *"A cheerful heart, is good medicine."* Proverbs 17:22. Laughter improves your blood circulation, exercises your abdominal muscles, increases your heart rate, expels stale air from your lungs, aids digestion and releases muscle tension. After a bout of laughter your blood pressure drops to a lower level. According to laugh researcher William F. Fry, one hundred laughs provide the same cardiovascular benefit as ten minutes of rowing.[67] Laughter is good for you. While stressful situations release cortisol and aldosterone, laughter does just the opposite. It activates virus fighting killer cells and interferon-gamma, lowers your levels of the stress-related neurotransmitter adrenaline (epinephrine), raises your levels of immunoglobins and increases the pain-reducing neuropeptides such as endorphine.[68] Even anacephalic infants, born without a brain stem, appear to laugh when tickled.[69]

THE GIFT OF LITTLE THINGS Give yourself the gift of little things. Bring your full attention to a common task. If you are sweeping the floor pay attention to how your muscles are working, how many little silly things you are discovering in the pile growing with each sweep. Listen to the sound of the bristles of the broom. Notice how the floor looks. Write with your finger on the dusty furniture and see if anyone notices, then pass out dust rags and let the

67-69. Gamon, David Ph.D. and Bragdon, Allen D. (1998) *Building Mental Muscle: Conditioning Exercises for the Six Intelligence Zones.* Allen D. Bragdon Publishers, Inc, 252 Great Western Road, South Yarmouth, MA 02664.

kids erase your notes. When the shower steams up the bath mirror write "I love you messages." Make letters out of pancake batter and dish a child's name, on to their plate.

VISUALIZING The process of putting pictures into your mind and being able to retrieve them begins for most children at very young ages. Liz had to be taught to visualize. We begin very simply by choosing something she loved — her dog. Liz lay on pillows in the school room as I asked her to close her eyes and think about Beki, the dog. *"Tell me everything she could think of about her. Now imagine something Beki did that was very funny and try to make a movie of it in your head so you can see the whole thing happen again."* We practiced while driving in the car, sitting on the patio or in school. We advanced to visual field trips. Describe your room in detail. What is on the dresser? What is in the drawers? What color? We kept it fun. We stopped before frustration set in. In our minds eye we begin walking from the kitchen to the bedroom. What did we see on our walk? We added actions. The phone rings. What did Liz do? Mom knocked on the door. What did Liz do? How did Liz feel? We expanded into other areas of Liz's teen life — describing the yard, roller rink, park, schoolroom.

GET SOME SUNSHINE Place a chair by a window with sunlight. Take a five minute walk in the yard or sit outside and drink a cool glass of water. In cold weather enjoy hot tea on the steps.

BREATHING Focusing on my breathing helps me think before I act when I am under stress or anxious. During the day slowly fill your lungs, then slowly release the air. Imagine the air going in and out. Close your eyes and relax. Notice how your body feels. What sounds do you hear? What is the temperature? Is there a breeze? What do you smell? Take a moment. Sit in a comfortable chair, straighten your back, relax your shoulders and take a deep breath. Let the air "open" your chest. Hold the breath. Then exhale every last puff.

TENSION RELEASE Place your finger tips just in front of your ears and make all your facial muscles tight. Hold for five seconds and exhale and say ahhh. Let your jaw go loose. Repeat three more times first using half the original tension, then a fourth and finally an eighth.

DON'T OWN THE WORRY One of the gifts I was given was by the Australian culture was learning to acknowledge a situation as a worry, but don't lay claim to it. Statements such as "It's a worry" or "That's a worry" make it clear that it is something to ponder about, but you needn't get upset or increase your own personal stress level because of it.

RELEASE THE PAST According to Dominic OBrien, the past is a distant landscape, an unalterable vista. We should no more wish to change parts of it than we should wish the Himilayan peaks be covered with trees. It helps to think of the past as an academy of practical wisdom based on all our experiences positive and negative. An error in judgement, no less than a personal achievement, belongs in the archive of this academy, as a compass by which to harvest future directions of life. It is not a matter of debit or credit – instead picture all the archive files bound in covers of the same color, chronologically. We do not live in the past, its incidents excite no emotion.

PRAYER My relationship with my higher power (Jesus, Holy Spirit and the Father) is crucial in my daily walk to help me guideLiz. I am not capable of doing this on my own. I need inner peace. I need grace. I need patience. I need strength. I need forgiveness. I have found these tools when I pray. I have discovered that when life gets complicated, a session of weed pulling in my garden or snow shoveling while worshipping the Lord refreshes me (my girlfriend cleans her horse barns). Then I can face the heartache.

LEARN SOMETHING NEW FOR YOU   Find something you can do each day for 'you.' It doesn't have to take a long time. Use the minutes you have available. If you want to play an instrument – play in a five minute block of time when you can, you will notice the difference in your ability. If you are a gardener work in small blocks of time – piece by piece the garden will be beautiful. If you want to exercise - do leg lifts as you brush your teeth, roll your shoulders as you type at the computer, get some light 2lb. weights and lift them as you talk on the phone. If you have a significant other, take a class, participate in a hobby or go to a support group to be together, with other adults and have fun.

FOCUSING The work of Eugene T. Gendlin, PhD provides insight into helping you change thought patterns or behaviors in an healthy, effective way. If we can learn to divest a problem of its emotional charge, then we can find resolution and solution and limit the stress it places on our life. This method provides an opportunity to change perspective and use our library of past experiences and knowledge in wise and practical ways. His book *Focusing* (1982) can be found in libraries and is worth the read. When I deal with only one problem at a time and isolate myself from the other worries, I feel release and gain forward movement toward a solution. Following is a short summary of his method.

1. Clear a space. Find a quiet, isolated place. This is the shower in my home! Imagine a room filled with closed boxes of all your problems and troubles. Each problem is carefully wrapped and sealed so you must open it to deal with it. You can open only one box at a time. Ask yourself, how are you? What's between you and feeling fine? Don't open any of the boxes. Don't answer. Don't think. Just let your mind rest. Let what comes in your body do the answering. Don't do anything. Greet each thought that comes. Put each thought aside for a while, next to you. Ask yourself, except for that, are you fine?

2. Felt sense. Pick only one problem to focus on. Don't dwell on that problem. What do you sense in your body when you recall the whole of that problem? Sense all of that, the sense of the whole thing, the murky discomfort or the unclear body-sense of it.

3. Get a handle. What is the quality of the felt sense? What one word, phrase, or image comes out of how you are feeling? What quality-word would fit it best? I often find I am frustrated, lacking skills or don't know what to do.

4. Resonate. Go back and forth between the word (or image) and the felt sense. Is it right? If they match, have the sensation of matching several times. If the felt sense changes, follow it with your attention. When you get a perfect match, the words (or images) being just right for this feeling, let yourself feel for a minute.

5. Ask. What is it about the whole problem, that makes me so---------?

What is worst about this feeling?

What's so really bad about this?

What does it need?

What should happen?

Don't answer, wait for the feeling to stir and give you an answer.

What would it feel like if everything was OK? (Let your body answer)

What is in the way of that?

6. Receive. Welcome the word or idea. Be glad it spoke. It is only one step on this problem. It is not the last. Now that you know where it is, you can leave it and come back to it later. Protect it from your critical thoughts that interrupt.

7. Try another problem. Does your body want another round of focusing, or is this a good stopping place. Only you will know.[70]

70. Gendlin, Eugene T, Ph.D., *Focusing* (1988) Bantum Books

Our FAScinating Journey ©2004 Kulp

TEACHING TIPS - CHILD'S INTERESTS

Discover your child's desires

Lighting preference
- low light
- window light
- no light

Temperature preference
- open window
- air conditioning
- warm heat

Seating placement

Work
- alone
- with friend

Teach to Different Kinds of Processing

Visual	Auditory	Kinesthetic
Flashcards	Tapes	Dice and Cards
Pop-up books	Music	Clay
Slates	Oral reading	Games
Copy work	Educational videos	Computers
Board work	Computers	Construction
Diagrams	Direct teaching	Experiments
Workbooks	Songs	Manipulatives
Readers	Plays	Field trips
Magazines	Drama	Pop-up books
Letterwriting	Oral drills	Tactile flash cards
Storyboards	Interviews	Typing
Pantomime	Skip count	Writing in sand/air

GARDNER'S EIGHT INTELLIGENCES*

Howard Gardner teaches cognitive development at Harvard Graduate School

Musical/Rhythmic — Rhythm, music, melody. Incorporate music daily, tape record for listening, singing, recording, utilize rhythm and instrumentation.

Mathematical/Logical — Categorize, classify, work on patterns and relationships. Utilize manipulatives, games like checkers and chess, simple machines.

Body/Kinesthetic — Touch, move, interact. Physical challenges, spelling and grammar with dance, math with manipulatives, allow movement and interaction.

and don't forget to laugh and dance and play . . .

Spatial/Visual — Visualize, colors/pictures, map, draw, chart, diagram, puzzles

Linguistic/Verbal — Saying, hearing and seeing words. Listen, appreciate, reading outloud, spelling games, rhymes, tongue twisters, writing.

Natural — Explore, observe, collect, order. Explore outdoors, seek patterns and order within the world, collections, plants, animals

Interpersonal — Share, relate, cooperate, games that problem solve to figure out the knowledge or intent of another, discussion about social interactions.

Intrapersonal — Self-paced, individual, work alone. Express emotions, preferences, strategies, understand wishes, fears and how to cope, cozy quiet spaces.

*Exetensial intelligence is under consideration

TEACHING RESOURCES WE HAVE USED

BRAIN BUILDING

Can Learn - Toni Hager Neurodevelopment evaluations and home based programs. Site also includes ideas you can use immediately and product ideas. www.kidscanlearn.net

Brain Builder® -Working Visual and Auditory Memory Skill Building. www.advancedbrain.com

The Listening Program® Auditory Training Program. www.advancedbrain.com

Building Mental Muscle *Conditioning Exercises for the Six Intelligence Zones* by David Gamon.

How to Raise a Child with a High EQ *A Parents Guide to Emotional Intelligence* by Lawrence Shapiro, Ph.D. Dr. Shapiro also has a set of exceptional card games to help children which can be ordered through ChildsWork ChildsPlay at 1-800-962-1141.

The Everyday Genius *Restoring Children's Natural Joy of Learning and Yours Too* by Peter Kline.

PHYSICAL ACTIVITIES

Brain Gym® Physical exercises that enhance brain function. Edu-Kinesthetis, Inc., PO 3395, Ventura, CA 93006. www.braingym.com

Yoga for the Special Child Yoga exercises by Sonia Sumar. www.specialyoga.com

Games for Learning by Peggy Kaye. Peggy has also written *Games for Reading* and *Games for Math*. Super resources for keeping learning fun.

BOOST-UP and SMART A Chance to Grow. www.actg.com

LIFE SKILLS

Luke's Life List - Joyce Herzog www.joyceherzog.com Individualized Education Planner. Over 100 pages.

I Can Do It! A micropedia of Living on Your Own. Marian B. Latzko. 1-888-357-7654. The best independent living guidebook I have found. Budgeting, finance. roommates, renting, eating right, cleaning, laundry and more!

BASIC KNOWLEDGE

The Core Knowledge Series - E.D. Hirsch, Jr. *What Your 1st, 2nd, 3rd, 4th, 5th, 6th Grader* needs to know. Fundamentals of a good education. We used these throughout Liz's schooling. Liz began reading book one while I read book 3 aloud to her.

KONOS Curriculum Hundreds of activities to help children understand character traits. We focused one specific trait a month to understand the concepts of obedience, honesty, stewardship, honor, etc. www.konos.com

McGraw Hill Learning Materials The Spectrum Series for writing is an excellent tool to help a child begin to think about writing.

ART

All Simple Crafts Keep it simple, keep it fun. Start with preschool style activities and adapt to your older child's interests.

Drawing with Children
Drawing for Older Children & Teens
by Mona Brookes

Drawing on the Right Side of the Brain
by Betty Edwards

MATH

Math-U-See
Steve Demme Multi-sensory math program based on Build-Write-Say. Beginning through advanced levels of math.www.mathusee.com.

Key Mathematics
By Steven Rasmussen and David Rasmussen. An inexpensive series of workbooks to focus on specific basic skills areas: fractions, decimals, algebra, geometry, measurement, metrics. www.keycurriculum.com

Multiplication and Division
Computer Program written by my husband Karl Kulp.

LANGUAGE

Reading Works and Grammar Works
Jay and Jeanne Patterson RR2 Box 318, Henning, MN 56551 Multi-sensory step-by-step program for teaching your child to write, spell, read and do grammar. Based on *The Writing Road to Reading* by Romalda Spalding.

New Practice Readers
Phoenix Learning Resources. Graded readers for older students.

Bring Classics to Life
Academic Therapy has a wide selection of books for older struggling readers to help make reading fun. In additions to the classic series they have other areas of interest including mysteries and sports. www.academictherapy.com

McCall-Crabbs Comprehension Connections
Book series of on page stories to build and test reading comprehension. Spalding Education Foundation, 2814 W Bell Road, Suite 1405, Phoenix, Arizona 85053. (602) 866-7801 email: spalding@neta.com

Pathway Readers
Amish based readers that are black and white with easy to see text. Stories are wholesome - children are expected to obey and respect their parents and still have fun. Readers to 8th grade.

VISION

CVA, Classroom Visual Activities
A Manual to Enhance the Development of Visual Skills.by Regina G. Richards. Academic Therapy Publications. www.academictherapy.com

MAZES & PUZZLES

Dover Publications
has hundred of books the right size and reasonable priced. In addition they have wonderful paper dolls, paper models and realistic coloring books. www.doverpublications.com

HEALTH

The Complete Family Guide to Healthy Living
Dorling Kindersley books are wonderful to teach with and this book has been excellent in developing a health program for Liz.

Recovery 101: Lessons for Young Adults and the Young at Heart
Linda A. Meyer, PhD (370 pages)

MUSIC

Suzuki Music
A listening based music program designed for young children and very adaptable to children with special needs.

NUTRITION

Ancient Harvest Quinoa
Quinoa is an ancient grain of the Inca's. a fun substitute for ready made pasta. www.quinoa.bigstep.com

Omega Nutrition
Organic oils and health care products. www.omeganutrition.com

APPENDIX 5
FASD RESOURCES FOR FAMILIES
DEVELOPMENTAL SKILLS

It is my hope, that by providing these developmental outlines in one location, professionals with more skills and experience than I can utilize them in developing activities and programs for our special youth. Persons with brain injury follow the same developmental path as a normal person. It is on a different timeline. Thank you to the professionals who have compiled this developmental information. While ages have been designated as developmental milestones, I have chosen not to include them on the following pages.

Table of Contents:

THANK YOU TO THE PIONEERS

Appendix 5 is dedicated to the pioneers of developmental profile work. I am sure I have missed many talented and skilled people who also have shed insight into helping our special children. This is a work in progress and it will take the knowledge and love of many professionals in many areas of expertise. Children who have been prenatally exposed to alcohol have many areas needing remediation.

If we all join hands and share.

If we lay down our egos and

merge the power of our hearts and minds.

Then perhaps Liz's dream can come true.

"Mom, I want 95% percent of people affected with prenatal exposure to alcohol to be able to be happy and live successful lives. Not the 10% we have today."

Liz Kulp
January 2000

PRIMARY NEUROLOGICALLY-BASED CHARACTERISTICS ASSOCIATED WITH FASD

by Diane Malbin

Reframed interpretations and improvements resulting from application of alternative intervention.

When behaviors are understood as reflecting an underlying organic condition, interventions provide appropriate support and reduce frustration. Integrating understanding of this possible role of neuropathology in presenting behaviors dictates a different perception of the meaning of behaviors, and expands the range of interventions. The theme is 'trying differently', rather than 'harder.'

Common Traits Neuropathology	What you need to think. Reframed interpretation	What you can do Outcome adaptations
Memory problems	Understand frustration, fears	Provide external cues to help reduce fears
Forgetful	Identify poor short term memory	External supports, cues Build on strengths
Inconsistent performance	Recognize "off" days as normal	Understand, support, create flexible options
Slow cognitive pace	Understand need for adequate time	Provide adequate time for completion to increase success and reduce frustration
"Gaps", talks the talk, but can't walk the walk	Understand neurological disconnects	Revise teaching options Use task analysis to break into smaller steps
Can't link words with feelings	Recognize frustration, isolation	Alternative approaches e.g. art, music, dance to improve communication.

DV Malbin 1997

Common Traits Neuropathology	What you need to think. Reframed interpretation	What you can do Outcome adaptations
Fatigue	Rethink how behaviors show physical exhaustion	Adapt work schedule, load
Decodes, doesn't understand	See 'gap' between apparent and actual abilities	Check for congruence between words and acts
Confabulates	Understand attempt to fill in blanks	Use concrete language
May not generalize	See difficulty forming links and making associations	Reteach concepts in all different environments
Difficulty with abstractions, money, math, time	Concrete, literal thinker	Provide assistive technology (calculator, digital watch with alarm or pager for cuing)
Poor planning, sequencing	See inability to 'connect the dots'	Create structure
Difficulty predicting outcomes	May not understand consequences	Provide safety, prevent need for punishment
Impulsive, suggestible	Identify physically-based response	Recognize 'triggers' provide safeguards
Acts young for age	Recognize behaviors dysmaturity	Adjust expectations to meet developmental level Prevent burnout
Socially 'inappropriate'	Understand as neurologically based	"Think younger" model expected behaviors
Perseverative	Consider behavior as physically-based unmet need	Understand source, address underlying need
Physically oversensitive	Understand as neurologically-based	Adapt environments (clothing, fluorescent lights, noise, others)

DV Malbin 1997

THE FACE OF FETAL ALCOHOL SYNDROME

Features on the left side of the illustration are considered difinitive of FAS. Characteristics on the right side are associated with FAS, but not enough to determine the presence of the syndrome. These facial features only occur during specific days in pregnancy. If a mother does not drink at that time the discriminating FAS features will not appear.

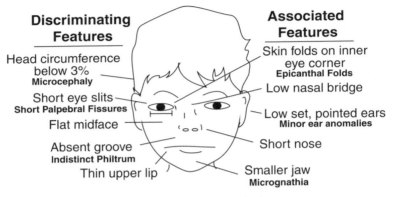

Discriminating Features

Head circumference below 3%
Microcephaly

Short eye slits
Short Palpebral Fissures

Flat midface

Absent groove
Indistinct Philtrum

Thin upper lip

Associated Features

Skin folds on inner eye corner
Epicanthal Folds

Low nasal bridge

Low set, pointed ears
Minor ear anomalies

Short nose

Smaller jaw
Micrognathia

In the young child. Streissguth and Little (1984)

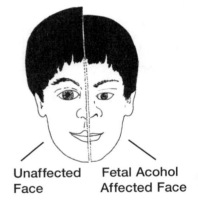

FAS/FAE "Age Appropriate" Timelines

The gap between developmental age and actual age widens during adolescence.

EXPRESSIVE LANGUAGE 20 YEARS	COMPRE-HENSION 6 YEARS	SOCIAL SKILLS 7 YEARS	MONEY & TIME 8 YEARS	READING SKILLS 16 YEARS	LIVING SKILLS 11 YEARS	EMOTIONS 6 YEARS

ACTUAL AGE 18 YEARS
PHYSICAL MATURITY 18 YEARS

Unaffected Face   Fetal Acohol Affected Face

Animal studies have shown alcohol exposure during the 20th or 21st day of conception to cause distinctive facial features. (Ed Riley, PhD). Central Nervous System damage can occur throughout pregnancy. (Ann Streissguth, PhD). If mom is not drinking during that time the baby will have a normal looking face.

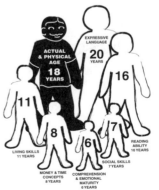

ACTUAL & PHYSICAL AGE **18** YEARS

EXPRESSIVE LANGUAGE **20** YEARS

16

11

8

6

7

LIVING SKILLS 11 YEARS

MONEY & TIME CONCEPTS 8 YEARS

COMPREHENSION & EMOTIONAL MATURITY 6 YEARS

READING ABILITY 16 YEARS

SOCIAL SKILLS 7 YEARS

HANDLE MODEL

Sensory-Motor Interdependency & Interaction
The Substrata of Mental Processing

Interhemispheric Integration

Lateralization
Dominance = file system
Laterality = central
computer control

Differentiation
Ability to move
one muscle or
a group alone.

Attentional
Priorities

Reading
Math
Spatial/Temporal
Orientation
(general)
Written
Expressive
Language
Oral
Expressive
Language
Visual
Perception
Constancy
Receptive
Language
Visual/Spatial
Integration
Auditory/Visual
Integration
Visual/Motor
Integration
Auditory/Linguistic
Integration
Binocularity
Auditory
Sequencing
Light Vision
Oral
Motor
Ocular
Motility
Audition Sound
Proprioception Body in Space
Muscle
Tone
Kinesthesia
Vestibular
Functions
Tactility Touch
Taste Gustation
Intuition
Ecosystem
Odor Olfaction
Maturation
Time, Nutrition

© 1992 Judith Bluestone

SENSORY INPUT				MOTOR INPUT		
VISUAL	**AUDITORY**	**TACTILE**		**MOBILITY**	**LANGUAGE**	**MANUAL**
Reading Ability to read 2nd grade material, 2nd grade math, Laterality noted.	**Understanding** Further understanding of language and abstract concepts. Laterality noted.	**Identify feel** Tactile identification of heads and tails of coins. Laterality noted.	7	**Walking** Skilled activities. Laterality noted.	**Talking** Use of 2nd grade vocabulary with good sentence structure	**Writing** Writing to 2nd grade level. Laterality noted.
Ability to identify symbols within experience.	Beginning understanding of language and abstract.	Tactile differentiation of miniature objects.	6	Walking and running in non aberrated cross pattern	5-8 word sentences with good articulation.	Efficient performance of bimanual tasks.
Ability to discriminate dissimilar and similar pictures.	Understanding 25 words	Tactile differentiation of medium size objects	5	Walking with arms held below the waist	25 words of speech and several 2 word couplets.	Bilateral and simultaneous cortical opposition.
Ability to converge eyes, simple depth perception.	Consistent ability to understand 2 words.	Tactile ability to discriminate 3rd dimension. Differentiate large objects and turn pages.	4	Walking unassisted without pattern for 10 steps.	Spontaneous use of 2 words.	Cortical opposition of either hand.
Vertical tracking, detail perception	Awareness of meaningful change in tonality	Perceiving and responding to gnostic separation. Ticklish.	3	Non-aberrated cross pattern creeping.	Meaningful and goal directed sounds with good tonality.	Volitional prehensile grasp.
Horizontal tracking, outline perception.	Consistent ability to react to threatening sounds.	Natural reaction to pain stimuli.	2	Non-aberrated cross pattern crawling.	Consistent vital crying in response to threatening sounds or events.	Ability to release object grasped.
Pupilary response. **Light reflex**	Responses to sudden loud noise. **Startle reflex**	**Babinski reflex**	1	Random motion of arms and legs **Move reflex**	Birth cry present. **Reflex birth cry**	Reflex ability to grasp object. **Grasp**

The research of Glenn Doman, *What To Do About Your Brain Injured Child* (1994) provided us a wealth of direction in developing a program to help Liz's neurological age begin to reach her chronological age, in addition to help develop the Hager Developmental Vortex.

THE OTENGENCY OF NEUROLOGICAL FUNCTIONS

Brain Stage	12 CORTEX	11 CORTEX	10 CORTEX
Avg Time Frame	6 years to Peer Level CONCEPTION Uniquely human physical and intellectual skills	5 years to 6 years CONCEPTION Uniquely human physical and intellectual skills	4 years to 5 years CONCEPTION Uniquely human physical and intellectual skills
VISION	All visual abilities equal to or above peers, consistent with dominant hemisphere.	Reading books.	Reading initial books.
AUDITORY	All auditory abilities equal to or above peers, consistent with dominant hemisphere.	Sophisticated concept of time and space.	Conception of sophisticated abstract language.
TACTILE	All tactile abilities equal to or above peers, consistent with dominant hemisphere.	Sophisticated stereognosis Sophisticated proprioception.	Concepts of solidity.
MOBILITY	All motor abilities equal to or above peers, consistent with dominant hemisphere.	Hop, skip, jump and other sophisticated skills.	Run and walk in complete cross pattern.
LANGUAGE	All language abilities equal to or above peers.	Sophisticated ability to express abstract thought.	Ability to participate in organized conversation. Proper articulation
MANUAL	All manual and writing abilities equal to or above peers, consistent with dominant hemisphere.	Writing many word spontaneously.	Writing words spontaneously.

AFFERENT SENSORY PATHWAYS — VISION, AUDITORY, TACTILE
EFFERENT MOTOR PATHWAYS — MOBILITY, LANGUAGE, MANUAL

Brain Stage	9 CORTEX	8 CORTEX	7 CORTEX
Avg Time Frame	3 years to 4 years CONCEPTION Uniquely human physical and intellectual skills	2 years to 3 years CONCEPTION Uniquely human physical and intellectual skills	18 months to 2 years CONCEPTION Uniquely human physical and intellectual skills
VISION	Reading sentences.	Reading phrases. Reading many words.	Reading several words. Identifying complex symbols.
AUDITORY	Conception of grammatical and idiomatic language.	Sophisticated concept of time and space.	Comprehension of basic directions.
TACTILE	Concepts of shape.	Comprehension of wordly information leading to concept of time and space	Comprehension of texture.
MOBILITY	Initial walking in cross pattern.	Walk and run with arms down, without cross pattern	Run and walk in complete cross pattern.
LANGUAGE	Structured sentences. Advancing vocabulary.	Initial sentences. Many phrases.	Initial phrases. Many new words.
MANUAL	Reproducing symbols and words.	Sophisticated bi-manual skills.	Bilateral simultaneous cortical opposition.

AFFERENT SENSORY PATHWAYS — VISION, AUDITORY, TACTILE
EFFERENT MOTOR PATHWAYS — MOBILITY, LANGUAGE, MANUAL

Sandler and Brown, 1980

We are indebted to the pioneering work of Sandler and Brown in helping us develop the Hager Developmental Profile and to A Chance to Grow School in Minneapolis for introducing us to this model.

Brain Stage	6 CORTEX	5 CORTEX	4 MIDBRAIN
Avg Time Frame	12 months to 18 months CONCEPTION Uniquely human physical and intellectual skills	9 months to 12 months CONCEPTION Uniquely human physical and intellectual skills	6 months to 9 months APPRECIATION MEANINGFUL
VISION	Complete convergence of vision. Identifying simple abstracts.	Initial binocularity.	Appreciation of fine detail. Seeing gross detail.
AUDITORY	Understanding many words and phrases.	Understanding several single words.	Appreciation of environmental sounds.
TACTILE	Initial stereognosis	Awareness of third dimension.	Proprioceptive ability as related to balance and space. Gnostic sensation.
MOBILITY	Walk with arms in primitive balance role. Free style. Cruising.	Functional creeping, culmination in cross-pattern. Pull to stand with fixed support.	Initial creeping. Assume and maintain quadruped position.
LANGUAGE	Structured sentences. Advancing vocabulary.	Word like sounds.	Range of expressive and meaningful sounds.
MANUAL	Primitive use of tools. Initial bimanual function.	Bilateral cortical opposition. Unilateral cortical opposition.	Mature bilateral prehensile grasp.

AFFERENT SENSORY PATHWAYS (VISION, AUDITORY, TACTILE)
EFFERENT MOTOR PATHWAYS (MOBILITY, LANGUAGE, MANUAL)

Brain Stage	3 MIDBRAIN	2 PONS	1 MEDULA (SPINAL CORD)
Avg Time Frame	3 months to 6 months APPRECIATION MEANINGFUL	Birth to 3 months PERCEPTION VITAL	BIRTH RECEPTION REFLEX
VISION	Seeing gross detail. Unified ocular movement.	Biocular outline perception.	Pupillary reflex.
AUDITORY	Localization of sounds.	Response to threatening sounds. Initial perception of sounds.	Startle response.
TACTILE	Localization of sensation	Awareness of temperature and discomfort. Early proprioception. Vital sensation.	Babinski.
MOBILITY	Functional crawling cummulating in cross pattern.	Initial crawling.	Complete movement of all extremeties
LANGUAGE	Experimental use of sounds.	Vital sounds.	Birth cry.
MANUAL	Initial prehensile grasp.	Bilateral vital release.	Bilateral grasp reflex.

AFFERENT SENSORY PATHWAYS (VISION, AUDITORY, TACTILE)
EFFERENT MOTOR PATHWAYS (MOBILITY, LANGUAGE, MANUAL)

Sandler and Brown, 1980

We are indebted to the pioneering work of Sandler and Brown in helping us develop the Hager Developmental Profile and to A Chance to Grow School in Minneapolis for introducing us to this model.

Stages of Development

(Carol Stumpf, CFS
Tamara Piwen, CFW)

1. **Identify** make a list of skills that your child needs to develop. For each one write down a fun activity to help the child develop that skill.

2. **Introduce** the skill through play, discussion and modeling of the desired response.

3. **Cue** the child what to say and do regarding the new skill.

4. **Self-talk** have the child cue themselves with self-talk.

5. **Roleplay** practice the skill through modeling and role play.

6. **Reinforce** the new skill through practice.

7. **Teach** the child to reinforce himself through self-talk.

8. **Provide opportunity** for the reinforcement of the skill in daily play.

Steps of Skill Development

(Carol Stumpf, CFS
Tamara Piwen, CFW)

1. **Teach** the child to recognize their negative response to a problem or situation.

2. **Show** them that their response is NOT beneficial to them ("How did it work for you?")

3. **Break Down** the response into manageable parts.

4. **Learn** new ways to respond to the problem.

5. **Decide** to stop acting in ways that hurt themselves and others.

6. **Choose** a more healthy response.

7. **Learn** to recognize when a situation arises or will arise.

8. **PRACTICE** new responses. Practice. Practice. Practice.

9. **Expect initial** partial or complete failure.

10. **Celebrate** small successes.

Promoting Play for Children

(Carol Stumpf, CFS
Tamara Piwen, CFW)

Pick and choose those that will work best for your child. Not all will work with all children.

1. **Participate** there is no plaything more interesting than an adult. Adult participation enriches the experience for the child.

2. **Importance** play is the equivalent to work for a child.

3. **Variety** give the child a variety of different ways to play and learn.

4. **Safety** provide a safe play area and safe play materials.

5. **Rules** Eliminate the amount of rules needed for play.

6. **Media** make thoughtful choices to children's media. Preview media you are unsure of. Read the warning restrictions.

7. **Match the developmental and emotional age of the child** not the chronological age.

Blom's Taxonomy Hierarchy Thinking Skills

(Benjamin Blom)

LOWER LEVEL THINKING

1. Knowledge
- **recognition**
- **recall)**

To remember information you have learned. **Remembering** facts, terms, definitions, concepts, principles.

What? Who? – list, name, define, describe, order, recite, list, record, recall, label, reproduce, match, repeat, underline, state, recognize, relate.

By – Books, facts, events, TV, radio, newspapers, magazines, films, tapes, CD's and movies

2. Comprehension
- **translation**
- **interpretation**
- **extrapolation**

To understand the meaning of things learned.

Explain. How? Why? – interpret, summarize, give examples, predict, translate, arrange, locate, indicate, describe, restate, sort, classify, translate, express, discuss, extrapolate.

By – Diagrams, puzzles, log stories, games, journal, reports, task cards, illustrations, drawings

3. Application
- **implication**

Using information in a new way to solve a problem.

Apply – compute, solve, modify, construct, sketch, practice, illustrate, measure, schedule, choose, use, demonstrate, prepare, operate.

By – diagrams, model illustrations, photographs, sculpture, model stories, diorama, scrapbook, puzzles, mobile, collect, map

HIGHER LEVEL THINKING

4. Analysis
- **elements**
- **relationship**
- **organization**

To break down knowledge into parts and show relationships among those parts. Physical, historical, functional descriptions

Examine. How? What? – analyze, diagram, question, appraise, test, calculate, discriminate, distinguish, categorize, compare, criticize, contrast, experiment, inventory.

By – graphs, charts, surveys, events, diagrams, objects, reports, commercials, puzzles, questionnaires.

5. Synthesis
- **unique communicate**
- **plan or set**
- **abstract relations**

To produce something original from elements and components of previous knowledge. To bring together.

Organize. Bring together – arrange, design, prepare, assemble, formulate, propose, collect, manage, set up, compose, synthesize, create, plan, write, construct, modify, conduct.

By – stories, news, articles, poems, games, magazines, TV shows, cartoons, recipes, plays, songs, machines, puppet shows, hypothesis, advertisements

6. Evaluation
- **internal evidence** (logical accuracy, consistency)
- **external evidence** (application of external criteria)

To make judgments based on pre-established criteria.

Support. Why? Why not? – appraise, estimate, select, argue, evaluate, assess, judge, value, attack, predict, score, compare, rate, defend.

By – polls, group letters, surveys, recommendations, evaluations, panels, simulations, discussions, news items, court trials.

Blom's Taxonomy allowed us to help Liz answer questions and figure things out without excessive frustration.

Visual Processing

(Deborah Zelinksy,
Mind Eye Connection)

1. **Orientation of body to time and place** relies on inner ear signals calibrated to gravity and reflexive eye movements. Jumprope, jacks, martial arts, gymnastics, dancing.

2. **Organizing space and time** awareness of movement, location, size, shape, color, detail, depth perception, laterality, directionality.

3. **Selective attention** deciding on a target to concentrate on and allowing the rest to be background.

4. **Visual memory recognition** being able to recognize something in front of you that you have seen before.

5. **Visual memory recall** being able to recall from memory something you have seen.

6. **Usage of memory**

7. **Visualization** being able to create something in your mind using more than one memory.

8. **Creativity** being able to create in your mind new information with previous memories.

Vision

1. **Balance – vestibular** the ability to maintain an upright position without falling over. Sit, stand, balance one foot, hop one foot, skip.

2. **Gross motor** large muscle movements. Roll over, crawl and creep, sit, pull to stand, walk, run, pedal trike, walk up and down stairs alternate feet, ride two wheel bike without training wheels.

3. **Fine motor** small muscle movement. Transfer object hand to hand, grasp object, pincer grasp, throw objects, scribbles, copies circles, buttons clothes, catches ball.

4. **Bilateral coordination** the ability to be aware of and use both sides of the body separately and together. Important in balance, gross motor coordination and directional sense

5. **Visual acuity** clearness of vision

6. **Eye movements** tracking, voluntary or induced movements

  a, **Gross pursuits** – follow a moving target.

  b. **Fine pursuits** – mazes, smooth eye movements to follow a printed target.

  c. **Gross Saccades** – abrupt voluntary shift in fixation. To move eyes from chalkboard to desk.

  d. **Fine Saccades** – abrupt voluntary shifting of eyes along a line of print in book with a rapid and accurate return to the next line.

7. **Eye teaming** using both eyes together and at the same to accurately determine what is seen.

  a. **Fusion** – two eyes see only one image.

  b. **Lateral and Vertical posture** – no abnormal deviation in, out, up, down,

  c. **Stereo vision** – being able to use both eyes together in 3-D

8. **Accommodation** focusing. Being able to maintain a clear picture when shifting form one distance to another (desk to chalkboard)

9. **Laterality and Directionality** Internal and external spatial concepts such as right, left, up, down, **Laterality** being aware of internal coordinated right, left, up, down on self. **Directionality** being able to project this set of coordinates into space. (Letters, forms, numbers)

10. **Visual analysis skills** used in recognition, recall and manipulation of visual information.

11. **Visual motor integration** integrate vision system with motor system.

12. **Auditory Visual integration** integrate vision with auditory system.

Functional Developmental Growth

(Dr. Stanley Greenspan
www.stanleygreenspan.com)

Symbolic play and conversation is the safe way to practice, reenact, understand and master the full range of emotional ideas and experiences.

1. **Regulation and attention** Interest in all the sensations of the world, focuses and attends to sights and sound remaining calm. Help child look, listen, move, respond and calm down.

2. **Engaging in relationships** Emotional relating, expressiveness and signaling. Shows pleasure and delight. Play with child to encourage pleasure and delight.

3. **Interacts purposefully and two way communication** Child initiates communication and can exchange communication with another person. Follow your child's lead to exchange gestures, emotional interests about the child's ideas. Join child in perseverative play. Do not treat avoidance or "no" as a rejection. Help your child deal with anxiety–separation, fear, getting hurt, loss, etc – using gestures and problem solving. Play toddler games peek-a-boo, I'm going to get you. Expand, expand, expand, play dumb, make the wrong moves do whatever it takes to keep the interaction going. Use sensory-motor play – bouncing, tickling, swinging and so on – to elicit pleasure.

Pursue pleasure over other behaviors and do not interrupt pleasurable experience. Try to be as accepting of your child's anger and protests as you are with his more positive behaviors.

4a. **Simple problem solving and forms a sense of self** Child can show you what he needs or wants - point to door or toy.

4b. **Complex problem solving and forms a sense of self** Child can use a continuous flow of gestures to get needs met and can copy your words or actions

5a. **Creating Ideas (words and symbols) to convey intentions and feelings** Child can imitate familiar pretend action, feed or hug a doll. Interact with child's play and encourage conversation. Have props available to allow child to build a symbolic world. Allow your child to discover what is real and what is not. Respond to the child's real desires with pretend actions. If the child is thirsty offer an empty tea cup and

invite to a party. If the child lies down on the floor, cover with a blanket and sing a lullaby. Get some small figure that can represent people your child knows and role play with them. Use puppets. When the child climbs on the sofa pretend it is a mountain or when the child slides down a slide pretend she is sliding into the ocean and watch out for fish. Expand as long as you can.

5b. **Creating Ideas (words and symbols) beyond expressing basic needs** Creative play becomes more elaborate. Engage child in long conversations about desires, interests and complaints. Use gestures as props. Substitute one object for another when doing pretend play - pretend the ball is a cake and the spoon is a candle. As you play elaborate on intentions – who is the driver, where are we going, when will we get there, who will we see or what will we do. Insert obstacles into the pretend play, a truck blocks the road and the child must negotiate to get around the truck. You get into an accident. A doll falls and needs a

Stages of Change
*(Carol Stumpf, CFS
Tamara Piwen, CFW)*

doctor. Create symbolic solutions for situations. Talk directly to the cars or dolls and become a role player. Cry when a doll gets hurt, cheer when a car wins the race. Match your tone of voice to the situation. Use urgency and whisper to the child encouraging him. Use play to help child understand situations which may have frightened her. Work on reality and fantasy. Drama, drama, drama.

6a: Creates logical bridges between ideas

Child can use words or symbols to express and explain likes and dislikes. Can engage in pretend play with another person. Good guys and bad guys. Let your child be the director, play needs not to be realistic but you can encourage logic. Focus on the pretend play – what characters do we need, what props, what is the problem, what will be the beginning, what will be in the middle and what will be at the end. Make up different tones for the characters - one may have a spooky, mean or angry voice, one may have a childlike voice and one may be an old grandpa. Discuss with your

child good guy/bad guy, separation/loss, and any other emotion the child may need to work on – anger, jealousy, fear, closeness, bossiness, competition. Talk about ideas and feelings of these characters as you participate in the drama and later as you interact in normal daily living.

6b: Creates logical ideas between three or more emotional ideas

Child can explain reasons for desire or behavior. Child can make logical conversation with three or more give and take situations about a variety of topics.

Reading Dr. Stanley Greenspan's books **The Child With Special Needs, Building Healthy Minds** *and* **The Challenging Child** *will provide you with ideas and insight to help your child who has been prenatally exposed to alcohol. Dr. Stanley Greenspan's ideas and floortime opened the door to Liz's imagination and fantasy role play. We began at level one and reprocessed all the steps in a manner that a teen could enjoy.*

1. **Pre-contemplation** The young person is unaware or under aware of their problem and does not intend to change.

2. **Contemplation** The child becomes aware of the problem and gives serious thought about changing behavior.

3. **Preparation** The child begins to have strong intentions about change for the future.

4. **Action** The child sets a standard and begins to modify behavior to overcome problems.

5. **Maintenance** The child works to keep behavior to the standard that he has set. Much recognition and reinforcement will be needed as the child struggles to maintain gains in positive behavior. Behavior change will continue only if the environment encourages and supports the child's efforts.

Language Development *(Laureate's Linguistic Hierarchy www.laureatelearning.com)*

1. Interpreted communication

Child does not understand any words. Begins to focus on caregiver's speech. Cries, coos, and expressions are interpreted by caregiver.

2. Intentional Communication
Expresses intent primarily through eye gaze. Comprehension of words as abstract concepts emerges. Complex gaze coupling develops.

3. Single words

Comprehends objects names as symbols of basic categories, understands verbs, uses single words in combination of gestures and environment to communicate.

4. Word combinations

Child is using 150-200 words. Comprehends a core vocabulary. Two-word combinations emerge. Word combinations describe here and now environmental events.

5. Early Syntax

Short simple sentences. Combining words but not talking in sentences - lacks grammatical refinement and complexity. Comprehension goes beyond the here and now.

6. Syntax Mastery

Speaks in sentences but makes grammatical errors. Uses simple and complex sentences. Masters most grammatical constructions. Limited comprehension about abstract relationships among words.

7. Complete Generative Grammar

Learning to read and write, masters irregular verb form.

Visit

www.laureatelearning.com for developmental language software to help your child.

Social Language

(Gesell)
1. **Small sounds,** coos, vocalizes, listens, speaks
2. **Identifies objects,** verbs, asks "why?", short sentences.
3. **Combines** talking and eating, complete sentences, imaginative, dramatic
4. **Language** major form of communication
5. Verbal **language predominates**

Self Talk

(Lawrence Kohlberg)
1. **Self entertainment,** repeat words and rhymes
2. **Own voice** – talk to the air about yourself
3. **Own voice** – questions about self and answer them
4. Begin **internal thoughts** and mouth words
5. **Inner dialogue** is entirely silent.

Auditory Processing Levels

1. **Auditory object recognition** speech sounds, words, melodies, familiar sounds
2. **Complex feature detectors** phonetic features, owl mating calls, bullfrog mating calls
3. **Simple feature detectors** timbre, pitch, loudness.

Many children who have been exposed prenatally to alcohol appear to have high functioning verbal skills.

Auditory Processing
(Swain)

1. Sensation
Ability to identify the presence of sound.

2. Discrimination
Determining differences in sounds – essential in reading, spelling and following directions.

3. Localization
Ability to determine the origin of the acoustic signal.

4. Auditory attention
The ability to direct and sustain attention to auditory stimuli.

5. Auditory figure-ground
The ability to identify signal over other signals.

6. Auditory discrimination
Necessary to discriminate among words and sounds that are similar.

7. Auditory closure
The ability to understand the whole word or message when a part is missing.

8. Auditory synthesis
The ability to blend isolated phonemes into words.

9. Auditory analysis
The ability to identify phonemes or morphemes in words.

10. Auditory association
The attachment of meaning.

11. Auditory memory
The recall of the acoustic signal after it has been labeled and stored and then recalled.

Therapeutic Listening Programs: Tomatis Method, Samonas, The Listening Program, Listening Ears

Language Development
(New Visions - Moriss)

1. Pre-speech
Play with sounds and voice before saying first word. The babbling voice of a baby reflects the timing and intonations of its caregiver. Learn to express joy, excitement, pain, disappointment through vocal play and movement. Movement and speech are closely linked. Infants initially vocalize primarily when moving. Dynamic stability and mobility create the foundation for respiratory-phonatory-articulatory competence.

Marvelous Mouth Music recordings allow a child to go back to pre-speech in the context of musical fun.

Visit: www.new-vis.com

Speech production Levels of difficulty:
(New Visions - Moriss)

1. **Spontaneous sounds**
2. **Emotional sounds**
   (cry, laugh, cough)
3. **Environmental sounds**
   (motor puh, puh)
4. **Animal sounds**
   (moo/cow)
5. **Short sounds**
   require less breathing
6. **Same consonants**
   (bah, bah, bah)
7. **Mixed consonants**
   (bah-boo-bee)
8. **Simple contact of lips**
   (m, p, b, w)
9. **Front of tongue**
   (t, d, n)
10. **Back of tongue**
    (k, g, ng)
11. **Gentle contact of teeth and lip** (f, v)
12. **Higher level of coordination between tongue, lip and jaw movement**
    (s, sh, z, zh, ch, j, th, l, r)
13. **Consonant blends***
    beginning of words (fl, st, sl, pr)
14. **Consonant blends***
    end of words (fl, st, sl, pr)

* New Visions does not separate these

Developmental Tasks
(Robert Havighurst)

1. Infancy & Early Childhood
Learn to walk, talk, eat, control elimination; learn sex differences, modesty, social language, physical reality, begin to distinguish right from wrong, forming concepts, begin to develop a conscience.

2. Middle Childhood
Learn physical skills to achieve competency in games, activities, getting along with peers, healthy attitude about self, learn appropriate sexual and social roles, develop skills in reading, writing, math, develop perceptions of everyday life and incorporate abstract concepts, develop a sense of conscience, morality, and values, begin to achieve personal independence, develop social attitudes toward groups and institutions.

3. Adolescence
Achieving more mature relations with peers of both sexes and social and sexual roles, learning to accept ones body and protect it effectively and satisfactorily, achieving emotional independence from parents and other adults, preparing for adult life and economic independence, acquire a set of values and ethics, develop an ideology and social responsibility.

4. Early Adulthood
Selecting and learning to live with a mate, deciding to begin or not begin a family, manage a home, begin employment, taking on civic responsibility, and engage in congenial social group activities.

5. Middle Age
Assisting adolescents in becoming responsible, productive adults, achieving adult social and civic responsibility, reaching and maintaining satisfactory career performance, develop adult leisure activities, committing oneself to an intimate relationship, accepting and adjusting to physiological changes in midlife, and adjusting to aging parents.

6. Later Maturity
Adjusting to decreasing physical strength and health, retirement, and reduced income, and the death of one's spouse, establishing explicit affiliations with peers, adopting/ adapting social roles in a flexible way, and establishing satisfactory physical living arrangements.

Play
(Bruce Perry)

1. Brainstem
Establish self-regulation
- Peek-a-Boo
- Tactile Play
- Taste Play

2. Midbrain
Sensory-motor integration
- Large Motor
- Fine Motor
- Music
- Rhythm
- Cadence
- Finger Play*

3. Limbic
Facilitate social-emotional
- Win-lose
- Teams
- Turns
- Sharing

4. Cortical
Encourage abstract thoughts
- Humor
- Games
- Arts
- Crafts
- Language

* Perry places finger plays in Brainstem, but it is basically a 7-11 month midbrain function.

Faith Stages
(Fowler)
1. **Intuitive**
2. **Mythical**
3. **Synthetic**
4. **Reflective**
5. **Conjunctive**
6. **Universalizing**

Social Stages of Play

(Carol Stumpf, CFS
Tamara Piwen, CFW)

1. **Unoccupied** Children watch others at play, but do not enter play.

2. **Onlooker** Children watch others play, may talk to them or ask questions, and move closer to the group.

3. **Solitary** The child plays alone with materials even if others are sharing the same area. He doesn't change his play or interact with others.

4. **Parallel** A child materials like those nearby.The child does not try to influence the other children's activities. She plays beside rather than with the other children.

5. **Associative** Common activities occur between children. They may exchange materials. Everyone in the group does similar things, but there are no specific roles or shared goals.

6. **Cooperative** Children cooperative with others in the group to construct or produce something

Occupational

(American Occupational
Therapy Association)

1. **Occupational Performance Enablers** Subskills: Sensory Perception, Sensory Integration, Motor Coordination, Psychosocial and Psychodynamic Responses, Sociocultural Development, Social Language Responses.

2. **Activities and Tasks of Occupational Performance** Skill areas: Self-care/Self-maintenance, Play/Leisure, Work/Education, and Rest/Relaxation.

3. **Occupational Roles** Worker, Student, Volunteer, Homemaker, Parent, Son, Daughter, Mate, Sibling, Peer, Best Friend/Chum

Daily Living

(Gesell)

1. Recognizes bottle, holds spoon, holds glass, controls bowel

2. Feeds self, helps undress, recognizes simple tunes, no longer wets at night

3. Laces shoes, cuts with scissors, toilets independently, helps set table.

4. Enjoys dressing up, learns value of money, responsible for grooming

5. Interest in earning money

6. Concern for personal grooming, mate, family.

7. Adjusting to changes of middle age.

8. Adjusting to changes after middle age.

Physical/Motor

(Gesell)

1. **Reflexes to posture** Head sags, fisting, gross motion, walking, climbing

2. **Balance** Runs, balances, hand preference, coordination

3. **Coordination**, more graceful muscles develop, skills develop

4. **Energy** development, skill practice to attain proficiency

5. **Rapid growth**, poor posture, awkwardness

6. **Maintenance** Growth established and maintained

7. **Middle Age** Alterations begin to occur in motor behavior, strength and endurance

8. **Older Age** Alterations in motor behavior, strength and endurance

Ego Development

(Erik Erikson)

1. Basic trust vs Mistrust

To mature an infant must acquire a sense of basic trust and overcome a sense of basic mistrust.
Socioemotional development dependent on building a solid foundation here.

2. Autonomy vs Shame and Doubt

As infants gain trust of their caregiver and the environment, they discover they can exert control. They discover a sense of automony and develop will.

3. Initiative vs Guilt

Conscious control of the environment enhances mastery and competence, resulting in a sense of initiative. A balance between initiative and passivity results.

4. Industry vs Inferiority

The determination to achieve mastery is a major theme of this phase of development. Acquiring a sense of mastery overcomes a sense of inferiority.

5. Identity vs Role Confusion

A sense of identity in adolescence signals mastery of childhood crisis. Identity of development is closely linked to mastery of skills and achievement of competence. Acquiring identity overcomes role confusion.

6. Intimacy vs Isolation (Young adult)

Acquiring a sense of intimacy in relationships reinforces affiliation and reduces isolation. Differentiation occurs in a persons pattern of development by choice, influences by socioeconomic expectations.

7. Generativity vs Stagnation (Maturity)

Acquiring a sense of generativity forestalls a sense of self-absorption stagnation. Generativity refers to society at large and the combination that the mature adult can offer the next generation in terms of "hope", virtue, and wisdom.

8. Ego Integrity vs Despair (Old Age)

Memory

(Dominic OBrien)

1. Sensory Memory

Raw information gathered from our senses – sight, hearing, taste, smell, touch. Unconscious level and almost immediately discarded. A tiny percentage is selected by the monitored process and sent to short-term memory.

2. Short-Term Memory

Active or working memory. Holds information 10-20 seconds. Vital to any activity that requires conscious thought. Can normally hold only 7 pieces of information simultaneously – numbers, shapes, words, images which are then replaced with new information. If such a memory is sufficiently powerful, surprise, due to intense concentration, repetition or emotion it can become long-term memory.

3. Long-Term Memory

Permanent or reference memory.
a. **Explicit** (declarative) names, things, recognize, facts, events, birth, death.
b. **Implicit** (procedural) acquired skills – ride bike, roller blade, ice skate.

Friends
(Zick Rubin)

1. Egocentric stage
Seek friends they can use, who have toys they want to play with or personal attribute they lack. Believe friends think the same way they do and become upset if it is not so. Friends are others who are simultaneously engaged in the same activity. Best friend lives the closest.

2. Need fulfillment stage
Friends meet a need away from family. Typically have trouble having more than one friendship. "You're not my friend, John is." Value friends as individuals, rather than for what they have or where they live.

3. Reciprocal stage
Friends are in pairs, group or cliques are networks of same sex pairs. Concerned with fairness, who does what for whom. Invitation for sleepover must receive an invitation for sleepover, sharing a treat must get a treat the next day.

4. Intimate stage
Passionate sharing of ideas, emotions, conflicts and problems. Concerned about the person behind the facade and his or her happiness.

Groups
(Lawrence Shapiro, PhD)

1. Like to be around groups of other children of **either sex**
2. Like to be around groups of children of **same sex.**
3. **Group membership** enhances confidence and skills, Scouts, baseball team.
4. **Secret clubs** to define who can and who cannot be a member.
5. **Same sex groups** talking about opposite sex. Pressure to conform and be like each other.

Compassion

1. **Outburst** Baby is self absorbed.
2. **Synergy** Baby sees another baby crying and cries too. One baby is angry (happy) and so it the next baby.
3. **Sympathy (with passion)** See another person and feel with the person.
4. **Compassion** See another person in distress and have passion to do something about it.
5. **Abstract compassion** Expand passion from people they know to include groups of people they haven't met. Outreach to homeless, hungry, etc. (Referred to as empathy also)

Morality
(Lawrence Kohlberg)

1. **Preconventional Morality** Emphasis on external controls, standard of others. Seeks to avoid punishment and receive rewards.
2. **Morality of Conventional Role Conformity** Begins internalizing environmental standards. Starts to exercise judgment on what is "good" and identify with roles of authority figures who are judged to be good.
3. **Morality of Anonymous Moral Principles** Control of conduct is internalized as to standards and reasoning.

Ego Stages
(Loevinger)
1. Presocial
2. Symbiotic
3. Impulsive
4. Conformist
5. Individualistic
6. Autonomy
7. Interindividual

Self Stages
(Kegan)
1. Incorporative
2. Impulsive
3. Imperial
4. Interpersonal
5. Institutional
6. Interindividual

Cognitive Development
(Jean Piaget)

1. Sensorimotor stage
Infants mature from primarily reflexive beings to more neuro-physiologically organized beings through play experiences and interpersonal interaction. They experiment by banging, biting and pulling on things to learn how their world behaves and how to interact with objects. They learn the existence of the world beyond themselves.

2. Preoperational stage
Child develops a representational system and uses symbols such as words to represent people, places and events. The child can ask for a cookie even though the cookie was not in sight. This is the beginning of being able to think beyond what you see, hear, touch, smell or taste and is the beginning of abstract ideas. Egocentrism is a factor in this stage.

3. Concrete Operations stage
Child begins to understand and use concepts to deal with the immediate environment and solve problems logically when related to actual events and objects. Conservation is a major cognitive skill learned at this stage – objects remain the same in different contexts as long as nothing is added or taken away. Reading and writing development allows for more sophisticated abstractions. Drawings can be used to show complex ideas. Empathy begins to emerge to allow for understanding of another person.

4. Formal Operations stage
Competence is achieved in abstract thinking and the ability to handle hypothetical situations, consider multiple possibilities and systematically solve problems. The child can sketch out an action play (like a diagram for a soccer play) and can visualize simple mechanical relationships.

Understanding of Effort vs Ability
(Lawrence Shapiro, PhD)

1. **Can Do** Children believe if they try harder they can succeed at almost anything.

2. **Focus** See that effort is only one part of success, innate ability is also important. They still focus on effort to be successful.

3. **Compensate** Aware that a person with less ability can compensate with more effort.

4. **Ability** alone is necessary to achieve.

5. **Adaptation** Aware that a person with less ability can compensate with more effort, adaptations or special training in some cass.

Violence Prevention Six Core Strengths
(Bruce D. Perry, MD, PhD)

1. **Attachment** - being a friend
2. **Self-regulation** - thinking before you act.
3. **Affiliation** - joining in
4. **Awareness** - thinking of others
5. **Tolerances** - accepting differences
6. **Respect** - respecting yourself and others

Jungian Stages
(Grant)

1. Random functions
2. One function dominates
3. Alternative two functions
4. Develop third function
5. Integrate shadow function
6. Four functions deliberate

Humor
(Paul McGhee)

1. Peek-a-boo, smiles, **physical comedy**
2. **Nonsense,** Physical incongruity (shoe on head, sock on nose), nonsense words
3. **Verbal statements,** misnaming something (calling daddy mommy)
4. **Knock, knock jokes,** riddles
5. Ready made **jokes and riddles,** may be sexual or aggressive in nature.
6. **Puns and double meanings.**

Mind Development
(Jean Piaget)

1. **Sensory-Motor:** playing with toys teaches us how objects behave and how we react to them.
2. **Pre-Operational:** Early experiences with language lay foundations for the representation of ideas as symbols, making the leap from written word to meaning.
3. **Concrete-Operational:** Begins to understand the experiences of others around us. Development of empathy opens new doors for learning.
4. **Formal Operational:** Math, word puzzles, sophisticated symbolic manipulation

Needs that Motivate Human Behavior
(Abraham Maslow)

1. **Biologica (Physiological) needs (primitive – survival)** act or action to instant reward, immediate gratification, hunger, thirst, emotional sustenance

2. **Safety needs** act or action to reward, some delay, need to feel secure and out of danger

3. **Belonging (Affiliation) needs to** act or action is enjoyed as much as reward, delayed gratification, belong, love and be accepted

4. **Esteem needs** act or action means more than reward, striving for achievement, competence, approval and recognition

5. **Intellectual (Cognitive) needs** quest for knowledge, understanding, push for exploration, personal growth and discovery, thinking, understanding.

6. **Aesthetic needs** Search for symmetry, order, beauty, sense of justice, helping others, giving, spiritual.

7. **Self-Actualization needs** drive toward self-fulfillment and realization of ones potential.

7. MY GIFT

6 SPIRITUAL
Religious beliefs, feelings, self expression, giving, expression of love, art, music, beauty, sense of justice

5 INTELLECTUAL
Self awareness, personal growth and discovery, learning, thinking, understanding

1-4 PHYSICAL WORLD
Touch, taste, feel, smell All things: clothes, cars, houses, money, drugs, alcohol, popularity, friends

Maslow Flow Chart

FASD RESOURCES FOR FAMILIES
BASIC BRAIN NUTRITION

This information is not intended as medical advice. It is intended to give you an initial knowledge of the types of nutrition to help a brain function. Proper nutritional fuel is often critical for a vulnerable or injured brain person.

PROTEINS are the building blocks of neurotransmitters. It is essential to eat enough protein in balanced amounts with fats and carbohydrates. The protein needs of each individual vary. Too much protein for some people can restrict 'brain protein.' Not enough protein will result in a protein deficit. There are many sources of protein and protein combinations to provide adequate protein sources. Proteins eaten alone on an empty stomach can pick up dopamine and acetylcholin nuerotransmitters.

COMBINATIONS OF COMPLEMENTARY PROTEIN SOURCES INCLUDE *pasta / cheese, bean soup / corn bread, rice / lentils or blackeyed peas, corn tortillas / beans, barley / cheddar cheese, zucchini / rice / tomatoes*

BEST PROTEIN RESOURCES *Fresh cold-water fish, low fat cottage cheese, free-range and drug free poultry, eggs, hard cheeses, low fat low lactose yogurt, beans, seeds, nuts. (organic and grass fed lean red meat contain rich sources of minerals, protein and B-group vitamins and though costly you may decide is worth the extra money).*

AMINO ACIDS AND ENZYMES

AMINO ACIDS are the building blocks of protein. There are over 20 different amino acids found in animals and humans. There are eight 'essential amino acids' from which we can make the rest of the aminos our bodies need. If we get enough of these essential eight, our nutritional needs for daily protein will be met.

ENZYMES are chemical catalysts that are needed to change chemicals into organs, cells and hormones. They are manufactured in the body from amino acids, plus vitamins and minerals. Without a particular enzyme, any one of thousands of chemical changes needed in the body won't operate. You need a balance of protein, vitamins and minerals to continue to manufacture enzymes. For example, take an elderly woman eating only white bread and tea for each meal or a teen eating only junkfood and sodas. Each day they are using up protein already in the body to rebuild cells. They are not adding any protein to the diet nor getting any real vitamins and minerals. Even if they suddenly start eating steak, milk and eggs poor nutrition leads to poorer nutrition their body has stopped producing 'protease' the enzyme needed to break down protein, lactase the enzyme to break down lactose, phosphatase to breakdown calcium and galactase to breakdown glacactase. In other words, she can no longer digest and utilize this food with higher nutritional value. Providing enzyme supplementation canhelp kick start enzyme production, but it takes time.

CARBOHYDRATES are made from carbon dioxide and water by green plants in the sunlight. Sugars, starches and fibers are the most common carbohydrates. They enhance neurotransmitters. Most people think of carbohydrates as grains and high starch vegetables like potatoes. Carbohydrates also include lower starch (3%) vegetables like *asparagus* or fruit like *strawberries* or higher starch (20%+) vegetables *beans, corn, yams and potatoes* or fruit like *bananas, figs and prunes*. Lower starch fruits and vegetables release glucose (sugar) slowly into the bloodstream, as do whole grains and legumes. Potatoes and rice release glucose quickly causing power surges in some people and then a let down. If glucose levels fluctuate, mental confusion and dizziness may occur.

3% – SLOWEST RELEASING VEGETABLES *asparagus, bean sprouts, beet greens, broccoli, cabbage, cauliflower, celery, chard, cucumber, endive, lettuce, mustard greens, radishes, spinach and watercress.*

3% – SLOWEST RELEASING FRUITS *cantaloupe, rhubarb, strawberries, watermelon, melons and tomatoes.*

6% – SLOW RELEASE VEGETABLES *beans (string), beets, brussels sprouts, chives, collards, dandelion greens, eggplant, kale, kohlrabi, leeks, okra, onions, parsley, peppers (red), pimento, pumpkin, rhutabegas, turnips.*

6% – SLOW RELEASE FRUITS *apricots, blackberries, cranberries, grapefruit, guava, melons, lemons, limes, oranges, papaya, peaches, plums, raspberries, tangerines, kiwis.*

MULTI-VITAMIN Insure your child's vitamin and mineral intake with a high quality daily multi-vitamin. Liz takes an intensive care, easy absorbable multi. Her vitamin is designed to include high levels of B vitamins, vitamins E, C, folic acid and selenium.

Research studies now show a strong correlation between aggressive behavior in children and deficiencies in nutrients such as niacin, pantothenic acid, thiamin, vitamin B6, vitamin C, iron, magnesium and tryptophan. Before changing your child's medications, try a daily multi-vitamin, one preferably without artificial colorings.

For more information, read the Crime Times article at http://www.crime-times.org/98a/w98ap2.htm

WATER SOLUBLE VITAMINS

B VITAMINS: Essential for cognitive function, helps to improve memory and assists in brain development. Prenatal exposure, encephalitis, stroke, prolonged drinking or vitamin B deficiency can cause damage to the hippocampus and thalamus. The effect may be good recall of past and normal short term memories, but they are unable to recall what they had for breakfast, last hours class notes or what spelling words they had just learned. Their procedural memory seems unaffected and the person may become steadily more competent and faster at performing a task, even though they do not remember ever doing it.

B1– THIAMIN – Changes carbohydrates to glucose into energy or fat and helps to provide energy to the brain, heart and central nervous system. It helps prevent nervous irritability; necessary for a good appetite.

RICHEST VITAMIN B1 RESOURCES *whole grain, nuts, legumes, yeast, liver, beans, peas, soy products, fish, and pork.*

B2 – RIBOFLAVIN – Transports hydrogen; is essential for the metabolism of carbohydrates, fats, and proteins; helps keep the skin and eyes in a healthy condition.

RICHEST VITAMIN B2 RESOURCES *lean meats, nuts,. liver, brewers yeast, leafy green vegetables, whole grain cereal, cheese, fish, eggs, milk*

B3 – NIACIN – Needed to convert food into energy, maintains normal functions of the skin, nerve tissue and digestive system. Can help lower LDL (bad) cholesterol. Reduces allergic reactions and supports sugar metabolism.

RICHEST VITAMIN B3 RESOURCES *fortified cereals, breads and grain products, meats, fish, poultry, nuts, grain products, peanuts*

B6 – PYRIDOXINE — Essential for brain function and the production of red blood cells. Aids in the immune system. Essential to protein, amino acid and carbohydrate metabolism. This is found in most foods naturally but a problem may be in the malabsorbtion.

> **RICHEST VITAMIN B6 RESOURCES** *yeast, liver, crabmeat, brown rice, meat, fish, wheat bran, germ and grains, vegetables, white and sweet potatoes, eggs, poultry, bananas*

B12 – CYANOCOBALAMIN – Helps to build and maintain the central nervous system. Important in the production of dopamine (energy) and serotonin (well-being). Necessary for production of red blood cells and normal growth.

> **RICHEST VITAMIN B12 RESOURCES** *clams, shellfish, meat, eggs, green vegetables, orange juice, yogurt, cheese, eggs, milk, fortified breakfast cereals.*

FOLATE (FOLIC ACID) Necessary for the production of RNA and DNA (the building blocks of cells) and normal red blood cells. Helps to lower homocysteine levels and prevents some birth defects. Helps relieve depression.

> **RICHEST FOLATE RESOURCES** *Fortified rice; pasta, breads, cereals, and grains, poultry, lentils and beans, green leafy vegetables, avocados, papayas.*

VITAMIN C – ASCORBIC ACID Protects against infection, assists in healing, helps maintain strength and elasticity of blood vessels. Enhances iron absorption. It is so important to the brain that it is found in concentrations of 15 to 100 times higher than elsewhere in the body. It is one of the most active and abundant antioxidants in the body. Stress hormones deplete it, since vitamin C is needed to synthesize them. Water, heat, light, oxygen and cooking all destroy vitamin C. When cooking steam lightly. Smoking one cigarette destroys 25 mg and aspirin triples the excretion rate of vitamin C.

> **RICHEST VITAMIN C RESOURCES** *orange juice, rose hips, guava, kiwi, black currents, kale, parsley, red peppers, brussel sprouts, broccoli, collards, cabbage, white and sweet potatoes, citrus fruits, tomatoes, artichokes, swiss chard, strawberries*

VITAMIN K – Necessary for blood clotting, aids in bone formation, helps regulate levels of calcium.

> **RICHEST VITAMIN K RESOURCES** *Brussel sprouts, kale, broccoli, spinach, lettuce, cabbage, turnip greens*

FAT SOLUBLE VITAMINS

VITAMIN E Protects fatty acids in the blood stream and improves overall blood circulation including blood to the brain. It is the primary fat-soluble anti-oxidant in the brain. Heat, oxygen, freezing, and chlorine destroy vitamin E.

> **RICHEST VITAMIN E RESOURCES:** *seeds, nuts, soybeans, eggs, brown rice, oats, fresh wheat germ, peanut butter, sweet potatoes, mangoes, sunflower oil*

ANTIOXIDANTS

ANTIOXIDANTS Help to clean the brain. These are foods that produce healthy chemicals that clean the brain from free radicals that cause cell deterioration. They act like a rust cleaner that keeps rust off brain matter. Vitamin E and C, beta carotene, lipoic acid, coenzyme Q10, grapeseed and pinebark extract are antioxidants.

> **RICHEST ANTIOXIDANT FOOD RESOURCES** *Blueberries, strawberries, cooked kale, raisins, raspberries, apples, grapes, cherries, prunes, blackberries, garlic and raw spinach. Mangoes and sweet potatoes contain high levels of vitamin E and C, plus beta carotene.*

CYANIOXIDANTS – PINE BARK (pycnogenol) and GRAPE SEED Has 20 times the antioxidant activity of vitamin C and 50 times that of vitamin E. It can cross the blood-brain barrier and can stay in the blood stream for up to 72 hours. Few other antioxidants cross this barrier and none do it as well.

MINERALS

CALCIUM necessary for teeth and bones, where most dietary calcium is found. The rest moves in and out of cells allowing conduction of impulses between nerves and contraction of muscles. Aids in heart regulation, blood clotting, muscle contractions and relaxation. Excess calcium depresses magnesium levels.

> **RICHEST CALCIUM FOOD RESOURCES** *cooked bones as in canned salmon or sardines, sesame seeds, tofu, dairy products, yogurt, turnip greens, broccoli, milk, blackstrap molasses, spinach, broccoflower.*

CHOLINE current research indicates a mother's choline intake may influence the development of the memory center in fetal brains.[71] Helps maintain healthy cellular structure and functions, plays role in muscle control.

71 Zeisel, er. Al: Chlorine: Needed for normal development of memory. Journal of the American College of Nutrition 2000, 19 (5): 528

RICHEST CHOLINE RESOURCES *eggs, milk, fish, whole grains, liver, iceberg lettuce, cauliflower, peanuts*

IRON is essential to the production of red blood cells. Aids in manufacturing amino acids, hormones and neurotransmitters. It strengthens the immune system. An iron deficiency in babies and children can have significant and permanent effects on brain development. Iron is a vital component for fueling our bodies, carrying oxygen to the brain and helping our newborns reach their greatest potential. Iron is deposited in the brain – it is part of the brain structure and an essential nutrient for mental development. Newborns have three times the ratio of iron in their bodies as adults. Babies have very high iron needs, because they grow so rapidly. Infants who are iron deficient can suffer from altered behavior, reduced immunity, slower language, gross and fine motor development, and reduction in IQ. Most babies are born with enough iron stores, these last four to six months. Breastfed babies rarely lack iron, not because there is a high concentrate of iron in breast milk, but because the iron in the breast milk is readily absorbable. A US study of nearly 5,400 children 6 to 16 found those who were deficient in iron were more than twice as likely to score below average on standardized math tests than their more well nourished peers.[72]
NOTE: If you believe you need to supplement iron, use caution. Get a blood test. Some of the symptoms of iron deficiency are the same as iron overdose. In addition, not all iron supplements are the same. Some are dangerous. Too much iron can make you sick or KILL A CHILD Evidence is showing that children with 'pica' – eating dirt (geophagia), lead paint, or ice (pagphagia) often show iron deficiencies. Symptoms of iron deficiency include listlessness, fatigue, memory deficits, sore tongue, reduced cognition.

RICHEST IRON RESOURCES *organ meat, liver, red meat, poultry, mussels, oysters, tofu, legumes such as lentils, kidney beans and chickpeas, eggs, enriched breads and pasta, nuts.*

MAGNESIUM Important for bone development and protein building; necessary for energy production, muscle relaxation and maintenance of heart health and function. Activates almost all the key enzymes needed for your neurons to create energy from glucose. Low levels of magnesium can cause the nerves to fire too easily even from mild stimuli. This can result in noises sounding too loud, lights too bright, and emotional reactions on the

72 Reuters Health, Sunday, July 8, 2001

edge. Magnesium deficiency in children is characterized by excessive figit-ing, anxious restlessness, psychomotor instability and learning difficulties in the presence of a normal IQ (Magnesium in Health and Disease, Seelig, 1980). Magnesium seems to absorb better in combination with folic acid and vitamins b6 and B12.

RICHEST MAGNESIUM RESOURCES *nuts, meats, tofu, milk, beans, bananas, apricots, legumes, yogurt, whole grains, leafy green vegetables, avocados, brown rice, carrots, citrus fruits.*

SELENIUM Acts as an antioxidant to help protect cells from damaging free radicals. It works in synergy with vitamin E to protect polyunsaturated fats from becoming oxidized. It is necessary for thyroid function. Helps with moods. It is a detoxifier of heavy metals that damage the brain. It binds mercury, lead, arsenic and cadmium which disrupt brain chemistry.

RICHEST SELENIUM RESOURCES *Grains, garlic, meats, seafood, tuna, soybeans, molasses, cashew nuts, brazil nuts, breads, oatmeal, soynuts, pasta, poultry, shellfish, sunflower seeds, cabbage, celery, mushrooms, onions*

ZINC is a component of every living cell in the body. It is essential for the structure and function of over 50 enzymes. Is needed to maintain proper levels of vitamin E in the blood. It is important for growth, sperm produc-tion, night vision, appetite, sense of taste and smell, immune system func-tioning and wound healing. Zinc deficiency may make children irritable, tearful, sullen and have gaze aversion (Moyhahan, Zinc Deficiency and Disturbances of Mood and Behavior. Lancet, 1:91, 1976) Chineses studies with school children show improved performance in memory, reasoning, perception and eye-hand coordination with additional zinc intake. Beef and lamb have a high zinc content especially in kidneys and liver meats.

RICHEST ZINC RESOURCES *oysters, seafood, red meats, poultry, nuts, whole grain breads and cereals, tofu, eggs, milk.*

Additional information can be found at www.betterendings.org including recipes our family has adapted to support Liz.

NATURAL NEUROTRANSMITTER ENHANCERS

DOPAMINE AND NOREPINEPHRINE have an energizing effect. When your brain is producing these chemicals you are alert, highly motivated and have fast reaction times. It is believed to play a role in working memory function. Low levels produce: depression, lethargy, trouble focusing, negativity, mental fuzziness. To enhance eat high protein snacks which have the amino acid tyrosine which boosts the synthesis of dopamine and nurepinephrine. Less than half the size of a typical restaurant portion is all you need (3-4 oz.) will help you feel more energized, alert and assertive— *fish, shellfish, skinless chicken, lean beef, egg whites, low fat dairy products, dried legumes, tofu, soy products.* Because these foods are basically pure protein they work relatively quickly. Avoid fatty foods as they divert blood from the brain to the digestive tract and take a very long time to digest. Avoid simple carbohydrate snacks *(breads, pasta, cakes, candy).*

SEROTONIN has a calming effect and its presence boosts concentration, relieves feelings of anxiety and makes you feel drowsy. Low levels produce: worry, moody, emotional, rigidity, irritable. Some scientists believe that low activity of serotonin can lead to underlying ability to handle powerful feelings which can result in impulsive acts, aggressive behaviors and suicidal tendencies, in addition to creating high risk behavior tendencies. To make serotonin your brain needs a supply of the amino acid tryptophan – found in *turkey, milk, meats, poultry, fish.* Like tyrosine it is found in proteins but eating more protein will not increase its level. In fact a high protein diet depletes the brain's tryptophan supply. To enhance serotonin eat a complex carbohydrate snack without added protein. Within about 30 minutes of eating a carbohydrate meal you will feel calmer and more relaxed. One to one and one half ounces is all many people need – *whole grain, crackers, bread, potatoes, pasta, popcorn, pretzels, rice.*

NOTE: *Eating the carbohydrate without protein is crucial. Doing so triggers an insulin release which shunts some of the amino acids from the blood to other organs. Tryptophan, however is left behind in the blood. With less competition from other amino acids, it can easily enter the brain.*

CAUTION Tyrosine and tryptophan can be dangerous if taken in pill form.

FASD RESOURCES FOR FAMILIES

OUT OF THE BOX IDEAS
that have helped our family.

MANAGE
ANGER Drink a cold glass of filtered water or suck on an all natural fruit popsicle. Mix up in a blender of fruit, ice and yogurt smoothie, then make the rest into popsicles for later or anger emergencies.

TIME OUT A pup tent or large box filled with blankets, cuddle toy and/or pillows is a safe recluse to regain composure.

GAIN ATTENTION Clap hands to a beat or try this: Clap one time if you hear me. Clap two times if you hear me. Clap three times if you hear me.

GAIN QUIET Speak in whisper, mouth words or turn down lights.

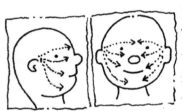

HEADACHES
TRIGEMINAL MASSAGE We use this massage when Liz is stressed, frustrated, has a headache or needs to regroup.

This shows where your trigeminals are.

1. Beginning at the top of the ear lightly tap three times along each of the pathways.
2. Next wiggle your fingers and lightly touch along the trigeminal pathways.
3. Then press lightly along the pathways.
4. Finally make little pressing circles along the pathways.
5. Finish by lightly touching the pathways, holding and hugging child.

SHOULDER AND NECK MASSAGE Use the same series of touching as the trigeminal massage. Roll your shoulders and neck to loosen tight muscles.

ROLLING WHEELS Use a small toy car or truck to drive up and down shoulders, neck and around top of head.

WASHCLOTH (cool or hot whichever feels better) and a dark quiet room.

RELAX

BATHE Epsom Salt Bath. Add 1 cup of epsom salt to a tub of water and soak. Shower off after bathing. **BATH & BODY WORKS** has a wide variety of calming scents in soaps, shampoos and bath oils. Stress Relief Pulse Point Serum made from eucalyptus and spearmint oils in the aromatherapy line can be massaged on temples if a headache is beginning.

BAROQUE MUSIC (Mozart, Handel, Bach, Vivaldi) Initial research in the 60's by Georgi Lazanov (Bulgarian Psychologist) and further scientific research has shown that a slow, relaxing temp of one beat per second can sometimes affect memory recall and learning. In addition, high frequency, nature sounds have been shown to stimulate electrical brain activity.[73]

AROMATHERAPY (www.naha.org or www.csh.umn.edu) Smell bypasses the thalamus region of the brainstem and connects directly with neurons in the cortex creating a direct route to our memory.[74]

Essential oils are highly concentrated and need to be used with care and applied 'only' by the drop. Do not use directly on the skin and dilute before using. Grapeseed, almond or hazelnut oil are good carriers for them. They can be used in potpourri or in a tea kettle to scent a room, add to a candle or spray mister, sprinkled on a tissue you can put in a little plastic bag in your purse, added to bath water, unscented lotions or shampoos. In addition natural scents can be used as insect repellents or in scenting laundry.

Rose, Lavender, Chamomile (Roman/German) – calming

Grapefruit, Orange, Lemon, Tangerine or Lime – uplifting, cheering, refreshing

Juniper Berry – easing tension Eucalyptus (Citriodora) – aids concentration

Jasmine – creativity OR Hyssop – alertness and clarity

NIGHT MARE SPRAY: Fill a spritz bottle with water and add a few drops of jasmine, lavender, chamomile or ylang-ylang. Provide bottle to your child to spray away night time monsters and fears.

SOUND SLEEP A humidifier with jasmine, lavender, chamomile or ylang-ylang. When Liz has a cold we add eucalyptus. The humidifier makes it easier to breathe and also adds a soft white noise. Additional sound sleep ideas: time in the sun, a day outside, a quiet evening, a hottub, sauna or bath, a medically certified magnetic mattress, natural nutrients to encourage sleep (melatonin).

73.-74. O'Brien, Dominic; Learn to Remmber, 2000, London

INFORMATION ON FASD FOR FAMILIES AND FRIENDS

Parenting Ideas from Families in the Trenches

We need you! Children with brain injury need non-judgmental, loving friends and relatives who accept them as they are, encourage but not demand growth, and rejoice in strengths and accomplishments no matter how small.

What every child with FASD needs?

- Unconditional love.
- Acceptance.
- Attention.
- Supervision.
- Patience and understanding.
- Wisdom.
- Structure / environmental controls.
- Redirection.
- Help to slow down when getting out. of control (deceleration).
- Someone who believes they are capable.

Ways to help our child grow

1. Praise their strengths.
2. Acknowledge their expression of frustration.
3. Respect their fears and difficulty with change.
4. Understand that behaviors may be a can't do it not a won't do it.
5. Talk to them as a person - not someone who is stupid.
6. Keep from comparing them with others.
7. Keep from joking, teasing or putting them down.
8. Keep yourself from telling them, "you will grow out of this."
9. Get involved in their interests.
10. Find out what they are trying to learn and think of fun ways to join.

We need your help. It is exhausting to raise a child who has prenatal brain injury. Consider learning how to provide respite for us. Please understand this is a brain injury not an issue of 'bad' parenting and our child is not a 'bad' child.

We may have to avoid

- Holidays and birthdays
- Circus, concerts, movies, sport events
- These events may be too much for our child to handle.
- New people or visitors in the home are a change in routine and may be difficult for the child.

Things to remember

1. Poor impulse control is a brain injury issue and frustrating behaviors are most likely not intentional.
   - Keep your cool and refrain from yelling.
   - Why? Because the child is more than likely not misbehaving, but unable to understand certain things.
2. The child may not be able to do two things at once. For example: If you are eating or playing a game the child may not be able to talk.
3. The child may not be able to use their feet and hands at the same time.
4. View behavior problems as a disability that can be dealt with, rather than disobedience.
5. Think stretched toddler, our child may look like other children their age, but trust us when we tell you supervision issues, responsibility issues and amount of freedom. It is for your protection and our child's safety.

Our FAScinating Journey ©2004 Kulp

Tips on communicating with a child with FASD

1. Find a quiet place to talk.
   Why? Large, noisy and busy areas are hard to communicate and function well in.
   a. Turn off radio or TV.
   b. Close door.
   c. Move to quieter area.
2. Began talking with simple topics.
   a. How is your dog?
   b. What did you eat for lunch?
3. Talk about things the child likes.
4. Stay on one topic.
5. State one sentence at a time.
   a. Make it easy for the child to participate in a conversation by asking yes and no questions.
   b. Remain still or walk at the same speed as the child when talking.
6. Keep sentences short.
7. Instead of asking why, use words like where, how, what, who or when. Why will send their brain in a house of mirrors.
8. Allow time for child to respond, refrain from hurrying child.
   a. If our child can not get the right word, don't fill in, give clues or description or ask the child to point.
   b. Repeat a point using different words. Keep information simple.
9. Give them choices to ease decision-making, but still allow independence of choice.
10. Be an active listener.
    a. Give frequent eye contact.
    b. Look for gestures.
    c. If understanding is unclear, take a guess (are you talking about . . . Oh now I get it.)
11. Look through the child's eyes.
    a. How we look at things or understand things may be totally different from how they understand something.
    b. Consider watching Forrest Gump with Tom Hanks to get an idea of concrete thinking.
       For example if you tell our child to handle it, they may only think about touching it.
12. Tell others if you learn better ways to talk with our child so all can benefit.
13. Avoid behavior which winds our child up. Such as tickling, wrestling and pillow fighting.
14. Sit or squat next to our child, do not stand over.
15. In a group, make sure the child is placed so conversation can be around them.
16. May not be able to express needs such as thirst, hunger, going to toilet and may fidget instead.

"Embarrassed? No, I've never been embarrassed. Why would I be embarrassed?"
   Because the child had a hot foot. a dirty tennis shoe had just landed ten feet away, hitting an older woman on the back of the leg. His logic was that the person who was hit was dumb to be standing in the way.

"You can only buy something under $10."
   An armload of clothes later, the teen assumes you will purchase all she has found as long as each is under $10.00

Controlled failures

We allow our child to fail at times so that she/he learns the consequences. We offer Plan A and Plan B. Plan A allows the child to do it the way he chooses. Plan B provides another way to handle a situation. We role play both plans. We discovered 'real life' experiences provided better opportunity to make a permanent memory, so sometimes we allow him to try his way and fail. Once the choice is made, we provide the supports to help him learn from his choice.

Controlled successes

Provide opportunities for your child to succeed.

- A carnival game that allows every child to win.
- Visit to the amusement park on Mother's Day when all the other mother's are doing something else and there are no crowds.
- Short periods of time at an event and then leave to integrate child in regular community life -
  - Circus to see the lions.
  - Sunday worship and leave before service.
  - Parade to see one marching band.
  - Museum to see dinosaurs.
  - Library to get one book.
  - Restaurant to have desert.
  - Grocery shopping to get less than ten things
- Set an attainable goal and break into very small steps and show progress to a larger goal on a posted chart with stickers

Think different birthdays

Birthdays can be very overwhelming:

- Let the child pick out their own presents and don't wrap them. The energy of the surprise may be hard for child to handle.
- Start the day with a special breakfast and a few tiny presents.
- Wear matching family T-shirts on holidays, community events and birthdays.
- If you do have a party keep it organized and simple.
- Have the child pick their favorite dinner

Think different holidays and events

- New Years Party on the child's time zone while they're still awake. Make a time capsule using a can with a lid. Write a New Years wish. Put a picture of the child, favorite toy, food, color, story. Open the capsule next New Year to see how much they have changed.
- Adopt a family for a holiday, visit a shelter to deliver presents
- Have a holiday tea party with the family - tea, cookies or appetizers
- Make a paper chain the child can rip off a chain per day to count down to the holiday or write a number count down on a calendar and cross off days.
- Valentines Day everyone in family writes or says three nice thing about every other family member.
- Thanksgiving Trees from Nov. 1 to 31 secretly place paper leaves with notes of thanksgiving on a bare twig tree.
- Have a pajama day. Stay home, goof off and do things together.
- Develop a bedtime or wake up ritual.

FASD RESOURCES FOR FAMILIES

JUVENILE JUSTICE
Help To Work Through The System.

Runaway Teens The National Runaway Switchboard (1-800-621-4000) has helpful services and information. One in seven kids runs before the age of 18.

What should a parent do when a teen runs away:
- Call the police immediately and have them enter your child into the National Crime Information Center Missing Person File.
- Call the child's social worker or SOS line if the child is in foster care.
- Call everyone the child knows and to help you including the school.
- Use instant caller ID and tracers
- Don't leave your phone unattended. Call forward to your cell phone if you are going to be out.
- Search your teen's room, bank accounts, credit cards, pagers and cell phone records for clues.
- Take care of yourself. The stress and terror can be overwhelming.

When the teen returns home:
- Be warm and welcoming. Many teens stay away because they are afraid of the return confrontation.
- Allow time to settle in. You'll all be emotional and probably need a rest.
- Get necessary medical attention.
- Call back anyone you've contacted while your teen was on run to let them know he or she is home.
- Talk with your teen. Look for ways to prevent a repeat runaway.
- Seek all necessary assistance.

You're Busted! *To arrest someone, the police need 'probable cause' to believe a crime was committed and that this suspect did it. A judge rules on the facts, not the police officer. To convict someone of a crime, the court must find "beyond a reasonable doubt" that the defendant committed the crime - a high standard.*

Most parents talk to a child about smoking, sex, drinking, grades, getting a job, learning to do chores and dating. Also teach your child how to deal appropriately with a security officer, police officer or similar authority figure. A young person who has thought about this issue is better prepared to handle it if the experience occurs.

The American Civil Liberties Union's "Bustcard" recommends:

- Be polite and respectful, lower your voice, speak slowly.
- Stay calm. Do not get into an argument with the police. Never run away.
- Keep your hands where they can be seen. Never touch an officer.
- Write down everything you remember (officer's badge and patrol car numbers, witness names, etc.) as soon as possible. You can ask for their business card politely.
- Attitude is can be the difference between going home and Juvenile Hall.
- Ask for a lawyer when it is "CLEAR" you are under arrest or not free to leave the scene. If you are "REALLY" arrested, don't make any statements without a lawyer present.

A Trip to the Police Station If your teen ends up in the police station, by his own hand, what should you do? Your job is to protect and advocate for your teen. Some parents think a night or two in jail does some good for a teen, most juvenile justice professionals would disagree with this idea.

- Be polite
- Listen carefully to what the police have to say. Make no verbal attacks on the teen or the police.
- Get the facts, find out the names of the officers handling the case. Try to ascertain just what happened.
  - Did my child make any statements? Get copies
  - Did he/she take a sobriety/drug test? Get the results
  - Who is the complainant?
  - Were their any witnesses?
  - Was there property damage?
- Be careful about what you say to the police. Children in foster care have confidentiality issues. In an effort to cooperate it is possible to say too much.
- Call the child's social worker or SOS line to determine what to do if the child is a foster child.

RECOMMENDED READING Tools for Succcess, Working With Youth With Fetal Alcohol Syndrome and Effects in the Juvenile Justice System, (2002) Prepared by MOFAS and written by Susan Carlson, JD, research by Lisa Brodsky. This books provides professionals and parents the tools they will need to help youth with FASD who are dealing with juvenile deliquency issues and the criminal justice system. To order visit www.mofas.org

A Trip In Front of a Judge If your teen is in detention or appears in front of a judge

- Make contact with the child's social worker if the child is in foster care.
- If the child has a disability and is need of special education services, be sure to make this known in writing. Provide IEPs, past hospitalizations, medical and school records to social services.
- If consequences are being imposed that havebeen tried previously and failed, make this information known.
- Follow court procedures. Be respectful and non-emotional.
- Advise the teen to be respectful in behavior and appearance.

Books by Jodee and Liz Kulp

Kulp, Jodee: *Heart Break* 2003. Support workbooks for a person with FASD or other brain injury working through the grief of heartbreak. **FREE ONLINE** (A gift from Better Endings)

Kulp, Liz and Kulp, Jodee: *The Best I Can Be: Living With Fetal Alcohol Syndrome or Effects.* 2000. Discover what it is like to live with Fetal Alcohol. Join Liz as she lets you become a part of her life. $12.95 *(plus s&h)*

Kulp, Jodee: *Families at Risk: A Guide to Understanding and Protecting Children and Care Providers Involved in Out-of-Home or Adoptive Care.* 1994. 416 pages of valuable information on living and loving high risk children. Special sections to help protect children and prevent and survive allegations of maltreatment. $29.95 *(plus s&h)*

Kulp, Jodee: *Journey to Life* 1986. A poetic journey of an adult ahild of alcoholics growing into personal and family renewal and restoration. *"I can not give up my past. I shall not forget. But forgive. And let go in respect for myself and living."* $5.00 (plus s&h)

Upcoming books:

Kulp, Liz, *The Frozen Truth.* Liz takes the reader in this book through the truth of growing up as a teen with FASD.

Kulp, Jodee, *The Whitest Wall*, a mystery intertwined with characters challenged by the realities of FASD.

Trainings, Presentations and Workshops

Allegations: Prevention and Survival. Three hour to two day trainings to help foster and adoptive families face the reality of potential allegations of child maltreatment. Presentation includes information on national and international statistics, family and child risk factors, actual review of a real allegation, how to appeal, the emotions of allegations and building support teams. Training session is fun, fast paced and very informative. Research is based on work done with *Families at Risk* and years of providing allegation support services.

FASD - There is Hope. Overview and training on teaching strategies and worksheets Jodee Kulp developed to help Liz cross bridges to be able to write research papers, handle math more easily and learn to read, write and spell. Plus family and social ideas that have helped the Kulp family enjoy life with FASE, embrace the community and cope.

Website. Better Endings website **www.betterendings.org** is filled with up-to-date and practical information to help families and professional live with, laugh and love children who have been affected by prenatal alcohol exposure. **Free Online Worksheets and Workbooks to help persons with FASD.** New Beginnings offers hope for families.

Keynote addresses are available.

Special 20% Off Discount!

Order a copy of this book with this form or online at:

http://www.moangels.com/store   coupon code BE030304

2nd Edition: Our FAScinating Journey:
Keys to Brain Potential Along The Path of Prenatal Brain Injury

_____in softbound at $20.00 (regularly $24.95) ISBN 0-9637072-4-8

Plus take advantage of other publications at savings

_____ Families at Risk in softbound at $25.00 (regularly $29.95)

_____ Best I Can Be in softbound at $10.00 (regularly $12.95)

Cost of books _____
Outside US/Canada/Mexico Add 20% _____
POSTAGE & HANDLING _____
(US first book add $5.00, _____
each additional book add $2.00
Outside US: $6.00 for first book
and $2.00 for each additional book)
SUBTOTAL _____
SALES TAX _____
(MN Residents please add sales tax)
FINAL TOTAL _____
(US Dollars, please convert using
current currency exchange rate)

___PAYMENT ENCLOSED $
___PLEASE CHARGE MY CREDIT CARD

___ Visa ___MasterCard ___Discover

Account #_____

Exp Date _____

Signature_____

Prices in US dollars and subject to change without notice.

SHIP TO:

Name _____

Institution _____

Address _____

City _____

State/Zip _____

Country _____

Telephone _____Fax_____

Email _____

We will never share or disclose your data as we regard such actions as an invasion of your privacy.

Order from your local bookstore or directly from:
Better Endings New Beginnings
6289 Brunswick Avenue North
Brooklyn Park, MN 55429
763-531-9548
books@connetworks.com

Visit our website

Hope for the Future

Better Endings New Beginnings
www.betterendings.org

Our website provides a variety of additional tools to help professionals and families help the children they care for and love.

Please visit and feel free to share our tools too help others.

ADAPTATIONS

• Family friendly ideas to encourage growth for your child and family

ALLEGATIONS

• Ideas to work through misunderstandings regarding your child and family

EDUCATION

• Ideas for homeschool families and public school teachers to help make learning easier for children with FASD

NUTRITION & ENVIRONMENT

• Brain changing easy recipes
• Safe cleaning products
• Non-Alcoholic Beverage Recipes
• Nutrition ideas and links

RESOURCES

• To support services
• Store
• Free FASD Workbooks

TRAINING and WORKSHOPS

• Allegations: Prevention and Survival
• FASD: There is Hope

For more information:

Better Endings, New Beginnings

6289 Brunswick Ave. N.

Brooklyn Park, MN 55429

763-531-9548

Our FAScinating Journey ©2004 Kulp

I AM ONLY ONE.

BUT I AM STILL ONE.

I CANNOT DO EVERYTHING.

BUT STILL

I CAN DO SOMETHING.

I WILL NOT REFUSE TO DO

THE SOMETHING   I CAN DO.

HELEN KELLER

THANK YOU FOR YOUR LIGHT!

Epilogue from Liz

It has been five years since I found out why life was so hard for me. Finding out didn't change how hard life is, but it did make me believe I was not a bad person. One thing I hate is when people say "don't use fetal alcohol as an excuse," that is all well and good to say, but they don't know how hard I am trying or what it is like to be me. When I ask a question, it is because I don't understand, not because I have not been listening, sometimes there is a blank space and I can't get across it. When I am accused of something I did not do, I want to punch someone, there is no place to go for help when people think you do something and you don't do it.

I may look really normal and I work really hard to maintain and that is really stressful and sometimes I get so frustrated. Sometimes the stress just all builds up, especially when different people put different expectations on me all at the same time. I catch an attitude when people expect more of me than I can give, but I also don't want to expect less of myself. I am creative and I have my own style and I try really hard to look the best that I can.

I like to be with friends at school, but I hate school because learning is so hard. One of my teachers is non-judgmental and walks me through the process so I understand it piece-by-piece and slow enough so I can stay with him, but he doesn't treat me like I am a little child. I do really well in his class and I respect him, because he respects and believes in me. I will be glad when I graduate and look forward to having my own life and place to live with roommates. I don't like to be alone, I am a people person. I don't like it when my parents worry about me, they worry too much.

One of my dreams is to be a dancer and a rapper. I like getting attention when I perform and I like to write my own lyrics about real life. I need to write from my soul. Some dance steps are really hard to learn, but I keep working and working and working on it until I get it. I am working on writing a new book called "The Frozen Truth" about being a teen and becoming an adult with a hidden brain injury. It will take a long time, but I will work on it little by little. I like doing presentations on FASD because I like to answer questions and give my opinions on things. I hope my book "The Best I Can Be" helped others. Today, kids come up to me and say things like "you don't look like you have any problems, you know my mom drank too." I feel safe to them and say "I can just do the best I can."

Peace out

Liz

Our FAScinating Journey ©2004 Kulp